ORGAN THEFT LEGENDS

ORGAN THEFT

VÉRONIQUE CAMPION-VINCENT

LEGENDS

UNIVERSITY PRESS OF MISSISSIPPI

OCM 58546739

JACKSON

Publication of this book was made possible in part by a Hemingway Translation Grant from the Book Office of the French Embassy.

www.upress.state.ms.us

Designed by Pete Halverson

The University Press of Mississippi is a member of the Association of American University Presses.

First English edition 2005

⊗

Library of Congress Cataloging-in-Publication Data

Campion-Vincent, Véronique.
    Organ theft legends / Véronique Campion-Vincent.
        p. cm.
    Includes bibliographical references and index.
    ISBN 1-57806-593-3 (cloth : alk. paper)
    1. Organs (Anatomy)—Folklore. 2. Theft—Folklore. 3. Body snatching—Folklore. I. Title.
    GR489.C33   2005
    398′.353—dc22   2005005446

British Library Cataloging-in-Publication Data available

CONTENTS

ACKNOWLEDGMENTS

The author thanks all those who helped her in her research, especially by sending her texts: Pierre Bénichou, Yves-Marie Bercé, Lucian Bois, Rolf Wilhelm Brednich, Jan Harold Brunvand, Peter Burger, Dr. Bernard Cohen, Jo-Ann Conrad, Georges Cuer, Delfeil de Ton, Jean-Pierre Digard, Steven Fluss, Mark Glazer, Didier Houssin, Bengt af Klintberg, Todd Leventhal, Eduardo Mackenzie, Jean-François Mayer, Mithra Moezzi, Antoinette Molinié, Christine de Parscau, Claude Pernet, Jean-Bruno Renard, Myriam Tebourbi, Paolo Toselli, Olga Vincent, Renaud Vincent.

She also expresses her gratitude to the following organizations:

Etablissement français des greffes, Paris. In 1995–96, the French Establishment for Transplants sponsored this author's study *La greffe, la rumeur et les media. Les récits de vols d'organes* (Paris, April 1996), to which the present work owes a great deal.

La Maison des sciences de l'homme, Paris. This, the author's place of work, has given her precious support, both administratively and intellectually.

INTRODUCTION

I have long noticed that fiction goes far beyond the realm of literature, cinema, and the arts, the genres to which people believe it is limited. . . . Fiction appears everywhere; it shows itself in religion and in science, and likewise in activities which are apparently very well inoculated against it. Politics . . . is one of the most favourable areas for what is fictional and imaginary.

—MARIO VARGAS LLOSA, *Le poisson dans l'eau. Mémoires.* Paris, 1995

Having been systematically studying contemporary legends and rumors from the viewpoint of the social sciences since 1987, I followed and analyzed instances of the Baby Parts Story almost as soon as it appeared. These narratives, originating in Central America and alleging that international adoptions were being misused for secret illegal organ transplant operations, were reported in the international media from the end of 1986 onwards, but seemed to have disappeared after a series of well-documented denials during the summer of 1988. However, they continued, and were enriched from other cycles of collective narrative concerning stolen eyes and stolen kidneys. In 1993, these accusations were repeated in documentary films on TV, which had a great impact and aroused controversies and denials. At the time of writing (1997), organ theft stories are more topical than ever.

Organ thefts are now no longer presented as mere gossip, but as facts—incontrovertible, frequent, and systematic. Indeed, the international trade in human organs and tissues, which is perfectly real, is perceived as theft. The same is true of the equally real cases where international adoption goes very wrong. We know that the trade in human organs and tissues is based on the "voluntary" sale of living organs by the poor, and on exploitation of the dead. There is evidence that this is common in India ("voluntary" sale) and in China (where the corpses of people condemned to death are exploited), but it also occurs sporadically in other countries. Instances of misuse of international adoption constitute one particular category within a complex of many situations where the poor and weak are exploited, which can be grouped under the general heading of trafficking in human beings. Such types of trafficking do not run smoothly. They often lead to conflicts, accusations, scandals. Though the trade in organs and children is rarely made explicit or analyzed in the public media, the accusations and scandals, by contrast, are exploited by media systematically based on sensationalism; immense publicity is given to any shocking assertion, for example, without regard to the status of the person making it. Thus the interpretation that sees abuse in selling and trading in human organs and tissues, and in international adoptions, receives support from the media and institutions, turning organ theft stories into facts accepted as true.

Until now, this subject has inspired hardly any objective, analytical studies seeking to understand why such highly implausible narratives and allegations have gained widespread acceptance.

My objective is to make people understand how a collective belief is born and develops—more precisely, how and why there arose a conviction that the theft of organs (particularly children's organs) is systematically carried out nowadays. The alleged facts were repeatedly denied, in detail and authoritatively, every time there was a major outbreak of the rumors; ten years after the allegations were first reported in the international press, no solid evidence has been produced to support them or to demonstrate that any system is involved (since the examples cited have either collapsed, one after another, or could not be verified, and remained isolated). Yet even so, belief in organ thefts persists and grows steadily more widespread, reaching much broader sections of the population in 1997 than in 1987.

It is necessary to analyze how the terms in which these accusatory narratives are presented give them strength. So (without being myself misled by it) I will adopt the emotional vocabulary of the mass media and the general public, not the precise specialist vocabulary used by the medical profession to describe the features of transplants. One example, to show my approach: I will speak of the crimes attributed to those who steal eyes as "organ thefts." This description involves inaccuracy, for although the eye is indeed an organ, the cornea transferred in a transplant is simply a tissue. Yet this distinction is irrelevant at the level of the narratives that will be analyzed. The accusatory narrative speaks of the plucking out of an eye, the mutilation of this symbol of the personality, this seat of vision and of the soul. Someone transmitting such a horror story never even thinks about the difference between an organ and a tissue, between an eye and a cornea, even if he or she belongs to the small fraction of the population with enough knowledge to make these distinctions. To understand why these narratives are convincing, we must re-create their emotional power; we must choose to adopt (without being misled) the commonsense definitions which stir the emotions, rather than medical definitions.

In my first study of the topic, in 1990, I made an assessment on the future of the Baby Parts Story which was later disproved by events; I said at that time: "This story is no longer legitimate, and has joined the ranks of anti-American stories of minor importance."[1] I soon realized my error, for the French version of that article, published two years later, put this phrase in the conditional tense, and concluded by foreseeing some developments:

> What this article describes and interprets is simply the first episode in an ever-evolving cycle. In 1992, tales of abduction and mutilation hold center stage. One can readily recognize in the local panics, and in the anecdotes about fake boutiques and miraculous last-minute rescues which recur in abduction stories, episodes which appeared during former panics about the white slave traffic. As for mutilation stories, they mostly feature stereotyped anecdotes about stolen kidneys, but the motif of eyes plucked out is still often present, especially in Latin America. . . . Rather than Western governments, it is now the Mafia (a guilty organization about which one can say what one likes, without fear of contradiction) which is accused and fingered by the low-grade media, TV fiction, and scandal sheets which publicize this story.[2]

It was largely in order to understand the reasons for this error, and to analyze the factors that explain the dynamics of the collective belief in organ thefts that I resumed work on the subject in 1995.

This work is based on a considerable corpus of press articles of every level. These texts, though often simplistic and full of distortions, merit analysis. News items circulated by the media, read or seen thousands of miles from where they occurred, are most often superficial and decontextualized, i.e., cut off from the social network within which they are meaningful and understandable. More-over, the logic of the media draws them towards what is sensational and shock-ing, to the detriment of any commentary. An important cause of distortion is the concern of the media to anticipate what they assume the general public wants, and to supply at least as much entertainment as news. Yet these superfi-cial, decontextualized, and deformed news items are for the general public their main sources of information on distant parts of the world. They therefore feed the perceptions which are the real object of this investigation.

This work also examines the products of mass culture, whether fictional or documentary, which relate to the belief in systematic organ theft. The subject has become a commonplace, and we cannot claim to cover everything, but will indicate the first important examples which proved influential, those which launched a fashion rather than simply exploiting it.

ORGAN THEFT LEGENDS

CHAPTER 1

NARRATIVES AND THE LEGEND

I must start by justifying my use of the terms "narratives" and "legend" in preference to "rumors," which is the more usual one in France. Certainly the theme of organ theft is a perfect incarnation of a classic rumor—one which denounces and reveals ghastly secrets, unmasks sinister plots, and carries a strong connotation of protest and of opposition to the elite. However, instead of drawing together all rumor phenomena within a single word, as is the French custom, I have chosen to use a differentiated vocabulary to distinguish between different stages of development.

The term "narratives" is preferable to "rumors" because this is not a matter of short, simple statements such as "there is a trade in organs," or "organ theft does happen," but of stories which include several significant details, and where the narrator tells his hearers who the participants were. So these are indeed narratives. Moreover, far from belonging to the fictive world of fairy tale, these narratives claim to be giving information, to be relating authentic facts, and those who tell them are expressing beliefs. So this is a "legend," a narrative genre whose main characteristic is that the narrators assert its truth, while another characteristic is the arguments to which this assertion gives rise.

Diverse though they are, organ theft narratives correspond to a legend, to a body of beliefs which can be summarized thus: organized criminal groups engaged in the organ trade are using large-scale kidnapping and murder, preferably of children, in order to supply human organs to a vast network of professional but criminal medical personnel, who practice clandestine transplants, bringing huge profits to themselves and to those in the trade.

Organ theft narratives appeared towards 1985, at first in Latin America. At a time when transplants on children were still rare, the first two scenarios concerned children; this clearly indicated that they were reactions to other situations, particularly the child trafficking and abductions involved in international adoptions, and also that they included powerful elements of fantasy.

In their first versions, the scenario was of pseudo adoptions, in which children left poor countries only to die upon operating tables, not to be welcomed into loving families; it is commonly referred to as the Baby Parts Story, since organs taken from these children were allegedly used as "spare parts" in transplants (see below). Scenarios of this type aroused an official controversy, with accusations and denials. Here, the narrative is the primary material for a controversy where institutions and pressure groups clash face to face.

Existing alongside these scenarios, there were narratives about kidnappings and mutilations, committed either singly or by sinister ambulances making raids on poor city districts, with the purpose of gathering eyes for transplants; murder might or might not be involved (the eye thieves).

There then appeared narratives about kidnappings and mutilations which were analogous but which chiefly concerned adults (usually men); they were sometimes set in poor countries, sometimes in the great cities of Europe or the United States, but the victims were tourists or businessmen originating from the rich countries. They would awake from unconsciousness to find that one kidney had been removed; this story has been named the Kidney Heist. It is mainly this theme which circulates orally in Europe. Stories of kidney theft are no longer told only about adults but also about children who disappear in large amusement parks such as EuroDisney, and are sometimes found again with one kidney gone—or so it is alleged. For France's neighboring countries (the Low Countries, Germany, Italy) Paris is a frequent setting for the disappearance and/or mutilation of tourists.

PSEUDO ADOPTIONS—THE BABY PARTS STORY

1987–1988

The Baby Parts Story—so called by the United States Information Agency (USIA) in the reports it circulated in order to combat this accusation—was reported in the international press at the beginning of 1987. It is a "pseudo adoption" scenario, alleging that children taken or bought from impoverished mothers are destined to be cut up and used in organ transplants when they reach the foreign country where they were supposedly to be adopted. The places where these accusations appeared were the countries of Central America (Guatemala, Honduras, Costa Rica); the countries accused of profiting from this horrible trade were, in the first place, the United States, but also, very soon, Western European countries and Israel.

The first accusation appeared in the press on January 2, 1987. That day, in the Honduran daily paper *La Tribuna*, Danilo D. Antunez was interviewing Leonardo Villela Bermudez, the secretary-general of the Junta nacional de bienestar social (JNBS), a national agency for social assistance. The interview commented upon the recent discovery in San Pedro Sula, the chief city of Honduras, of four secret *casas de engorde* (literally, "fattening houses") where thirteen very young children were waiting to go abroad for adoption. Their origins were unknown and regarded as suspicious, for, having been taken or bought from impoverished mothers, their presence in the *casas* was the result of a monetary transaction. Bermudez explained to the journalist that foreigners pretending to want to adopt disadvantaged children for humanitarian reasons were selling them on, so that they could be cut up and used for organ transplants in the United States; he quoted prices of ten thousand U.S. dollars per child. The article appeared under the alarming headline *En el estrangero: ninos hondureños despedazados para traficar con sus organos* ("Abroad: Honduran children dissected for the organ trade"). Bermudez repeated his accusations the same day on local TV (Vica) and radio (Radio America).

The very next day, Bermudez wrote to *La Tribuna* denying his reported statement, saying that though he had repeated the speculations of certain social workers, he did not himself accept them. This denial was rejected by the journalist, who said he had a tape where Bermudez was indeed speaking in his own name, but it was supported by Bermudez's superior, Miriam de Acona, honorary president of JNBS and First Lady of Honduras. The accusations were picked up in the Latin American press, but the denials were not.

A month later, on February 5, 1987, new accusations arose in Guatemala in the same circumstances. Fourteen children (eleven of them newborn) had been found in a *casa de engorde*; the accuser was a police officer, Baudillo Hichoz Lopez, and the price quoted was twenty thousand U.S. dollars per child. Lopez issued a denial next day, which was confirmed by his superiors.

5

Once again the press (now worldwide, not just in Latin America) only reported the accusations, not the denials. The article which really launched the baby parts affair appeared on April 5, 1987, in *Pravda*. It spoke of thousands of Honduran children being sent to the United States, where they were used as organ donors for children of rich families; it was retransmitted by Tass news agency, and went all around the world. In France, this information was given by *L'Humanité*[1] and by *Témoignage Chrétien*.[2]

In 1988 the spread of the accusations was reinforced by two new allegations, rapidly followed by denials.

The first was made in January 1988 in Guatemala. Once again the accuser was a police officer, who withdrew his declarations to the press the very next day. The accusations had followed the discovery of an adoption agency that was obtaining children by illegal means, and was organized by two Israelis in the city of Santa Catarina Pinula; the price of a child was estimated at seventy-five thousand U.S. dollars by the paper *El Grafico*. The American and Israeli embassies in Guatemala issued statements reinforcing the denials of the policeman and his superior officers. Yet in two articles (January 27, 1988, February 6, 1988) *L'Humanité* made no mention of the denials but repeated the assertions of *El Grafico*, alleging that the Israeli couple had admitted selling hundreds of children to North American and Israeli families whose own children needed an organ transplant.

The second allegation became known on August 7, when Angel Campos, a judge in Paraguay, commenting on the discovery of a clandestine orphanage containing seven Brazilian babies, told the press that an inquiry led one to think that these babies were destined to be killed and dissected in clandestine hospitals in the United States, where their organs would be preserved for use in future transplants. The embassy denied this on the ninth, but the repercussions of this shocking assertion, made at a season when news was scarce, were considerable. In France, the allegations made by Campos were repeated not only by *L'Humanité* in its usual tone[3], but by *Le Figaro*. At first the latter did consider it possible that secret networks for organ transplants existed in the United States (August 9, 1988, *"Greffes d' organes: le monstrueux trafic"* ["Organ Transplants: A Monstrous Trade"]), but then it reported the denial, while still affirming that a trade in human beings for transplant was very real, and needed investigation (August 11, 1988, *"Trafic de bébés: les Etats-Unis démentent"* ["Baby Trafficking: The United

States Denies"]). *Le Monde*[4] reported both the allegations and the denials, followed by an editorial note stressing the persistence of rumors concerning such trade, the shortage of available organs at a time when transplants were developing so fast, and finally the technical reasons making the allegations implausible.

Thus in 1987 and 1988 four incidents, similar in structure, occurred in Honduras (January 1987), in Guatemala (February 1987 and January 1988), and in Paraguay (August 1988). In each case we see that after the discovery of secret orphanages containing babies that had been kidnapped or bought, a middle-ranking official makes comments on the affair (Bermudez is secretary-general of the official social assistance agency in the Honduras, the police officers in Guatemala belong to financial brigades, Campos is a judge in Paraguay). These men declare to the press that the children were to be cut up abroad for use in transplants. Next day, or a few days later, these officials withdraw their declarations, stating that they had no proofs of their allegations, were building hypotheses, were repeating the speculations of their colleagues or of social workers. Soon these denials are reinforced by the superiors of these middle-ranking officials. Yet the denials are ignored by the press, whereas the earlier assertions are taken up, and soon go around the world.

It is appropriate to decode these incidents. The assertions made to the press reflect beliefs which have sprung up throughout all Latin America since the mid-1980s. These beliefs involve the existence of organized gangs of organ traffickers, to whom the popular press quickly gave an emotive name: *organ mafia*.

The denials are never spontaneous, but reflect vigorous activity by the diplomatic services of the United States, which enjoys a dominant neocolonial status in Latin American countries, and is directly involved in assisting the anti-Marxist guerrilla movement (the Contras) in Guatemala, Salvador, and Nicaragua. This great power considers it necessary to clear itself of accusations which put it in an odious light. However, the denials seem hardly convincing to local public opinion, which habitually has little trust in statements from official authorities, and may even interpret a denial as an irrefutable proof that there is indeed something to be concealed.

As for the discovery of clandestine orphanages, these are linked to a real fact, namely the intense trade in children, which is itself created by the growth of international adoptions flowing into the rich countries: the United States and Canada, Western Europe, Israel, South Africa. Certainly, most of these adoptions follow normal procedures, yet for very poor countries they represent such an important source of income that they have attracted criminal activity.

Finally, the accusations that children are being sacrificed for the sake of transplants are related to the increase in these operations, in which immense progress was made after cyclosporine (which began being commercially produced in 1983) had allowed better control over tissue rejection, that having been a limitation on surgical techniques since the 1950s.

Two tendencies in the press, pro-Communist and pro–Third World, endorsed these accusations all over the world.

Reactions from politicians soon followed. As early as May 5, 1987, the Italian Radicals presented to the European Parliament a project for a resolution condemning the secret traffic in babies' organs. The project was rejected, and was turned into a written question to the Brussels Commission, which replied on July 23, 1987, that no such traffic existed. A year later, however, an accusatory motion presented by Danielle de March, a French deputy affiliated with the Communist Party, was adopted by show of hands in the European Parliament on September 15, 1988. This motion, "expressing condemnation of the traffic in organs of Third World babies," took up once more the incidents in Honduras and Guatemala, accusing Israel and the United States. Here are some extracts from that motion, namely the three paragraphs of accusation, and the appeal to European governments:

> The Parliament of Europe (A) Being profoundly shocked by the discovery on Saturday January 23 last [1988] at Santa Catarina Pinula (Guatemala) of a *casa de engorde.* "fattening house" in which were eleven babies bought for $20 each and aged between eleven days and four months; (B) Considering that when arrested José-Luis and Michel Rotman, who ran that house, declared that children never stayed more than a fortnight in that center and that they were sold for $75,000 to American or Israeli families whose children needed an organ transplant; . . . (D) Considering that in March 1987 a "fattening house" was closed down in Ciudad Guatemala and that its records mentioned that 170 children had been sold abroad between October 1 1985 and March 31 1986, the majority having been sent to the United States for the removal of their organs; . . . 3. Calls upon

the governments concerned to immediately adopt administrative and legal measures to prevent all forms of traffic in, and violence towards, children.[5]

Nongovernment organizations for human rights were very naturally concerned about these accusations, but the majority remained cautious. In this first phase one can see the outline of attitudes which will be found again, without much change, eight years later in 1995. Some organizations stress that there are no proofs, but that one cannot rule out the possibility that the accusations are based on facts; it is common, however, for their statements in carefully measured terms to be distorted by the press. This happened to Defence for Children International (DCI), which was quoted in a distorted way by *Izvestia* in an article which stated emphatically: "There is only one step from America's arrogance and its racist contempt for the Latin-American peoples to complete cannibalistic licence."[6] DCI then came under insistent pressure from America aimed at obtaining a formal denial of the statements attributed to it, and produced this in its newsletter for January 1988.[7] Although in this case the distortion came from a propagandist paper, distortions by sensationalist papers in search of striking headlines were to prove far more frequent.

Other organizations, notably the International Association of Democratic Lawyers (IADL), were convinced, and loudly proclaimed that all these horrors were real. Nevertheless, the United Nations Human Rights Commission in Geneva did not accept the accusations presented to it as early as 1988 by Renée Bridel, an observer from IADL. These organizations were accused of being instruments of Soviet propaganda, but their conviction and their actions survived the disappearance of the USSR. And though there was only a small nucleus of convinced organizations in 1988, they would be far more numerous in 1995.

All through 1988, numerous American institutions[8] were denying accusations of a trade in baby parts based on murder, pseudo adoptions, and the complicity of medical personnel and administrators. These denials were obviously the result of vigorous propaganda activity by the US Information Agency, which considered that the Russian KGB had played a decisive role in exploiting, if not actually creating, the story. In a report to the House of Representatives in July 1988, the USIA gave much space to the Baby Parts Story among the anti-American stories launched or supported by the

Soviets. The KGB replied to accusations on this point by a letter of protest from the deputy health minister, Alexander Baranov, to the president of the Foreign Affairs Commission of Congress; three years later this pediatrician explained to a journalist of the *Nouvel Observateur* that he merely signed this document, which had been drawn up by the KGB.[9]

The resolution passed by the European Parliament in September 1988 was obviously a blow to the Americans, but during September and October 1988 other non-American sources did reject the baby parts accusations. The first to do so was the International Federation for Human Rights (IFHR), a French human rights organization, which published a report from two lawyers after an inquiry in Guatemala. The report concluded that there existed a substantial trade in children in the country, or the region, giving rise to numerous illegal adoptions based on kidnapping or purchase, but that no proof of a trade in organs had been found.[10]

Next, the international press publicized the letter sent by Richard Schiffer, joint secretary of state of the United States, to Karel de Gutch, chairman of the European Parliament's Committee on Human Rights, protesting against Danielle de March's motion. The first article was American, but it was followed by important articles in the quality papers of Europe, completely discrediting the story.[11] An article in *Le Monde* brought two letters in reply. One from Joe Nordmann defended the IADL, whose president he was at the time. This star Communist barrister had represented *Les Lettres françaises* in 1951 in their lawsuit with Viktor Kravchenko; he had been very harsh towards the witnesses from the Gulag cited by Kravchenko, and had asserted (without convincing the judges) that there were no concentration camps in the Soviet Union. His protest was printed on November 1, with a comment from the editor of *Le Monde* stressing the absence of any proof of traffic in baby organs. Danielle de March's defense was published on November 24, and the editorial commentary emphasized how misleading was the way she confused child trafficking and organ trafficking: "Organ trafficking would be akin to assassination, whereas child trafficking generally sustains adoption networks, a practice one may disagree with, but which even so is in a very different category."[12]

In June 1989 the American administration sent a detailed and fully argued letter to the European Parliament, and allegations about pseudo adoptions hardly figured again in the media until 1992. Yet accusatory rumors were still developing, though it was the related tale of the eye thieves which was dominant in Latin America, while in our own regions the stories of the Kidney Heist appeared and developed.

1992–1996

After a comparative respite of two years, from 1992 onward allegations about pseudo adoptions in Latin America were once again repeated in the media. They were strengthened by the tension surrounding the topic of adoption in many East European countries, where the collapse of the Iron Curtain led to a sharp increase in the international demand for children to adopt, and gave rise to child trafficking. Romania and Albania in particular, which contained numerous abandoned children living in orphanages where conditions were very harsh, were besieged by people wanting to adopt, after their political regimes were liberalized. There were very widespread suspicions that adoptions were being criminally abused for the benefit of pimps, perverts, or organ traffickers. Such suspicions against foreigners were often expressed publicly by the authorities in these countries, and even though they generally mentioned the original allegations merely as hypotheses, the stories were always presented as certainties in the media.

Reports of any arrests of agents organizing illegal adoptions became distorted when given in the European press. In Brazil, where it seems that networks of illegal adoption are constantly being "dismantled," one after another, old accusations against Italy were repeated more and more strongly. A good example of how such pseudofacts are created is the old affair of the three thousand "disappearing" children, which was denied as soon as it appeared in 1990 but was still circulating vigorously in 1995. These elaborations are typical of the way in which the media and the authorities interact over accusations of the baby parts type.

THREE THOUSAND BRAZILIAN CHILDREN "DISAPPEAR"

In 1990, two Italian judges had been conducting an inquiry in Brazil into an illegal adoption network run by a former priest, Lucca di Nuzzo, operating in Salvador de Bahia, which had sent some two thousand children to Italy; on returning to Rome, they informed the press of their suspicions. Were all these children really living with adoptive families, or had they been used for the organ trade? While admitting that "they found nothing to make one suspect that children had been sold for organ transplants by any Italian couples," they asserted that their suspicions were justified by "the fact that the home region of most couples who have adopted children from Bahia is the Campagnia" (the four Italians arrested as agents of the network also came from there), because that region is dominated by the criminal organization called the camorra, which "goes in for all kinds of lucrative activities."[13] The Italian press confined itself to expressing suspicions, but the popular British press (picking up the information next day, very probably from Brazilian sources) gave a figure of three thousand children sent to Italy by this network, asserting that there had been numerous disappearances and that these Brazilian children, after passing through Italy, certainly ended up by being welcomed into secret clinics in Thailand and Mexico.[14] In 1991 Paul Barruel, professor of theology at São Paulo and member of a commission of inquiry investigating this adoption network, repeated these accusations. He talked of four thousand passports supplied for children sent to Italy by the network between 1984 and 1990, but stated that the Italian authorities declared that they had only registered the entry of one thousand Brazilian children; three thousand must therefore be missing. He accused the camorra of having used those who had disappeared.[15]

These statements of 1990 and 1991 reappeared in the accusatory article printed in August 1992 in *Le Monde Diplomatique*. Now, that article served as a source for the report of the European Parliament in September 1993. Having thus gained a foothold in institutions, the hypothesis which had been reported in the popular press and the allegations of the theologian Barruel became transformed into realities. However, in December 1994 Todd Leventhal (information officer for the USIA) established that the Italian government had carried out researches in 1990 at the request of the American embassy. The number of children of Brazilian origin entering Italy during the period 1986–89 had been recorded at that time by the Italian authorities. There were 2,869 of them (507 in 1986, 626 in 1987, 786 in 1988, 950 in 1989). Leventhal thinks it reasonable to estimate the adoptions in 1984–85 at 300, and those for 1990 at 1,000. This brings the figure to more than 4,000 (2,869 + 1,300 = 4,169), and the mystery of the 3,000 disappearing children vanishes away.[16]

In 1994 in Guatemala accusations about baby parts, which had never ceased circulating since the media reports at the beginning of 1987, led to several hostile actions against foreigners. However, by that time the allegations against these foreigners were more often about kidnapping than about pseudo adoptions, so these dramatic events will be considered below, alongside the accusations about the theft of eyes.

As soon as they appeared, allegations about baby parts and about the abuse of international adoptions for criminal purposes were taken up in popular fiction.

By the time they reached the media, allegations about baby parts had been taken up by authority figures, and became elaborations upon popular narratives. To find "raw" popular narratives we must turn to the rumors about eye thieves, a parallel and counterpart to those about pseudo adoptions and the Baby Parts Story.

KIDNAPPINGS AND MUTILATIONS; EYE THIEVES

Narratives about eye thieves appeared in the mid-1980s in the Andean regions of Latin America, and also in Central America and Brazil. They are stereotyped accounts of kidnapping followed by mutilation. Unlike the old anecdotes about the white slave trade, they rarely involve miraculous rescues, but tell how the kidnapped child tragically reappears mutilated, scarred, blind, or with only one kidney; in his pocket is found a large bundle of American banknotes (or some petty sum in loose change), together with a grimly ironic note, "Thanks for your eyes" (or "your kidney"). These are indeed ghastly tales! Sometimes there is, as well as the tragic return of the child, a scene showing the odious kidnappers themselves. They are foreigners, dressed in black leather and armed with machine guns, who emerge aggressively from big, black, gleaming cars, or from red ambulances.

A few short paragraphs in the press reported briefly on these anguished narratives. There was one in Colombia in mid-1987, before the Baby Parts Story began to spread: "A group of children playing football in the street in a poor quarter of Medellín was interrupted by the arrival of a gleaming Cadillac. Two people got out and carried off one of the children. The child came home a few days later with a dressing and a bandage over one eye;

doctors said that a skilful surgeon had removed one of his corneas."[17] The presence of these narratives in Argentina was noted in August 1988 and again at the end of 1991. In August 1988 an article presented a study by a group of psychologists, the *Causas y Consecuencias de la Asociacion Psiconalitica Argentina*, proposing an interpretation of the eye thieves story as a "modern myth" (a term proposed by Marie Bonaparte in the 1940s). They considered that this myth was a response to the real "disappearances" which had occurred during the period of state terrorism which Argentina had recently endured, the history of which could not yet be written.[18]

Two sensationalist articles by Maria-Laura Avignolo were published almost simultaneously in England and France at the end of 1991. They begin by telling a sad tale of kidney theft:

> Oscar has dark hair and a sad smile. He had wanted to become a footballer, but that was not to be; a year ago, when he was 11, he was snatched from the street, bundled into a car, and whisked off to a private clinic where he was anaesthetised.
>
> He was dropped off at his home in a shanty town outside Buenos Aires six weeks later with $400 (£220) in his pocket. Then he showed his mother the scar, telling her he did not feel well. It was discovered after medical checks that one of Oscar's kidneys had been removed. He had become a victim of a growing scourge in Argentina: the human-organ traffickers.
>
> Such was his mother's fear that she hesitated to tell the authorities. "The same people from this town might be the ones who are handing children over to the traffickers," she said.
>
> The demand for human kidneys for transplants is so great that the traffickers can sell them for up to $45,000 each. Some organs are said to go to the United States and Europe, others to Brazil. Some are bought locally in Argentina; only 10% of demand for kidney transplants can be met by the official transplant center. . . .
>
> Tales of lunatics and beggars being killed for their organs are legion, but hard to verify.

The French version of the article, but not the English, includes the following sentences:

> For two years there has been talk in Argentina about children being kidnapped and later recovered bearing a scar and minus one kidney. But this may be a

case of collective fantasy, a gigantic rumor which is circulating in most South American countries. The lack of authenticated evidence leads one to think this is so.[19]

The article also mentions voluntary sales of organs, which are illegal and scandalous but do happen, and quotes Health Minister Julio Cesar Araoz, who asserts that there is indeed a trade in organs and in children, and alludes to a conflict involving the parents of a young woman who died in the operating theater and whose organs had been removed (they had filed a lawsuit against the hospital). He concluded by announcing that he himself, his family, and all cabinet members would publicly donate their bodies, in order to launch an educational campaign promoting organ donation.

This article is typical in the way it juxtaposes material of very different kinds. Thus, it contains the transcription of an oral narrative which is very moving but for which evidence is very flimsy; some apparently better based facts about offers of voluntary sale of organs, but no firmly based indications as to whether these offers became a reality; some worrying paragraphs on child abductions and the illegal removal of donor organs in hospitals; and, in conclusion, some paragraphs that stress the implausibility of the other "facts" presented, and give "balance" to the article. The journalist has built up the whole thing into a single sequence of ideas, which, however, does not stand up to analysis.

In Mexico, official inquiries were set up in 1990 and 1992, in view of persistent rumors about children being kidnapped and their organs stolen. Their conclusions were that child trafficking was very real, but that it was directed towards illegal adoption or prostitution, not secret organ transplants.

Of the episodes described next, those from Brazil and Peru have been the subject of in-depth studies, while those from Guatemala had dramatic consequences.

BRAZIL

We know of the rumors about the theft of children's organs which arose in the northeast of Brazil in the mid-1980s from the work of the American anthropologist Nancy Scheper-Hughes, who visited the region several times from 1982 to 1989, to do fieldwork there. These are versions of the eye thieves story which are even worse than the norm, for here there is no mention of the child being found again, mutilated but alive; only corpses of children or young adults reappear after these kidnappings. Scheper-Hughes writes:

> I am referring to a rumor which first surfaced on the Alto de Cruziero (and throughout the interior of the state) in the mid-1980s, and that has been circulating there ever since. It concerns the abduction and mutilation of young and healthy shantytown residents (especially children), who are eyed greedily for their body parts, especially eyes, heart, lungs and liver. It was said that the teaching hospitals of Recife and the large medical centers throughout Brazil were engaged in an active traffic in body parts, a traffic with international dimensions.
>
> Shantytown residents reported multiple sightings of large blue or yellow vans, driven by foreign agents (usually North American or Japanese), who were said to patrol poor neighbourhoods, looking for small stray children, whom the drivers mistakenly believed no one in the overpopulated slums and shantytowns would ever miss. The children would be nabbed and shoved into the trunks of the vans. Some were murdered and mutilated for their organs, and their discarded bodies were found by the side of the road, or were tossed outside the walls of municipal cemeteries. Others were taken and sold indirectly to hospitals and major medical centers, and the remains of their eviscerated bodies were said to turn up in hospital dumpsters.
>
> "They are looking for 'donor organs,'" my intelligent research assistant, Little Irene, said. "You may think that this is nonsense, but we have seen things with our own eyes in the hospitals and in the public morgues, and we know better."[20]

Scheper-Hughes notes that newspapers in Pernambuco denied these rumors circulating among the poorer population, often in mocking tones. These denials, however, simply reinforced the rumors and indeed even acted as confirmation (as often happens): "Yes, it's true, they are reporting it in Recife," one of her informants told her, adding, "Now what will become of us and our poor children?" and bursting into tears.[21]

The vivid description by Scheper-Hughes is based on good knowledge of the people among whom these rumors were circulating; she had spent the equivalent of fourteen months living in the region, spread over twenty-five years. She conveys the climate of anxiety generated by these horrific narratives:

> The stories had reached such proportions that my attempts one morning to save little Mercea, Biu's perpetually sick and fussy three-year-old, backfired when I attempted to get her into the back seat of a taxi, even as she was carried in the arms of Xoxa, her older sister. As soon as I gave the order "To the hospital, and quick!" the already terrified little toddler, in the midst of a severe respiratory crisis, began to choke, scream, and go rigid. "Does she think I'm Papa-Figo [the Brazilian bogeyman]?" the annoyed cab driver asked. No amount of coaxing could convince Mercea that her tormented little body was not going to be sold to the ghoulish doctors. Biu had instructed her little girl well: "Don't let *anyone* take you outside the house."
>
> Even more children than usual were kept out of school during this period, and others were sent away to live with distant kin in the *mata*. Meanwhile, small children, like Mercea, who were left at home while their mothers were at work in the cane fields or in the houses of the wealthy, found themselves virtual prisoners, locked into small, dark huts with even the wooden shutters securely fastened. On several occasions I had to comfort a sobbing child who, through a crack in a door or shutter, would beg me to liberate her from her dark and lonely cell.[22]

However, Scheper-Hughes shows equally clearly that these rumors aroused much argument, and that there was no lack of skeptics within the poor communities themselves.

> "Bah, these are stories invented by the poor and illiterate," countered my friend Casorte, the new Socialist manager of the municipal cemetery of Bom Jesus, in August 1989. "I have been working here for over a year," he said. "I arrive at six in the morning and I leave at seven at night. Never have I seen anything. Where are the bodies, or even any traces of blood left behind?"[23]

PERU

Late in 1988, for about ten days at the end of November and the beginning of December, the whole of Lima, the capital of Peru, was filled with rumors about eye thieves. Groups of foreign-looking men, dressed as doctors but armed with machine guns, were said to be roaming the poor districts by car. They would force children to get in, take their eyes, and then let them go again, with their faces hooded and bandaged, and an envelope containing money and a thank-you letter in their pockets.

The rumor started in the district of El Salvador, where people confidently stated that four foreigners, two white and two Negro (not Amerindians, therefore) had attacked a school. The same day (November 30) it spread to all working-class districts in Lima. Towards 10:00 a.m. hundreds of parents invaded the schools to fetch their children away from the danger. The children, terrified and crying, went with them, without really understanding why.

The eyes were supposed to be being sold abroad to pay off the international debt that was crippling Peru at that time—a time when many unpopular austerity measures were also afflicting the population.

A few years later, the novelist Mario Vargas Llosa was to describe these panics, which his hero, the police officer Lituma, takes to be a worrying symptom:

> "There's something bad going on in this country, Tomasito . . . How is it possible for a whole district of Lima to swallow such falsehoods? Gringos in luxury limos kidnapping five-year-old kids to tear their eyes out with high-tech gadgets! If some crazy women spread such talk, well and good—Lima too must have its Doña Arianas. But for a whole district to believe it, for the people living there to fetch their children home from school and go rushing off looking for foreigners to lynch, well, don't you find that incredible?"[24]

As no concrete evidence appeared—no corpses, no mutilated children— the media and the public authorities worked hard to deny the stories, and issued numerous statements. But this truth, coming from a remote official source, was worth very little in comparison with the confident assertions of one's own neighbors, and it only aroused skepticism, for the poor know their government, and are aware that it often lies:

> Far from quieting the population, the skeptical or ironic articles appearing in the press and the solemn denial made by the Health Minister on television only increased the feelings of terror. How much credibility can one give to a Minister's assurances, when set against the testimony of a horrified neighbour?[25]

At that time, the Marxist guerrilla organization called the Shining Path was in the ascendant. As early as September 1987 in Ayacucho, a town where the Shining Path had deep roots, there had been rumors that there were cut-throats about, sent by the government to strip the fat from Amerindians' bodies and sell it abroad to pay off the debt. These 1987 cutthroats resembled the traditional vampire figure of the *pishtaco* more closely than the eye thieves of 1988 did, because what they took was the fat, not organs, and because they did not specifically target children. But, like the eye thieves, they were work-ing for export abroad, which is a modern trait of the *pishtaco*.

There was an immediate reaction to these frightening rumors. At Lima, two lynchings were only narrowly avoided in the Cantogrande district. One incident involved three young French tourists visiting that district; a crowd besieged the police station to which they had been taken for their own safety, yelling for their deaths. The other involved researchers from a nutritional studies institute who were studying diarrhea in children, and who were saved in the nick of time after being denounced as eye thieves. The previous year, the rumors at Ayacucho had also led to some trouble; vigilantes had formed street patrols, and a young shopkeeper had also been lynched.

Peruvian researchers analyzing the case of Lima[26] were chiefly concerned to note characteristics specific to that country which could account for the emergence of the eye thieves rumor: the strong influence of a population still very Amerindian in culture, mass poverty, a population caught up as hostages in the savage conflict between the army and the Shining Path guerrillas, a renewal and adaptation of such traditional Peruvian motifs as the *nakaq* and the *pishtaco*. What must make us pause, however, is that this outburst of eye thieves rumors will be found again in countries with very different character-istics: Colombia and Guatemala, but also Brazil, Mexico, and Argentina.

GUATEMALA: LYNCHINGS IN 1994

At the end of December 1993, classic eye thieves narratives were circulating in Guatemala City, the capital of the country. John Shonder, an American work-ing in that country, tells the stories, and explains why he did not believe them:

> I first heard the story from my secretary in December of 1993 in Guatemala City. She assured me that the body of a young child had been found at the side

of a road with its chest cut open and its heart and other organs missing. A note which said "Thanks for the organs" (in English of course) had been left in the chest cavity. In the next few weeks, the bodies seemed to multiply. Some people claimed that five had been found, some said seven. Other versions of the story replaced the note with U.S. currency, in amounts ranging from a few dollars to one hundred. Both the note and the money were sometimes said to have been found in the children's pants pockets instead of the chest. A completely different story concerned a street urchin found wandering around blind and dazed in Zone 1. When he was finally taken to the hospital, doctors determined that his corneas had been removed. This child's pockets had also been stuffed with American money. . . .

These stories were so grotesque—and so unbelievable—that I immediately took them to be urban legends. I also reasoned that if the bodies really existed, lurid photographs would be splashed across the front page of every newspaper in the city, in full colour. There is no press censorship in Guatemala, nor do the media subscribe to the same standards of taste (or self-censorship) which Americans are used to in their publications. The body of a child with its chest cut open would be no worse than photographs of accident victims and exhumed corpses which are published daily in *Prensa Libre, Siglo 21, El Grafico,* and other local papers. Of course no such pictures were ever printed, yet almost every Guatemalan I talked to had heard some version of the story, and believed it to be true.[27]

Graffiti saying *Gringos robachicos* (gringo child-stealers) appeared in the city. The rumors spread to other localities, and there were violent incidents in March 1994. First, on March 7, which was market day at the village of Santa Lucía Cotzumalguapa in the south of the country, an American tourist called Melissa Larson (aged twenty-seven, a fashion writer from New Mexico) was arrested in order to protect her from a crowd who were about to maltreat her, she having been accused of stealing children. She was transferred to a larger town, and next day a furious mob burnt down the police station and destroyed ten vehicles, in spite of the presence of five hundred antiriot police, since it was being said that she had been set free after paying a bribe of thirty-six thousand dollars. The army arrived to restore order, and some fifty wounded were counted. Melissa Larson remained in prison for nineteen days, and then was released and expelled from the country.

This incident became an important piece of information, whose treatment in the Guatemalan media tended towards sensationalism and reinforced the rumors, as John Shonder recounts:

Prensa Libre published a chart listing various organs and body parts along with their supposed prices on the black market. One of the television stations produced a particularly irresponsible "investigative report" on the issue. The scene I recall most vividly was when the reporter went to an orphanage to investigate illegal adoptions. In a room filled with cribs and crying babies, he picked up one squirming child by the legs and asked the social worker, "How much are this one's eyes worth? His liver? His kidneys?" This program seemed to do a lot to revive the rumor. It reinforced people's beliefs, and many cited it as "proof" that babies were indeed being kidnapped and killed for their organs. But in fact, no proof was ever presented, either by this program or by anyone else.[28]

Ten days later, the Swiss vulcanologist Thierry Stéphane was slightly injured; a crowd accused him and the team with whom he was working on the volcano Acatenongo, in the province of Chimaltenango, of being involved in child kidnappings.

Then, on March 29, came the most serious incident. June Weinstock (aged fifty-two, a journalist from Alaska) was taking photos of children in the market of San Cristóbal Verapaz (a town in the north of the country), and patted a small child's head. Suddenly a peasant woman screamed that her son had disappeared; a crowd gathered, and began beating the foreigner. The missing child reappeared, and the mother tried to stop the lynching, but in vain. Stripped naked, stoned, and beaten, June Weinstock was saved from death by the police who took her to hospital in a coma. She was sent home to Alaska by plane, but by the end of 1996 she still had not regained consciousness. The assault on her was filmed by an amateur and shown on Guatemalan TV, and later in the United States.

John Shonder writes of the reactions of the local authorities and of Americans to this dramatic incident:

Doctors appeared on television to explain the complicated procedures required to preserve organs for transplant, and that it was impossible for tourists to carry hearts and livers back to the United States in their luggage as some of the wilder rumors had claimed. . . .

Local newspapers then began to print editorials blaming the attacks and the rumors themselves on various groups. Some speculated that the armed forces were attempting to destabilise the country in order to overthrow the president, or that they were trying to scare away foreigners in order to resume covert military operations in the highlands. Other columnists blamed the guerrillas, who were already carrying out a campaign to cripple the country's economy. As the fastest growing industry in the country, tourism seemed a logical target.

In Santa Lucia and San Cristobal, where the violence had occurred, residents pointed the finger at a traditional target: the indigenous population. While these are for the most part ladino towns (meaning non-Indian), it was pointed out that both incidents took place on market days, when large numbers of Indians arrive from the interior to sell produce and crafts.[29]

The United States recalled the two hundred Peace Corps volunteers working in the country to the capital, and warned tourists to avoid Guatemala. However, the rumors continued.

John Shonder makes some interesting comments on one secondary cause of these violent events, namely the shocking attitudes of many American tourists, who seem to regard Indians as specimens in a zoo:

One of the few Guatemalans I met who did not believe the rumors had this theory: he said the country was paying the price for promoting its indigenous people as tourist attractions. . . . There is some truth in this. . . . Many times I have seen tourists in small villages giving candy to children, patting them on the head, and filming them with video cameras. During an Easter procession in Antigua, at the height of the baby-stealing paranoia, I watched a middle-aged American woman coo at a little indigenous boy, chuck him on the chin, and rub his hair. The child's mother was clearly uneasy, and dragged him away by the hand.

There's no getting round the fact that these children are very cute, especially when dressed in colourful indigenous clothing. But I have children of my own, and I would feel very uneasy if a stranger were to touch them or photograph them. Most people have sense enough not to do things like this in their own country. I don't think many would consider going to an Indian Reservation in the U.S. to photograph Native American children there. We recognize that this would be patronizing, as well as an invasion of privacy. Unfortunately, some tourists who come to Guatemala seem to leave their cultural sensitivity at home.[30]

CLOWNS AS KIDNAPPERS

In those years, new types of kidnappers appeared—no longer foreigners, but clowns. In Guatemala, after the violent incidents in March 1994, it was claimed that a man disguised as a clown had attacked a car, and soon bands of clowns were added to the list of suspects. Victor Lopez, president of the association of professional clowns in that country, explained to the press that he was reluctant to travel by car if he was wearing his costume or makeup.[31]

In April 1995 rumors about eye thieves swept through the impoverished suburb of Carapicuiba, near São Paulo in Brazil. For two months the police investigated alarmingly detailed statements: a trio of evildoers are enticing children into a Volkswagen car, killing them, and throwing their mutilated bodies onto the public highway. One of the trio is a woman dressed as a dancer, sometimes described as a blonde and scantily clad, and the other two are masked men dressed as clowns. None of these statements was confirmed, and the police dropped their inquiries.[32]

Lastly, in November 1995, a third episode involving clown kidnappers was reported from Honduras, another small country in Central America near Guatemala. The short article in an English newspaper describing this affair claimed that ten very young children really had been carried off by a clown who used to amuse children by his funny gestures, before seizing them and making off with them in a big black van. It said that more than sixty clowns had gathered in the capital to protest against these deeds, and had publicly burned their costumes.[33]

There is no doubt that we should consider the influence of mass popular culture as a major reason for the appearance of this new figure, for there the malevolent clown plays a great part, fitting excellently into the distorted world of the horror comic, often as a climax of horror. Over the past decade, clown kidnappers have been mentioned sporadically during panics in Britain and America. Evil clowns feature in works of fiction, while the same paradox can make a real-life criminal famous. Thus, the notoriety of John Gacy, the serial killer of adolescents operating near Chicago in the 1960s, is largely due to the disturbing photo that shows him in clown makeup at a children's party he had organized in his hometown.

In this survey of Latin American allegations about pseudo adoptions, abductions, and mutilations for organ thefts, priority has been given to setting out the narratives. However, it was impossible to limit discussion to narratives alone, for the elaborations and the actions to which they give rise must be taken into account. This shows the artificiality of separating narratives from behavior, useful though such separation may be for analysis.

VICTIMS IN RICH COUNTRIES; THE KIDNEY HEIST

THE RASH TRAVELLER

At the beginning of 1990, the story of the stolen kidney (Kidney Heist) appeared. This tells how a westerner passing through some distant country, either as a tourist travelling with his wife or a businessmen with his colleagues, is found wandering about, or lying in a hotel room, some time after becoming separated from his companion(s); he had left his wife while she went shopping or visited a museum, or had left his colleagues—often because he was following some attractive woman he had met in a bar. He does not know what has happened to him, is feeling distinctly unwell, and the wife or colleagues who rescue him arrange for a medical examination, generally after bringing him back to his own country. The doctors' diagnosis is unhesitating: he has had a kidney removed—and it is often added that the scar is remarkably neat.

The story, first collected by a clergyman during a conference in Brazil and published in a Danish paper in February 1990,[34] appeared that summer in Germany, where it aroused strong emotions. The misadventure was supposed to have happened to a couple from Bremen who were holidaying in Istanbul (the husband lost his way in the bazaar and was found a few days later on the beach), and the whole region was deeply upset by it. However, a Turkish journalist conducted an investigation in his own country after a German scandal sheet, *Bild der Frau*, told its readers this sad story of "Louise and Walter." On September 10 he reported to his readers that no complaint had ever been made to the police, or to the German consulate at Istanbul. Soon other variants appeared, pointing to other countries as dangerous (South American ones, Romania, Bulgaria), and some authorities took the affair seriously; for instance, an association of blood donors advised tourists going abroad not to take their donor cards with them, so as to make the work of the kidney thieves more difficult.[35] That summer, the story was also found in Australia; it was supposed to have happened in Los Angeles, a frequent holiday destination for Australians.[36]

This first scenario about the far-off country has remained in circulation up to the present (1997), sometimes with ingenious variants such as one told to Bengt af Klintberg on October 21, 1992, at Lerum in Sweden, by Marie Olofsson, a twenty-year-old engineering student who had got the story from a friend:

> A couple went on holiday to Brazil. While they were sunbathing on the beach a little boy came up to them and asked them to sign a petition to save the rain forest. They signed. Some time later they went to a bar near the beach for a drink. They both lost consciousness, and woke up lying on an operating table. In fact, the paper they had signed had nothing to do with tropical forests. It was an agreement that they were willing to donate their organs for transplant.[37]

This totally implausible narrative refers chiefly to the anxieties felt by tourists in a strange land, and the dangers which the good principles of the Swedes may lead them into (concern over the damage to tropical forests is very strong in northern Europe).

Just as ingenious is a gentler medical version set in India, which does not involve kidnapping but a fake operation. The story was told to a journalist, in the course of a simple appendicitis operation, by a hospital intern who had heard it on holiday in Goa. It concerns a young English tourist, travelling alone, who arranges to be admitted to a private clinic in Delhi for emergency treatment when she is suffering from an infection. There, it is diagnosed as acute appendicitis, and an immediate operation is needed to avoid peritonitis. She agrees, is well looked after, and goes back to England a week later. But when she stops the antibiotics, the pain returns, and she goes back into hospital. There they operate again, promising to follow exactly the course of her first scar (which is rather large), because the surgeon, who is from Sri Lanka, thinks that there may be some faulty scarring of the intestine after the first operation. She is then told that she had never had her appendix removed, but that a kidney is gone. The journalist telling the anecdote, who is a doctor contributing a "problems page" in a weekly paper, presents it as "perhaps apocryphal, but ringing horribly true."[38]

The same performance context, namely the passing of a narrative from one surgeon to another, is found in 1994 when the anecdote of the stolen kidney is transcribed in a comic.[39] But here the story told is set in New York. From the start of 1991, Americans began setting the Kidney Heist Story in their own crisis-ridden metropolis, perceived as a cosmopolitan and dangerous city. The narratives concern a group of men from some provincial capital (Washington, D.C., Chicago), travelling on business or having a spree. In March 1991 Jan Brunvand, the author of several books on urban legends (a term he invented in his first book, in 1981),[40] received two letters and a phone call from correspondents alerting him to this story:

> The first reached me in a letter dated March 8 from Felicia Strobhert of Stone Mountain, Georgia. She had heard it the previous day from a friend from Ohio, who had got it from a relative in Virginia.
>
> A few days later, on March 11, I received another version, told by Dan Werner from Manassas, Virginia, who had heard it that very day. Werner had heard tell that four business colleagues from Washington DC—three women and one man—used to go regularly to spend Thursday and Friday in New York on business. Sometimes they would stay on till Saturday to see a show, only going home to Washington on the Sunday. During one of these long weekends, the man stayed late in a bar on the Friday night, while the women went off on their own. They were a bit worried to hear nothing more from him, but on the Sunday morning he rang them at their hotel. "Please come and help me," he begged, and gave them an address. They rushed there in a taxi and found the man leaning against the wall of an apartment block, still wearing the same clothes as when they had last seen him on the Friday. He was sweating, and seemed dazed. They got him to hospital, where it was discovered that he had been given morphine, that he had 110 stitches in his abdomen, and was missing a kidney. According to the doctors, the operation "had been carried out by an expert."
>
> Two weeks later, on March 27, Joe Baldwin of Weymouth, Massachusetts, rang me. He had just heard the story from a colleague, and very much wanted to know if I knew it.[41]

At the beginning of 1991, the TV series *Law and Order* presented a fictional episode about a kidney theft in New York, with a very ingenious plot,[42] and press articles based on interviews with Brunvand identified the Kidney Heist Story as a new urban legend. Yet reports still arrived on Brunvand's desk: "I was still getting this story from people who hadn't seen the TV program, and had heard different details: the operation had been done at a dentist's, and the wound sewn up with dental floss; the incident had happened in New Jersey (or California); it was said that newly qualified surgeons were carrying out illegal kidney transplants to be able to pay off the bank loans they had taken out for their college fees."[43]

In Europe, the narratives were very soon set in neighboring countries, not distant ones. Thus, for northern Europe after 1992, it is mainly in Paris that the unfortunate tourist disappears, and doctors who later find him indicate that this is something that often happens there.

On May 22, 1992, the Dutch paper *Trouw* reported that pupils from the school Corderius d'Amersfoort, about to set off on a trip to Paris with their teachers, were anxious because it was said that a teacher had recently had a kidney removed in that city; the Dutch Embassy in Paris had to reassure them.

On June 6, 1992, when Peter Burger was appearing on television to talk about his book on contemporary legends which had just been published in the Netherlands, he met the PR officer of a hospital at Nimègue, who stated that he had several times replied to journalists who wanted to know if it was true that this hospital was treating patients who had fallen victim to the organ-stealing mafia of Paris. Burger then exposed the stolen kidney story as legend.

On July 14, 1992, *Brabant Nieuwsblad* reported that a bank director from Roosendaal in the Netherlands, visiting Paris with his wife for a few days, had allegedly been kidnapped from a bench near Notre-Dame, where he was sitting while his wife went shopping.

On September 30, 1994, the Danish paper *Horsens Folkblad* carried this report: a family from Horsens, visiting Paris after a camping holiday, left their sixteen-year-old son waiting on a bench while they went up the Eiffel Tower. By the time they got back he had disappeared, but next day they found him on the same bench, unconscious. The press attaché of the French Embassy in Denmark denied the story.

Other large foreign cities in nearby countries are indeed also involved, but it would be monotonous to list them, for this story spreads all over Europe.

CHILDREN, TOO

The tone changes once the Kidney Heist Story involves children. Once again, France is in the forefront, for the opening of the EuroDisney park supplied a focus for anxiety; as soon as it opened, narratives arose alleging that children disappeared there and were later recovered alive, but minus their kidneys. In July 1992 a group of children from Salzburg (Austria) cancelled their trip to EuroDisney (later named Disneyland) because of these stories.[44] Rolf Wilhelm Brednich, a specialist on contemporary legends, received a letter in September 1992 claiming that a child who disappeared at EuroDisney was later found again, lacking one kidney.[45]

Several press articles indicated allegations against EuroDisney.

Idag, August 8, 1992: two Swedish children have gone missing there; EuroDisney is concealing the affair; an editorial reports that the paper had received telephone calls on the subject two weeks after the theme park opened.

Nouveau Quotidien, March 3, 1993: several stories about children whose kidneys have been stolen; EuroDisney denies this, locating the rumor in Austria and Switzerland.

Leeunwarder Courant, June 21, 1994: two versions, concerning families from Friesia in the Netherlands; ironically, one family had won its stay at EuroDisney as a competition prize.

De Standaard, June 30, 1994: a twelve-year-old boy lost in the Paris metro, and a thirteen-year-old who disappeared at EuroDisney and was found in the Place de la Concorde six weeks later; irritated reactions from the PR staff of EuroDisney when rung by the journalist.

Privileging oral narration, I will quote in full a narrative collected in situ in Freiburg (Switzerland) by Jean-François Mayer on September 2, 1993:

Sitting round the family dining table, my father, my mother, and I, supper is drawing to an end and conversation touches on scattered subjects. A trip which one close relation is planning to take soon to EuroDisney is mentioned; so is a possible operation on someone in the family . . . Then my father joins in, saying he wants to tell us a story he'd heard that evening while shopping in the local supermarket. He was standing at the till when the store's loudspeakers broadcast an advertisement for trips to EuroDisney. Then the cashier turned to one of her colleagues to tell her about some people who had gone to EuroDisney and found that their child went missing while they were there. They went to the information desk of the park, where they were told there was no need to worry, they should just come back to the same spot in four days' time. So they came back four days later, and they did indeed find their child again, but he had had one kidney removed! And the cashier added: "And the same thing has just happened to some people I know, too!"

THE LOCALIZED NARRATIVE

In 1992, one begins to see rumors emerging which have little structure, are equally ready to speak of adults or of children, and mention classic sites for disappearances (car parks, supermarkets) as the settings for disappearances and recoveries caused by organ traffickers. In these narratives, only the site is indicated with precision. The circumstances of the abductions and the victims vary. Now there appears the theme of the van equipped as an operating theater, which fits in well with the idea that the victims reappear rapidly. These short-lived localized outbursts sometimes correspond to the feelings aroused by a real disappearance; however, they can also spring up without any particular circumstance to inspire them, or because of some quite trivial incident. This shows that the structure of belief is the major factor which accounts for such outbursts.

Républicain Lorrain, December 4, 1992: the site for the disappearances is a large car park at Moselle-Est; denials from the police and the local authority are noted.

Le Soir, January 26, 1994: this accuses Cora, a large store at La Louvière (Belgium), after the disappearance of a sixty-year-old woman; she was found drowned three weeks later.

Républicain Lorrain, May 4, 1995, and *Le Parisien*, May 6–7, 1995: there are rumors about disappearances and mutilations sited at the Auchan supermarket at Sémecourt (near Metz), with child victims; the subprefect issues a communiqué of denial, explaining the affair as a misunderstanding after an appeal was broadcast within the supermarket for a child who was missing for a few hours; the car park authorities complain.

Le Soir, May 10, 1995: this accuses a large car park, mentioning both adults and children as victims.

The rumors spreading through Belgium from the second half of 1995 onwards matched the anxieties aroused by the disappearance of two teenage girls and two little girls that summer. As we now know, the mystery of these disappearances was tragically solved in August 1996, when the criminal Marc Dutroux (who had already been found guilty of acts of violence against young girls some years previously) was arrested after two further abductions of little girls. His two latest victims were saved as a result of his arrest, but the remains of the four taken in 1995 were found buried in the garden of one of the many places where he had lived. The case eventually came to court, and Dutroux was sentenced in 2004 to jail for life.

Die Morgen on December 21, 1995, reported accusations from all over the west of Flanders (Belgium), accusing a gang of North African criminals based in northern France of carrying out operations on children kidnapped from crèches, schools, and large stores in a secret hospital at Auchan (the large store being confused with a locality). The victims were said to be returned to their parents, but minus one kidney.

The French-language TV channel in Belgium (RTBF) devoted a thirty-minute program to this outbreak of rumors on January 31, 1996, in their series *In the Name of the Law*, under the title "Smoke but No Fire." This report showed that the anxieties of parents and teachers centered upon phantom photographers who, it was alleged, were working in the region of Charleroi (Belgium) as pupils left school at the end of the day. The police, having been many times informed of this, carried out a thorough and serious investigation, without finding anything definite. These narratives often featured a green or white Mercedes registered in France, supposedly prowling along the children's regular routes. In the course of transmission, some police officers referred to there being many real disappearances of little girls, and to the justifiable anxiety which these unsolved mysteries aroused in the public.

This broadcast led one reporter to change his mind over the reality of organ thefts. This man, a correspondent on the Belgium TV magazine *Télémoustique*, had come to interview me in 1992, and at that time had not been convinced by my approach to stories about the theft of children's organs. But after the broadcast of January 31, 1996, he announced that he had modified his opinion:

> A few years ago, when I met Véronique Campion-Vincent in Paris, I did not believe what she was telling me. Even though this distinguished ethnologist carried every guarantee of credibility, I ended up telling myself she must surely be an agent of American influence! The explanation was that during the previous months I had accumulated a considerable dossier of reports on the organ trade, on the tragedy of those South American children cut up by sinister traffickers. And here was this Campion-Vincent assuring me that this was not credible, that these testimonies which the press had published in a burst of righteous indignation had not been tested. . . . I did publish her evidence, but played it down; really, I found what she was saying was outrageous! There were so many stories, all agreeing. . . . Well, I, like so many others, had let myself be taken in by a rumor![46]

In these localized versions of the Kidney Heist Story one can find some which take up again features of the classic stories about the white slave trade, claiming that organized groups of kidnappers operate in the heart of the city.

GERMANY AND ITALY

German-speaking countries proved particularly vulnerable to these narratives. Bengt af Klintberg, the author of books on contemporary legends in Sweden and Germany, has noted that almost all the letters he received reporting Kidney Heist narratives came from Germany, and it was in Germany that the story of the tourist couple in Istanbul appeared in the summer of 1990. Countries bordering on the Germanic region figure prominently in the corpus of texts collected, while in France the few narratives recorded come from regions near the border with German-speaking areas. Nevertheless, in 1995 we began hearing stories in the region of Paris which were aimed against EuroDisney.

As for Italy, this country proved even more vulnerable than German-speaking ones to stories about children kidnapped for their organs, but the

Italian narratives differ from those in the rest of Europe, which is why I present them separately. At first, even as early as the summer of 1990, Italy was accused by its neighbors of being a place where children disappear:

At the end of August 1990, as people were returning from holidays on the Adriatic beaches, the Austrian dailies (especially those in Carinthia) began getting dozens of phone calls asking why they were saying nothing about what had been going on in Italy as regards the trade in human organs. . . . The *Kaertner Tageszeitung*, the main daily in the region, sent a reporter to investigate. This man told a story about a little girl from Villach who, during a holiday at Lignano, had been found without a kidney. Many people explained to him that this happened to a thirteen-year-old child; they described the mother's despair, the exact position of the scar, the way the girl's face was swollen because of the anesthetics. They maintained that a letter had been found in her pocket, threatening her parents if they said anything. But nobody could tell him the girl's name, nobody knew any relatives of hers, and everyone had heard the facts from some third party. The police had heard tell of these rumors, but could not identify the child.

The journalist also heard tell of the attempted kidnapping of a little Austrian girl at Livigno, but this time he did track down the child and her parents, at Klagenfurt. One afternoon in late August, two women caught hold of the child in a playground, and began walking away with her. They had black hair, and seemed to come from some Mediterranean region. The desperate mother ran after them, screaming. The two women dropped their prey, and disappeared. Apparently the parents had received threats after returning to Austria. After publishing the story, the journalist too received threats by telephone, and, having discovered nothing, dropped his investigation.

These articles about the "organ mafia" and the real or presumed events at Livigno and at other centers on the Adriatic coast were taken up by many newspapers in Austria, Germany, and Slovenia. Reports about them crossed the Alps and reached Italy. Here in our country, they were interpreted as a fresh episode in the war waged against us to take away our summer tourists. Italian papers struck back, accusing the Austrians of unprofessional behaviour in publishing unverified information based simply on rumor and hearsay.

The mayor of Livigno and other civic authorities wrote vigorous notes of protest, and many daily papers sent their correspondents to Klagenfurt and

Trebnje, in order to teach their Austrian colleagues how proper journalists work, and how a serious investigation is done. Annoyed by this invasion, some Trebnje Gypsies, brandishing cudgels, chased a car full of Italian journalists. The story was dropped after two weeks.[47]

In Italy itself, stories appeared as early as 1989 at Bari and 1991 at Palermo, which are reminiscent of much older ones about white slave traffic (see below, pp. 170–75). These narratives are set in boutiques, and their victims are women, who, however, are not carried off to some distant spot but are operated on in the basements of the boutiques, or in lorries parked nearby. Narratives of this type are also to be found at Milan in March 1994.

Annamaria Rivera wrote in *La Gazetta del Mezzogiorno* on March 21, 1989:

These last few days people have been talking about women who, having disappeared mysteriously in the boutique at the back of such-and-such store, are supposed to have been killed and cut to pieces in order to take their organs for transplants. . . . A mysterious criminal organization arranges contacts with people needing organs, and on the basis of the requests they receive they proceed to obtain and despatch the organs required. The remains of the unfortunate women are destroyed in furnaces built for the purpose. All is discovered when a husband, becoming impatient while waiting for his wife, makes his way into the shop where he had let her go alone, only to be told that nobody has seen her. He goes directly to lodge a complaint with the police, who after a rapid investigation arrest the criminal gang.

At Palermo, in an elegant street in the historic center of the city, there is supposed to be a boutique with a mysterious basement containing an operating theater. That is where, allegedly, unfortunate customers are cut up for a vile trade in human organs. During the summer of 1991, on every balcony in the capital of Sicily, this was the only topic of conversation. . . .

From southern Italy, the legend spread to Milan. The rumor was circulating in March 1994, and was rapidly diffused from the Pavia region to the province of Alessandria; it asserted that the victim, who was saved at the last minute, was the wife of a shopkeeper in Stradella. He was forced to issue a denial. . . .

All these episodes take up old themes, adding the theme of removing human organs, a topic for heated debate in recent years. Whereas the legend formerly conveyed the warning, "Don't go into that boutique, you will be kidnapped and carried off to some Eastern country," it now declares, "Don't go into that boutique, you'll be cut to pieces and your kidneys, lungs, and corneas taken." [48]

In 1990, around Bologna, there were panics about eye thieves very similar to those in Latin America, involving black ambulances and attacks on schools. These narratives put the blame on Gypsies, and led to punitive expeditions against their encampments. Analogous narratives also appeared in Sicily, where the unsolved disappearance of a little girl in March 1990 had attracted much publicity, and reached Rome:

There is a black ambulance driving round the town to steal our children. Since early in the summer of 1990, there has appeared a sudden new series of "black" rumors, spreading slowly from the provinces to the cities (in this case, Rome and Bologna), and comprising two more or less simultaneous sub-waves. Their theme is one of the most characteristic generators of anxiety in today's urban society: the safety of children, and the dark forces threatening them, which are so hard to detect. According to a reconstruction published by *Il Resto di Carlino* on November 16, 1990, in numerous seaside resorts along the coast of Romagna there were very many attempts by Gypsy women to kidnap children, which were observed in public places and in shops, and came very close to success. Supposedly, the child-snatchers would try to hide small children under their large skirts, having lured them away from their mothers who had been "momentarily inattentive." In November, following a typical path of diffusion, the rumors clustered round a large supermarket on the outskirts of Bologna, the Hypercoop de Borgo Paginale. At the center of the event, as usual, was a Gypsy woman. Everyone was talking about it or had heard others talking about it, but there was no child missing in the district. These rumors, which led to protests from the Nomads' Association, occurred shortly before a series of bloody attacks on Gypsy encampments in the district of Bologna, confirming the truth of the remark that "gossip does not precede belief, but is its most obvious manifestation."

At the same period during the summer of 1990, but at the other end of the Italian territory, comparable rumors arose in Sicily: a gang was stealing children to supply a horrible trade in human organs. An article in *La Stampa* of November 29, 1990, reflected these rumors. However, the journalists only mentioned these reports long after they had first appeared, when the phenomenon had reached a stage of secondary development. The story about the ambulance would have arisen in connection with the disappearance of Santina Renda in March 1990 and the kidnapping of children in South America. We read in *La Stampa* how "At Cantarazzo people say the kidney thieves have struck already at some coastal town. At Foggia, they are certainly under surveillance. At Campobasso, mothers are alleging that a child was found dead in a neighbouring village. At Pescara, a case of sexual assault against a child was misinterpreted, giving rise to the conviction that the gang was operating in the neighbourhood. In the last few days, the rumors have reached Rome, where newspaper offices have received dozens of phone calls expressing alarm. And at Pomezia, people were so sure that they had detected false ambulance men that schools were besieged by groups of parents. It was said that the Schools Superintendent of Rome had sent a circular to all heads of schools, warning them against people lurking round schools in false uniforms. But no such circular exists. Some people added realistic details to enhance the narrative: 'Two people dressed as ambulance men, accompanied by two fake policemen, got out of the ambulance and asked for the child to be called, inviting him to go with them, on the pretext that his parents had been in an accident and were in hospital.' But there is no report of any child having disappeared."

Many speculations were put forward after a TV program in spring 1990, *Chi l'ha visto?*, devoted to the disappearance of Santina. Among other things, people talked of kidnapping by Gypsies, or by an organization of people trading in human organs. People also talked of a clinic on the outskirts of Rome where foreign surgeons had been pursuing this terrible trade over the last few months.[49]

Yet it is only in 1994 that anecdotes about kidneys stolen from adults are noted, in the north of Italy; they generally include the blonde temptress in the nightclub, and the lorry transformed into an operating theater:

Early in 1994, in February, a work colleague of mine (Eraldo Bologna, who lives at Mondovì in the province of Cuneo) alerts me to the latest version of the legend. It has been circulating in its own little corner for three months or so, and is very widespread. Everybody is talking about it and puzzling over many questions, especially over why the press is keeping silent. . . . In some versions, the unlucky young man is picked up by a pretty girl, in others by a whole group of girls. When the unfortunate man is recovered, he is in the emergency department of Mondovì

Hospital, or else in a hotel room. It is also said that the removal of the kidney is carried out in a camper-van containing all necessary equipment. Then the story began to spread. Still in February, another colleague (this one from Turin) informs me that his son learnt from his girl friend that only a few days previously, one Saturday evening, three boys who had gone to the Last Kingdom nightclub never came home. Then the hospital phoned their parents to tell them that they had had a kidney removed. The girl stated that this had been mentioned on RAI 3.

On the morning of March 12, 1994, Gianluca Ferrise, the correspondent of *La Stampa* at Alessandria, rings me: "Heard the latest? At Acqui, people are saying that at the Boccanegra, a nightclub on the border between the provinces of Asti and Cuneo, a young man lingered late in company with a pretty girl. He was put to sleep with a spray and carried into a lorry equipped as an operating theater, and there, it's said, he had a kidney removed." Ferisse understands perfectly well that this sort of thing is impossible, but he assures me that the mood in his district is quite paranoid. . . . Passing from mouth to mouth, this legend eventually reaches the press. In *La Stampa* of March 11, in the pages of local news from Asti and Cuneo, there appears an article by Gianni Martini on "The Beautiful Kidney-Thief." The young man's name is given, and that he lives in Imperia. Sure enough, there is somebody of that name living in that town. But he is perfectly well, and has both his kidneys. What's more, he often goes to nightclubs, especially the one so unjustly implicated.[50]

Italy is particularly conscious of news items from Latin America, which are widely repeated in the press, and also very receptive to anxieties about children; consequently it presents a very individual pattern of rumors, midway between narratives about eye thefts and those about kidney thefts. Moreover, these rumors appeared earlier in Italy than in other European countries.

ACCEPTANCE OF THE THREE TYPES OF NARRATIVE

These three types of organ theft narratives are topics for debate, as is characteristic of contemporary legends. Controversy occurs at every social level—which contradicts the contemptuous picture often presented by the authorities and the media, who set up a contrast between unanimous acceptance by the lower classes and general rejection by the elite. These horrifying narratives are passionately accepted, or equally passionately rejected. The choice between an often passionate and immediate acceptance or rejection is not so much based on the quality of the evidence offered, which is generally weak, as on emotion, the indignation such stories arouse in us. One cannot help but be moved on hearing them, so one accepts them spontaneously; yet feeling some uncertainty one turns to authority figures, whose attitude becomes the determining factor. In Latin America, numerous authority figures repeat and legitimate the narratives about eye thieves, which are also magnified by the international media in general; but things are different in Europe, where the authorities consistently deny the stories, and the media reject those set in our own countries (apart from the particular case of Austrian accusations against Italy). Consequently, in the case of the Kidney Heist Story acceptance is slight. Narratives set in distant countries are told almost humorously. The carelessness of the victim is stressed, and the businessmen to some extent deserves what happens to him, although variants involving a family of tourists do convey more distress.

However, when children are involved acceptance comes more easily. Here, it is not reinforced by authority figures, but by a whole corpus of traditional tales and beliefs (see below, pp. 164–67).

CHAPTER 2

FACTS AND THE LEGEND

Hostile attitudes towards medicine, both yesterday and today, have made public opinion more ready to accept allegations of organ theft and of the criminal activities by doctors which these imply. The accusations are made more plausible by the actual facts of a modern trade in organs, and also, above all, by the immemorial facts of violence and of a trade in human beings which has always existed.

CONFLICTS ARISING FROM ORGAN TRANSPLANTS

Organ transplants enable many patients to escape premature death and to return to normal life. They are therefore a legitimate medical procedure, enabling doctors to relieve suffering and bring a cure, as is their mission.

Yet these same transplants are disturbing, because they violate the frontiers of personal identity, and indeed of life. If an organ or organs are taken from a person who is brain-dead, and if the transplant operation succeeds, then the person whose organs have been taken is well and truly dead, but some parts of his or her remains—heart, liver, kidneys—go on living, but with a different identity. In the case of paired organs such as kidneys, or those such as the liver where it is possible to take part only, the donor can be a living person, usually a very close relative; but the most common practice in transplants is to use donors who are brain-dead, that is to say people whose brain is completely and irreversibly destroyed, but who, thanks to artificial respiration, still show signs of autonomic life: the heart is still beating, the chest moves, the body is warm.

This change in the criteria of death is a consequence of the improvement in techniques of reanimation. As early as 1968 the Ad Hoc Committee of the Harvard Medical School defined the concept of brain death[1], one of the objects of this redefinition of death evidently being to make the removal of organs morally acceptable. Yet even thirty years later, contrary to the expectations of the medical profession, this redefinition has not been accepted by society as a whole. Brain death is still a concept which the lay public find hard to grasp, as it contradicts the evidence of their senses. The idea is still shocking, still a breeding ground for suspicion. Well-intentioned moral leaders still regularly issue statements denying its legitimacy. Indeed, it is hard to dismiss the suspicion that death is being defined simply in terms of convenience when a recent article by authoritative specialists (the president and vice president of the Commission on Medical Ethics in French-speaking Belgium) states:

> In order for the transplant to succeed, the organ must be alive; in order for the transplant to be possible, the donor must be dead. The diagnosis of brain death is the ideal way to permit organs to be removed for this purpose. From then on, the implications of death are no longer purely a family concern and a matter of inheritance, for the corpse becomes an object of enormous value in the medical world.[2]

In France (a country which was a pioneer in this matter), the Caillavet Law of 1976 instituted a presumption of consent. This means that every person in a condition of brain death is presumed, unless he/she had expressly declared an objection while alive, to give consent to the removal of his/her organs. On the whole, countries in the Latin tradition have taken this option, whereas countries in the Anglo-Saxon tradition reject it, requiring an explicit consent to be given either by the person or, in the case of a sudden death, by the relatives. In Anglo-Saxon countries the law requires the doctor to put the request to the dying person or to the relatives. The very fact that it was necessary to adopt these rules shows that objections to the notion of brain death and to organ removal are not limited to the general public but also affect the medical profession.

There is no need to start an argument over the difference between the Latin and the Anglo-Saxon approach, for in both cases principles and practice are far apart. In France, in practice, doctors only apply the presumption of consent in conjunction with a consultation of the family, who are regarded as guardians of the deceased's wishes; presumption of consent is thus deprived of its hoped-for usefulness in ensuring the availability of organs. The practical effect of the text of the 1976 law was softened in 1978 by regulations as to its application, envisaging consultation with the family. The new law adopted in 1994 keeps the notion of presumption of consent, but adds immediately that the doctor must try to discover from the family what was the opinion of the deceased. Thus it is the family that decides, and the medical profession will not oppose them if they refuse.

Whether families should be told exactly how many organs have been taken remains a delicate question, opening a possibility of conflict. While the Caillavet Law was in force, the medical profession often interpreted the permission given by the family in a broad sense. For instance, besides taking several organs, one might also take tissues such as veins, arteries, and corneas. Since the latter affected the whole eyeball there was a risk that it might shock the family, in view of the symbolic value of the eye; so nothing was said about it, and a discreet prosthesis would be put in place. However, in doing this the doctors were setting themselves above the law. In fact, the Caillavet Law had not abrogated the Lafay Law of 1949, dating from before the notion of brain death. Transplanting corneas is an old technique, and in regulating it the Lafay Law had laid down that corneas could only be taken if there were instructions to this effect in the deceased person's will.

The so-called Amiens Affair is a case of legal conflict, which, it must be emphasized, was and remains exceptional. M. and Mme Tesnière were the parents of Christophe, a nineteen-year-old youth who was the victim of a traffic accident, and whose organs were removed at the Centre Hospitalo-Universitaire of Amiens, and in May 1992 they sued the hospital. Having obtained access to their son's medical records when they made a complaint against the person responsible for the accident (a complaint which the court did not uphold), they received a duplicate of the postmortem, and noted that in addition to the removal of the heart, liver, and kidneys, of which they had been informed, arteries, veins, and corneas had been taken too. The Tesnières turned to the media, and their complaint made a great stir. After an article in *Le Monde* headed "Death Violated," which launched the affair,[3] there was a televised debate chaired by Christophe Dechavanne, setting the parents, together with their legal advisor, media star Gilbert Collard, against Professor Christian Cabrol, president of France-Transplant, the organization responsible for transplants at that time. There followed magazine articles with inflammatory headings: "Latest News on Cannibalism,"[4] "Thieves Who Steal Sight."[5] Bernard Kouchner, health minister at the time, sternly called the surgeons to order: until a new law came in, one must explicitly ask consent from the family for any removal of a cornea. These new instructions resulted in a substantial decline in the supply of corneas in France, a decline which seemed not to have ended by 1997. In 1993 a book signed by the young man's father, *Les yeux de Christophe*, told the story of the Amiens affair. By 1996 the legal case had still not been settled, but Alain Tesnière had become a public figure; for example, his virulent testimony is the first item in a collection of papers on organ donation published in November 1996 in the Jesuit review *Etudes*:

> The history of organ transplants is an accumulation of facts which bring shame on mankind. . . . So long as people fail to understand that biomedical ethics are too serious a problem to be left to scientists and doctors alone . . . cannibalism will triumph.[7]

Organ transplants are carried out by the most advanced surgical services, whose work is often little understood by the public. Families of people in the state of brain death have to face the announcement of a brutal and unexpected death. Such cases are rare; in France, they amount to five per thousand of deaths in hospital. Those involved are generally young adults— victims of road accidents or of head injuries—whose deaths are to some degree abnormal, or even shocking, and whose families are frequently full of suspicion about the medical services. Did the doctors do everything possible to save their loved ones, whose loss haunts them?

When services of advanced surgery such as transplants are set up in countries with substantial social inequality, where large numbers live in poverty and have no access to even rudimentary preventive medicine, there arises a further area of conflict, the politics of health care. This problem was explicitly set out in South Africa after the major political changes in that country in the 1990s. On the occasion of an expensive heart-lung transplant operation which was carried out in spite of a moratorium on transplants, some people found it scandalous that within the same country there could be highly advanced medical services available to its former masters, and a very poor and patchy service for the rest of the people—a service largely inferior to that of Egypt. The governor of one distant province commented at the time that "the cost of two or three heart transplants equals that of a primary health care center which would be capable of caring for 10,000 people for a whole year."[8]

There have been a few cases where a dispute between the families of accident victims, who thought organs had been unjustifiably removed, and their doctors and hospital services have led to formal legal complaints publicized in the media. There was a case in the Philippines, for example: a lawsuit instigated in 1988 by the victim's mother, which led to further legal action in 1994. In Argentina there were numerous complaints about the hospital service in Córdoba, leading to the compilation of a dossier for possible prosecution. Most often, these complaints do not lead to guilty verdicts but to a judicial decision that there is no case to answer. Nevertheless, the media report these disputes in highly sensational terms.

We increasingly live in mixed, pluralistic societies where in many matters there is no true consensus of opinion. For public opinion to accept transplants, there has to be some recognized common ground where different social groups can exchange views.

CANNIBAL MEDICINE? SCANDALS IN THE PAST

The evolution of medicine has always meant that a corpse has a value to a doctor, whether for today's transplants or for yesterday's development in anatomy studies.

First, we can consider the old scandals connected to the rise of dissection and the body-snatching which accompanied it. From the Renaissance onwards, the development of anatomy was handicapped by a scarcity of corpses available for masters to study, and for the training of student doctors and surgeons. To mitigate this scarcity of anatomical material, doctors "had recourse to expedients whose shadow has darkened the history of anatomy: graves broken open to seize freshly buried corpses; bodies stolen from hospitals; bodies of those whom nobody claimed automatically taken for dissection; corpses of executed criminals bought from the executioners; expeditions by night to unhook hanged men from gibbets."[9] In France, the status of anatomy studies was recognized after an edict in 1730 ruled that medical faculties must offer both theoretical and practical teaching on this subject, but this recognition was slow to take practical effect. Officially, schools of medicine and surgery were supplied with corpses from hospitals, yet private operating theaters obtained their supplies chiefly by surreptitious exhumations; there were many incidents where surgeons (or those working for them) clashed with the police and the public, but these were usually not serious. It was only after the reforms of 1813 that the situation became normal.

THE LYON RIOT OF 1768

In a book about Lyon in the eighteenth century, Maurice Garden alludes briefly to an investigation into a riot at Lyon in November 1768:

> In 1768, the Oratory College was literally besieged by a mob, who then burst in and wrecked it, especially the buildings let out to the medical school. . . . The accusation current among the common people was that the Oratory was sheltering a one-armed prince, and that every evening children would be taken prisoner in the neighbourhood of the College, and would have an arm cut off to see if it fitted this alleged prince.[10]

Obviously, this extraordinary sentence about the one-armed prince and the arm cut off every day makes one long to know more. It also explains why Garden is quoted by Jean Delumeau and then by Arlette Farge and Jacques Revel in their books on mass panics and on crowd psychology.[11] Did not this turn the Oratorians into malevolent ancestors of our transplant surgeons? So I consulted Garden's sources, namely a dossier in the Superintendent's Archives, and the *Petite chronique lyonnaise* published in 1851 by Morel de Voleine on the basis of contemporary letters recounting the events.[12]

The Medical School was lodged in buildings belonging to the Oratory College, formerly owned by Jesuits who had been expelled five years previously. On November 27, 1768, it was the target of "a considerable riot" by people accusing the surgeons of abducting children:

> At four o'clock in the afternoon some two or three hundred people of the lower classes gathered outside the door of the Medical School, which occupies a building belonging to the College of the Oratory fathers. I happened to be passing

this gathering, together with the Intendent, so I stopped and asked what was the reason for this public disturbance; I was told that it was because the surgeons had been abducting children and keeping them alive but imprisoned, in order to dissect them.[13]

Towards four in the afternoon, more than five hundred people crowded in under the archway, armed with axes, and broke down the door of a former religious house now used as a college for medicine, surgery, and drawing. They claimed that children were being abducted, and that they were dissected alive in that place.[14]

The rioting had begun already; it spread from the medical school to the nearby college, and the authorities decided to order shots to be fired at the crowd to disperse it:

The Provost of Merchants and I having gone on foot to the Medical School, we found its door had unfortunately been broken down, and the crowd were carrying in triumph some old skeletons and some of the doorkeeper's linen, which happened to be bloodstained. Their fury grew more and more intense, and within less than half an hour over 15,000 souls had gathered. . . . Before long, the operating theatres and all the furnishings of the Medical School and the School of Art had been carried away and burnt. . . . All the doors were broken down, people were getting in from every side, threatening to set the place on fire and loot it; then the officers, seeing they could do nothing to remedy the situation, were the first to suggest to the Commandant that he should order the troops to fire. They were unfortunately obliged to do so, as a last resort; twenty-five people were gravely wounded, and six killed.[15] These strong measures naturally spread terror, and by ten at night the people had begun to disperse. . . . Seventeen of the chief rioters were arrested and taken to prison.[16]

The authorities immediately searched for the real cause of the riot, for they suspected a plot, and feared the enmity of a religious guild of artisans whose chapel had previously been housed by the Jesuits, but this was no longer the case with their successors, the Oratory Fathers.

Charges are being zealously drawn up. It appears that proof will be found of some plot hatched the previous day, but so far the only pretext we know of is the idiotic credulity of a few women, the dregs of the people, who were insisting that their children had been locked up in the Medical School in order to be dissected alive.

There have indeed been some comments which would suggest that there was also a plan aimed against the Oratory Fathers; you know, sir, that the building housing the Medical School belongs to their College, and furthermore that in the time of the Jesuits there was a guild of artisans there.[17]

Wishing to clear themselves of blame, the authorities also made inquiries in places where beggars who had recently been arrested were being detained:

A few people, who I dare say had evil intentions, have tried to ascribe these events to the actions of beggars, insisting that the lobby of the Medical School was used as a place to hold those who had been arrested in the course of that night. Monsieur the Provost and I, having been put in charge of that operation, thought it important not to allow this opinion to gain belief, and we took statements from the Captain of the Watch and all his sergeants, who assured us that (quite apart from the fact that they had never arrested any children) the only place used for temporarily holding beggars in was the Watch House by the Intendent's door.[18]

Suspicion centered on one of the accused men, Hubert Balmont, who had made rash statements allegedly announcing the riot one day in advance:

As for the plot, the only beginnings of proof is a statement by the wife of the doorkeeper at the Medical School that she had been warned the previous day that she would "notice a bit of noise tomorrow." She even recognised among the prisoners the man who had said this to her, but he did not admit it.[19]

The reply from Intendent Bertin in Paris was that these suspicions must be taken seriously, but that at the same time one must repress sedition severely, even if it had been caused solely by the belief that children had been abducted:

I see, Sir, from the details I read in your letter of December 5, that the accused man you are speaking of is the same who declared, at the time of his arrest, that somebody had come the previous day to tell him to be ready. It would be really extraordinary if this knowledge of his, taken together with the eyewitness evidence of the doorkeeper's wife that the accused himself had warned her in similar terms the previous day, were circumstances of no significance, and if the whole affair were the result of pure chance. Even so, it does not follow that unrelated views were the secret motive for stirring up the common people, while giving them as pretext this ridiculous idea about dissected children; rather, one may presume that after this idea had taken shape among the people several months ago, there were several individuals among them who premeditated and plotted the riot themselves, and it is these who must be identified and punished.[20]

The unfortunate man was tortured before being executed, yet denied any premeditation, or any plot. But, in addition to his rash statements, the circumstances of his arrest caused him to be suspected of belonging to the artisans' guild which had been turned out of the chapel, since he was found to have ornaments from this chapel in his possession:

> Several of the men entered through a breach in the wall into a chapel belonging to Trinity College which had formerly been used by the guild; soldiers followed them in and arrested eleven of them, two of whom were found to be carrying some items they had taken from the chapel, namely two flasks and two bobbins of thread. . . . Several witnesses testify that this same Hubert Balmont was stirring up the rioters, that he shook his fist under the nose of M. de la Verpillière, saying "You will give us justice," and furthermore that he was found carrying two glass flasks.[21]
>
> When he was arrested and led into a room at Trinity College, he said, in the presence of some of the most distinguished men of this town, that on the previous day someone had come to his house at eleven o'clock at night to advise him to be at the College gates next morning. . . . He said that when he was arrested he was terribly distressed, and so perhaps he did say what we have just repeated, but he protested to us that he had no recollection of this, and that in truth he had not plotted with anyone. We ordered the interrogator to administer the first turn of the rope, and we charged him to tell us whether he had not heard people saying, before the riot, that the chapel which used to serve the artisans' guild had been desecrated by putting an anatomy school in it. He said, with loud shrieks, "You can have me chopped to pieces, but I have nothing to say."[22]

Hubert Balmont was executed shortly after being put to the torture, pleas for mercy from Lyon being rejected in Paris. Another of the accused was banished, but all the other prisoners were released on January 16, 1769.

The scornful phrases of the authorities about a "ridiculous idea" and about "the idiotic credulity of a few women, the dregs of the people" attribute the belief in the abduction of children, and the riot this gave rise to, to ignorant levels among the common people. This is not borne out by the list of dead and wounded, which gives the trade of thirty-one out of thirty-seven people: fifteen are silk workers, including the unfortunate Hubert Balmont (three of them spinning-women, and two servants of silk workers); twelve are artisans, several being in the clothing trades (a hatter, a cobbler, two tanners, two drapers, a silk stocking maker, a woman making gold and silver buttons, a carpenter, a braid maker, a wig maker, a tailor); only four can be reckoned to belong to the lower working class (a day laborer, a basket maker, a tripe seller, a bird seller).

The dossier in the archives does not take up the story of the one-armed prince and the arms cut off every day from unfortunate children. Need we be surprised? Garden's source, the author Morel de Voleine, published his chronicle in 1851, but as proof of authenticity he refers in his introduction to letters contemporary with the events:

> This is not an imaginary construction, a fictional setting created to make readers swallow indigestible scraps from official files. This correspondence does exist. My late grandfather, a councillor in the Finance Court at Lyon, kept up a steady correspondence with M. de J., a Lyon man by birth, intelligent, moving in high society, and keeping in touch with news from the city and the court. This bulky bundle of letters and replies was preserved, and I picked out from among its informal gossip anything relating to our local history. . . . The correspondence I allude to begins in 1768 and ends in 1784.[23]

Immediately after telling the story of the riot, Morel de Voleine offers a few theories as to its causes (including hostility from supporters of the expelled Jesuits), but it is only when the inquiry comes to an end, a month after the events, that the story of the one-armed prince appears. In relating it, the letter writer stresses that it is an opinion of "the people," which the educated classes laugh at:

> [November 27] It appears that the College doorkeeper, pestered by local children, used to threaten roughly that he would have them dissected; it was

claimed that one of the rioters had recognised the corpse of his brother, who had died in hospital, taken to this place to serve as a specimen. . . . [December 30] A large number of the common people believe that the Oratorians are hiding among them a one-armed prince, and that every evening children are seized in the neighbourhood of the College, and they have one arm cut off, to see if it will fit the supposed prince.[24]

BLOOD, THE EXTRAORDINARY REMEDY

The mention of the one-armed prince places the riot in the context of a well-known series of legends about extraordinary remedies needed to restore a prince's health, and obtained by criminal actions; the perfect example is the bath of blood from the innocent—virgins, or children—to cure a leper king.

Abductions of children were very real in the Paris of 1750. Inspectors and police officers had received instructions to clear the city of children who had no family to claim them, thus taking further the policy of imprisoning vagrants which had been regularly pursued for decades, but they exceeded their instructions by arresting children of ten or twelve who were not vagrants, but were in regular work. As the police were paid by results for these arrests, though not much, they could double their profit by making the parents pay to have the abducted children released. These facts led to several serious clashes on May 22 and 23, 1750, culminating in the killing of a policeman named Labbé in St. Roch Street, his body then being dragged to the home of Berger, the lieutenant general of police, who was responsible for the operation to arrest "vagrants."

After this riot, the accusation of seeking the blood of innocent children as a remedy was made against the king, previously nicknamed "the Beloved," thus making a new Herod of him. In the book they wrote about this affair, Arlette Farge and Jacques Revel gave examples from history of the legend of this extraordinary remedy. It is told of the Emperor Constantine, miraculously healed of leprosy because he had refused to use this cruel remedy when his doctors suggested it; then it appears in some versions of the Grail Quest, where Galahad and Percival encounter a leprous lady who can be cured by a virgin's blood. The Grimms studied this motif in connection with the poor knight Heinrich Hartmann von Aue in a German poem from the end of the twelfth century.[26] As regards the riot of 1750, as for that of 1768, it is only through unofficial sources such as contemporary diaries and memoirs (e.g., by Ménétra, who was a child in 1750) that we learn of the rumor of the extraordinary remedy, the legend of blood—and they merely repeat it in order to reject it. Farge and Revel give these sources:

Barbier: "People repeat unthinkingly that the reason the children were abducted was that there was a prince who was a leper, whose cure required a bath, or several baths, in human blood, and that as there was no purer blood than that of children they were taken away to be bled in all four limbs till they died, which disgusted the populace. Nobody knows what gives rise to such fairy tales; that remedy was suggested in the time of the Emperor Constantine, who refused to use it. But we have no leprous prince among us, and even if there was one, one would never use such cruelty as a remedy." D'Argenson: "There is a rumor going round that the King is a leper and takes baths of blood, like a new Herod." The Marquise de Pompadour: "Talking of foolishness, I suppose you know about the folly of the Parisians? I don't think there can be anything so stupid as to believe that one wants to bleed their children to bathe a leprous prince." Ménétra: "At that time, a rumor was going round that one was seizing young boys and bleeding them, that they were lost for ever, and that their blood was used to bathe a princess suffering from a disease which only human blood could cure."[27]

Since the accusations associated with child abductions in Paris were linked to a wicked prince, princess, or king, this brings them close to the rumor which Morel de Voleine's grandfather reported in his letters as explaining the riot at Lyon. At the same time these legend-like narratives, whether dealing with blood as in Paris or more with surgery as at Lyon, are also implicitly blaming the medical personnel, the bleeders and surgeons, who carry out the evil wishes of the princess and supply the extraordinary remedies they demand.

In the case of the Lyon riot of 1768, the rumor did not arise from any real child abductions but from controversy over the status of the medical school, which had been set up a few years earlier in premises formerly occupied by Jesuits, driving out a guild of artisans from the chapel they had been using. Given the very widespread mistrust of medical schools, this controversial status was probably enough to revive the age-old tale of attacks on children. The authorities at the time were content to make only passing allusions to these awkward facts, preferring to put the blame on the stupidity of the general public rather than to analyze the real reasons why the rumor developed.

We find parallel attitudes today among the authorities when faced with narratives about organ thefts. Thus, it is very rare for the link between such narratives and the ethical disputes surrounding transplants to be mentioned in medical circles. As for American information services, their analyses of organ theft narratives concentrate on the role of deliberate disinformation, and neglect to discuss the instances of organ trading which make the narratives plausible.

BODY SNATCHERS IN GREAT BRITAIN

In Great Britain at one time, the only official source of anatomical specimens for surgeons was corpses of people executed for murder. This proved inadequate, but was not supplemented by unclaimed corpses from hospitals (as was the case in France), with the result that a real "profession" of body snatchers arose in the mid-eighteenth century. A body did not legally belong to any owner, so stealing it was nothing more than a misdemeanor; however, it was important that it should be a naked body which the body snatcher had stripped of all clothing or other objects and which had to be left in the grave, since stealing clothing or objects was a felony. However, public opinion would not tolerate thefts of corpses, so guards were set on graveyards, and clashes between them and the body snatchers became more frequent, while the value of a corpse rose from one or two pounds in 1800 to ten or sixteen pounds in 1828.[28] Despite their market value, corpses were rarely sold by the relatives, and there are many indications of the great importance the poor attached to having decent and dignified funerals.

In 1828, a parliamentary committee considered this question; its report recommended that one should cease dissecting corpses of hanged murderers, and make use instead of those of paupers who died in hospitals or workhouses and were not claimed by any kin. Their purpose in giving up the use of murderers' corpses was to confer new respectability on dissection. The idea of accepting voluntary bequests of bodies was considered, but set aside. In the words of Ruth Richardson, "the *Report* effectively recommended a redefinition of poverty—from being seen as a state of pitiable misfortune to one of criminal responsibility."[29] The proposed new law, known as the Anatomy Act, was rejected in 1829 because of opposition from the bishops in the House of Lords, since in this first version it did not envisage any religious funeral for dissected bodies; after amendment, it was passed in 1832. Debate had been heated, and fierce opposition, vigorously expressed, came both from personalities of radical and populist politics and from ultraconservatives. Present-day historians studying the passing of this law emphasize that the Anatomy Act came shortly before the New Poor Law of 1834, which considerably worsened the condition of the poor. The Anatomy Act was only one among several degrading treatments inflicted on the bodies of the poor, comparable to the humiliating pauper funerals instituted in the nineteenth century—anonymous burials in mass graves, any ornament or ceremony being forbidden, and where it was specified that the coffin be made of wood thinner than the norm. Dissection, it is argued, expressed symbolically the growing contempt for paupers:

> The poor, instead of being those who are with us always, and whose position was spiritually privileged, had become those who could not or would not sell their work, and so should be maintained at little more than starvation level, rather in order to ensure political stability than out of charity.[30]

The exclusive use of paupers' bodies continued for a long time in Great Britain. In London between 1832 and 1932 almost thirty-seven thousand bodies were dissected in medical faculties, and fewer than three hundred of them did not come from paupers unclaimed by their relatives.

BURKE AND HARE

Soon after the 1828 report, at the beginning of November that year, much distress was caused in Edinburgh by the discovery of sixteen murders committed in that city by the Irishmen Burke and Hare, who sold the bodies of their victims to Robert Knox, a famous anatomist. In the absence of material proofs (destroyed by Knox, who was not called to give evidence), the courts offered Hare immunity in exchange for his evidence, and prosecuted Burke for one of the murders. Both Burke's wife and Hare's had taken part in the murders, but Mrs. Hare was not prosecuted, and Mrs. Burke, though prosecuted, was not found guilty. On January 28, 1829, Burke was executed in front of a huge crowd, who demanded the deaths of Hare and Knox too. After the execution, Burke's body was dissected in front of an audience of students, and the remains put on display; over forty thousand people filed past to view them. Burke's skeleton is still kept in the Anatomy Museum of Edinburgh. Ten days later, on February 7, the publication of Burke's two confessions, and of a pamphlet said to have been written by the doorkeeper at the school of anatomy run by Knox, rekindled public anger.

Meanwhile Knox was still teaching and dissecting, without making the least statement in self-defense. His colleagues announced they were setting up a commission of inquiry, and the public, foreseeing a whitewash, grew indignant. A crowd gathered in front of his house on February 12 and organized the type of demonstration traditionally called "skimmington" or "rough music." An effigy labelled "Knox, associate of the infamous Hare" was throttled—the method of killing attributed to the murderers, allegedly with bandages used for setting broken limbs—and then cut to pieces, not burnt, as was usual in skimmingtons.

The discovery of these murders did much to convince people that a law making the use of body snatchers superfluous was urgently needed. Burke and Hare had not in fact previously followed this "profession," but had become murderers more or less by chance. They had been tempted by the fine price of ten pounds, which Knox's school offered them when they tried to sell the body of one of their lodgers who had died without paying her rent (Mrs. Hare kept a cheap boardinghouse). The next lodger who fell ill was made drunk, and then throttled; Knox's school paid them ten pounds for this second body; they went on as they had begun, and fifteen other murders followed—twelve women, two young cripples, and one old man, lured in off the street with promises of drink and shelter. Yet the idea that they started by snatching bodies and went on to murder has persisted, since it seems logical. Moreover, public anxiety was reinforced in November 1831, when a series of murders occurred in London, carried out by confirmed body snatchers. John Bishop and Thomas Williams were hanged in London on December 5 for three murders, but rumor said Williams had confessed to more than sixty. Edward Cook and Elizabeth Ross, who had killed an old woman, were also executed. Other similar affairs took place in several European and American cities in the nineteenth century, leaving persistent local memories.

Hostility towards body snatchers predisposed people to think of them as potential murderers, and rumor spoke of them even before any were discovered. The crimes of Burke and Hare inspired works of literature towards the end of the century, for in 1884 Robert Louis Stevenson, a native of Edinburgh, wrote a short story about them, entitled "The Body-Snatchers." In 1896 Marcel Schwob, a great admirer of Stevenson, entitled the final section of his *Vies imaginaires*, a set of sophisticated short stories in the biographical tradition of Aubrey, "Messrs Burke and Hare, Assassins." But it was above all in popular imagination that their murders left deep, enduring traces as a terrifying event. Nearly fifty supposed news reports and narrative songs, some still remembered nowadays, commemorate the grim exploits of Burke and Hare.[31] To this day, "burker tales," telling how the hero only just escaped sinister figures who were in fact murderous body snatchers, can be found in the repertoire of Scottish storytellers. The folklorist Sheila Douglas collected some in Perth in 1987 from traditional storytellers of Gypsy descent.[32] The verb *to burke* is still defined in current dictionaries in both literal and figurative senses: "1. To stifle or strangle someone in order to sell the body for dissection, as Burke did in Edinburgh. 2. To stifle or suppress (a scandal); avoid, silence (a question); suppress (a fact)."[33] Nowadays an allusion to Burke and Hare is a natural part of mass culture in Anglo-Saxon countries, currently available as a point of reference.

CANNIBAL MEDICINE? TODAY'S FEARS

In our own time, one can readily observe an alarmist, distorted, and overly dramatic vision of the progress of knowledge and the potential of medical treatment. Whether the matter in question is medically assisted conception and the ever more sophisticated techniques this involves; or the therapeutic use of human tissue; or the development of prenatal diagnosis; or the treatment of people in vegetative states and prolonged coma; or, finally, organ transplant—whatever the topic, one can very rarely escape sensational headlines, full of both amazement and anxiety at once. It would be absurd to deny that advances in medicine, especially those affecting the frontiers of life, pose multiple problems, especially in ethics. But alongside these real problems, and the many institutions devoted to describing and resolving them, this alarmist vision seems to create imaginary problems, and to foster a wholesale rejection of science which in recent years has spread considerably at many social levels.

MISDIRECTED MEDICINE

Medical science certainly becomes misdirected if it forgets the patient in focussing on the illness alone. Moreover, it is certainly true that in recent decades there have been several proposals put forward by doctors which viewed persons in the persistent vegetative state, or in prolonged coma, as mere instruments to be used for the benefit of others. An alarming instance of this possible future trend is the provocative article written in 1974 by Willard Gaylin, a psychiatrist who at that time was president of the Institute of Society, Ethics and the Life Sciences at Hastings (in New York State).[34] Gaylin proposed that the "neo-dead" should be used for teaching students, testing medicines, conducting experiments, banking blood, harvesting organs, and manufacturing antibodies by injection of viruses or bacteria.

Proposals which came close to instrumentalizing the patient were put forward in 1987 by the Frenchman Alain Milhaud, who advocated the introduction of a "living will," where the signatory would consent in advance to being a subject for experiments if he were to pass into the chronic vegetative state. This proposal was supported by the signed approval of about a hundred medical personnel. Previously, in 1985, Milhaud had voluntarily made public the fact that he had carried out an experiment on a young man in prolonged coma, a revelation which drew a reprimand from the National Ethics Committee.[35] The scandal broke out again in 1988 when, in the course of a judicial inquiry at Poitiers, it was revealed that Alain Milhaud had gone on to conduct an experiment on a second young man in prolonged coma.[36] This time, the Council of the Order issued a ruling suspending him, which was confirmed five years later by the State Council.[37] Clearly, when medical proposals become inhumane they are vigorously resisted from within the medical profession itself. As for Gaylin's nightmarish visions, they never became reality, and the medical community has not adopted them.

The theme of harmful science is old; an early literary manifestation is Mary Shelley's *Frankenstein: Or the Modern Prometheus*, written in 1817.

Medical horrors are a favorite target of authors writing for the popular market, including many who specialize in medical thrillers. I was interested to discover, while preparing the present work, that this theme in popular culture was echoed in the writings of intellectuals who give a highly negative picture of procedures for assisted conception, treatment of persons in prolonged coma, and, above all, of organ transplants. The writings in question are not all of the same level—far from it. They range from the legitimate posing of questions (for medical developments certainly can raise unprecedented ethical problems, or can increase the risk of mishaps) to militant, propagandist writings where medical developments are merely a pretext for setting out preconceived arguments. I have chosen to describe four such intellectual works, ranging from serious work to propaganda.

EMIKO OHNUKI-TIERNEY

An important and controversial article by Emiko Ohnuki-Tierney, "Brain Death and Organ Transplantation," appeared in 1994. It focuses on the problems posed by organ transplants (and their repercussions on the concepts of the person and of human nature) and by the notion of brain death as the death of the person.[38] This text, written as part of a symposium[39] and printed in the prestigious journal *Current Anthropology*, is by a woman anthropologist of Japanese origin, author of several works on that culture, and takes an anthropological and cultural approach. Its main argument is that "transplant technology leads to a series of transgressions of received categories in almost all cultures."[40] She takes Japan as an example, where there is a marked rejection of transplants from nonliving donors, and where the concept of brain death does not exist in law. Comparing Japan with China, she emphasizes that the Japanese rejected all elements of Chinese culture that threatened the physical integrity of the body: ear piercing, foot binding, castration of eunuchs. She reminds us how death is conceived of in traditional societies, and recognizes that, besides the Japanese case, certain features are universal: death is a cultural phenomenon which goes beyond the biological factors, involving an institutionalized series of rituals whereby social death changes the status of the dead person into that of an ancestor. The corpse is of crucial importance to this mourning process. Therefore the removal of organs constitutes "an act of transgression—it deprives the deceased of the final process that enables them to leave this world with dignity and as persons."[41] However, taking into account public opinion surveys in Japan which show increasing acceptance of transplants and the taking of organs postmortem, the author admits that the notions of brain death and organ transplants have a good chance of imposing themselves in Japan. Blood transfusions are widely accepted in that country, after strong initial resistance, and so are cornea transplants.

A secondary and more controversial argument in Emiko Ohnuki-Tierney's article is that what we call "giving organs" is not to be considered a "gift," since it can have no place within any social relationship. Reciprocity is the foundation of all social relationships, but in response to the gift of an organ, which by its nature is inalienable, no reciprocal counter-gift is possible. Furthermore, the fact that the origin of the donated organ remains secret, and that the assignment of organs to recipients is done by highly bureaucratic organizations, transforms organ giving into a mere transaction:

> It is the absence of a social relationship between donor and receiver that leads to the commercialisation of organ donation. Without the social context in which real social agents engage in a transaction, the organ—or any object, for that matter—becomes a candidate for commodification. Without a social agent, an object has no meaning. No restriction is placed upon the way its value is interpreted by the recipient. The most inalienable of all inalienable gifts thus easily turns into a commodity. This is happening in the "organ market", and in addition we are witnessing the rapid development of a black market in organs.[42]

It is the policy of *Current Anthropology* to invite authorized comments on its articles. Two anthropologists sent in remarks displaying strong hostility towards medical power. Taking up the notion of brain death, one of them states that there are no simple, clear, and universal standards within the medical community for diagnosing it:

> That diagnosis is, indeed, a result of negotiation among various interested parties in context—specific interactions—the recipient of an organ and his/her family, transplant surgeons in need of organs, third party payers unwilling to

pay for prolonged intensive care of "a dead brain in a living body"—in which the status of the donor as a potentially living entity works against the interests of all the others. Therefore the decision to declare brain death is a social act that occurs on various ways depending on shifting circumstances; it is not purely an exercise of neutral biomedical technology.[43]

The same hostility is indicated in the remarks of the second commentator, a specialist on Japan, for whom it seems that the fear of being sued is the only possible method of controlling the unbounded ambition of Japanese surgeons: "The most serious Japanese reason for rejecting brain death as a criterion for death is that the market for organs could provoke abuses of the system by physicians."

Some of that commentator's remarks seem perfectly applicable to the situation in France, where the doctors held sole power:

> There are serious economic, educational, and cultural barriers to Japan's adopting a Western-style adversarial doctor-lawyer relationship in which lawsuits and whistle-blowing are commonplace. Yet without such institutions, leaving the determination of brain death to professional interpretation of EEGs [electroencephalograms] is tantamount to sentencing organ donors to a clandestinely premature fate.[44]

Two surgeons also commented upon the article. A. S. Daar set out the precise differences between the chronic vegetative state, where natural breathing is still present, and prolonged comas, where artificial respiration is essential; he reminded readers that resolutions passed at the Ottawa Conference of 1991 ruled that only in the latter case could organs be taken. M. I. Lorber pointed out that ambivalent attitudes and cultural resistance to the idea of brain death are equally widespread in Western countries.

Responding to these comments, the original author stated that she was not opposed to transplants, but stressed:

> . . . the need for "cultural adaptation" to high technology, and the need for accommodation by medical specialists of human and cultural needs and emotions. . . . It is medical doctors, . . . and not we anthropologists, who can make significant changes in the development and delivery of the new medical technology for the benefit of humanity rather than for its exploitation.[45]

It seems that the changes Emiko Ohnuki-Tierney wished for are gradually appearing, at any rate in France, where people are beginning to accept that families express objections to the removal of organs, and to consider this legitimate, whereas previously such views were haughtily dismissed as outdated and superstitious.

DAVID LE BRETON

David Le Breton also takes an anthropological point of view, though in a far more polemical manner, in his book *La chair à vif. Usages medicaux et mondains du corps humain* (*Raw Flesh: Medical and Secular Uses of the Human Body*).[46] Here he develops arguments sketched in his previous works[47] and proposes a history of anatomy in the past and transplants in the present. He asserts that to take organs is a violation of the boundaries of what is sacred and human, as were the dissections in the past, and that transplant surgeons are successors to body snatchers.

The book has a polemical purpose, and from the start makes a head-on attack on biomedical science as a whole. Modern medicine, centered on sickness, the physical organism, and the body, "is historically based on opening up corpses, obstinately refusing to accept social values which affirm the sacred status of the remains of a human being."[48] Dissection imposes a distinction between a person and his or her body, the latter becoming valueless once he or she is dead. Yet this practice clashes with "the feelings of many who see the corpse as an enduring symbol of the man."[49] Physical medicine is not the only possible one, and the author rejoices in the new popularity of alternative medicine today:

> The crisis of confidence which medicine is currently undergoing, because it has wagered everything on the human body and abandoned the human being, has set free many other so-called alternative therapies, and has brought into increased favor the folk traditions of healing in our own societies, which have different conceptions of sickness and of therapeutic methods. There are many forms of medicine, each addressing itself to a different body. So the history of anatomy is not the history of the discovery of the one and only truth about the body, but just one version among innumerable others which feed one form of medicine among others.[50]

Maintaining this polemical approach, the chapter entitled "Removal and Transplants of Organs" is a wholesale attack on transplants, on the notion of brain death, and on how medicine, by concentrating on the body, has turned it into an object, a piece of merchandise. Le Breton writes about transplants, brain death, and the commercialization of the body as follows:

Transplants . . . pose terrible questions for society: whether it is morally permissible to take organs, and what is the anthropological status of a corpse. For the second time in the history of Western medicine, after the conflicts over anatomical dissection, the human body has become a coveted object and a source of disputes, causing divisions in medical and social discourse, forcing everyone involved to take up a position in the debate.[51]

Brain death is a concept that belongs to the learned culture of the medical world, it harshly contradicts the sensitivities of anybody outside this body of knowledge. . . . The notion on brain death is inherited from dualism; it is a purely biological view of humanity which obscures real existence. It is not the brain which thinks, lives, or wins affection, but the person. According to this logic, the death of the brain would be the death of the soul, and therefore the death of the individual too, as nothing would remain of the living man except his "body."[52]

Thus the body is subtly distinguished from the man, and reduced to a particular kind of machinery. . . . But to separate a man from his flesh and simply regard the latter as on a par with machinery strips the body of meaning and value. . . . In losing the dimension which gives it meaning, the body loses its moral value, while in contrast its technical and commercial value increases. A body is a rare commodity. Today the successes of medicine and biology (transplants, blood transfusion, prostheses, genetic manipulations, assisted conception, etc) have opened the way to new practices for which a great future is foretold. To regard another person as a body and not as a man is a fearful decision, encouraging all sorts of misuse. Morality and ethics are concerned with relationships between individuals, not between objects. To turn a body into an object leads implicitly to the following stage, where it is turned into merchandise. . . . Today, the commercialisation of bodies no longer spares the living.[53]

There follow three apocalyptic and denunciatory pages, where the whole mass of data about organ traffic is mingled together, every instance being apparently treated as equally valid. Although the author remains cautious about accusations of organ theft, which he still labels as rumors, he does use emotional and unrealistic phrases to evoke how the poor are cut in pieces, and includes the sinister figure of the mafia. "Men and women in good health . . . have no other means of survival but to sell themselves, organ by organ. . . ." This striking and emotive assertion, however, does not correspond at all to the real trade, where one buys a single kidney, nothing more. Yet the author repeated it on television in the autumn of 1995.[54] He continues: "Tourism for organ transplants seems to be prospering in Latin America, even if most of those countries have legislated against commercialisation of the human body. Next to prostitution and drug dealing, the trade in organs is one of the most lucrative forms of criminality today."[55]

This gift, for which nothing can be given in return, distresses the recipient. The author focuses on the difficulties some people feel in regarding the transplanted organ as truly part of themselves (which are real enough), but is reticent about the positive aspects of transplants. Reading him, one would easily forget that a transplant saves the patient from imminent death, often enables him or her to resume an active life, and is at least as much the result of a request by the patient as of the pride surgeons have in their skill.

Le Breton gives a great deal of space to the psychiatric troubles of certain recipients, which he appears to consider the normal reaction to having one's life unnaturally extended and incurring a debt one cannot repay:

> The recipient perceives the transplant as a wonderful present, which gives him a second lease of life. At this moment, he does not suspect what a poisonous gift he has just incorporated into his own flesh. . . . A transplant is the insertion of a new identity as well as of a new organ. Medical discourse, which insists upon the physical mechanism, is disproved by the way the recipient's personal identity is undermined. To integrate a transplant into one's self involves an interior crisis. . . . During the first phase, coinciding with the fear of rejection or infection, the new organ remains an intruder, a persecutor. . . . In the second phase, the organ begins to be perceived as one component of one's self. . . . In the course of time, interiorization occurs, the organ blends into the image of the body. . . . That is the normal course of events after transplants, but it does not exclude the persistent awareness of indebtedness and of alarming strangeness, nor of a general anxiety at having crossed the symbolic line dividing life and death. The lifelong need for daily immunosuppressive medication to combat

rejection of the transplant is a permanent reminder of how precarious is this alliance with the Other, and with death. . . . A not insignificant minority of individuals are affected by the insertion of a strange organ and by the intolerable debt. Many authors have described psychiatric complications following transplants. . . . [These mental troubles] show the devious ways in which symbolism asserts itself after all, in an operation which medical discourse would like to present as purely mechanical. . . . Written discussions on transplants, being always favorable, pass over these mental troubles in silence.[56]

The practice of transplants, according to Le Breton, is an example of the passionate denial of death which characterizes Western medicine:

Nowadays, the struggle against death is an essential and active principle in medical morality, and its social consequence is to increase the fear of death even further. Besides its social and cultural effects, this obstinate repression of death costs the patient not only his liberty but also a great deal of pain, for an outcome which is often uncertain. Postponing death is only a victory if its result is a lasting joy in life, or if it comes from a clear willingness to undergo this ordeal. . . . The task of medicine is not to "conquer death," as many doctors like to say, for if so it is permanently and basically doomed to failure; its task is the humbler one of relieving suffering.[57]

The chapter ends by assimilating the postmortem removal of organs to cannibalism:

People talk freely about "a shortage of organs" without seeing the obscenity of what they are saying, and without querying the moral significance of such a statement. . . . Organ transplants are not a sign of a generous society; on the contrary, they introduce a flaw into the social fabric, they alter collective morality, they lead one to wish for the death of a stranger, and they transform the essence of a human being into one material object among others. . . . In the name of life or of human solidarity (to use a hallowed phrase), the Western world has invented a hitherto unknown form of cannibalism.[58]

Le Breton waxes indignant over the admittedly provocative proposals of Professor François Dagognet, who said the obligations imposed by social solidarity meant that bodies should be nationalized postmortem.[59] He is just as indignant over certain very tactless remarks made by those in charge of transplants, putting blame on the public; for instance, Professor Cabrol, when he was president of France-Transplant, said that relatives who refuse permission for organs to be donated are condemning the potential recipient to death: "When parents refuse to give the organs of their recently dead child, they are condemning another child to death."[60]

Not everything Le Breton says is false; he has read a great deal, and defends his position with some skill. However, he completely overlooks the steps taken to guard against misapplication of medical procedures, as mentioned above. What is more, he seems to completely forget the interests of the patient himself, whom he represents as simply the subject of a medical experiment. To read him, one would think no doctor ever thinks of relieving his patient's suffering. This is a blatant distortion of the truth, and weakens the impact of certain just comments which he does make.

However, Le Breton was more moderate in a later article, published in the journal *Lumière et Vie* in 1995 in a special issue, "The body, organ donations and transplants."[61] After giving a good deal of space to the problems raised by the way transplants were organized in France in 1992 (though in more moderate and sober terms than in his article of 1993), he reports that the situation improved with the institution of the French Establishment for Transplants: "The lack of transparency and abuse of trust so frequent in past years, and widely reported in the media, seems to have been a major reason why people refused to donate organs. It is precisely from a wish for better control, and with the intention of restoring the confidence so severely undermined in France, that France Transplant was replaced in September 1994 by a State organisation, the French Establishment for Transplants."[62] Although Le Breton admits in his conclusion that "transplant medicine cannot be called into question,"[63] he remains extremely critical of the French system whereby consent is presumed, even though refusals are now officially recorded.

In these two publications, Le Breton makes a real contribution to the discussion; it is indeed necessary to understand the depth of resistance to postmortem removal of organs, and the possible pitfalls in communicating with the general public, which is difficult to manage. The anthropological problems raised are well expressed in the conclusion of his 1995 article:

> There can be no solution to the question of whether the body after death is a mere object or whether it is still a human being. . . . No position gives anybody the authority to give a firm, authoritative, and non-polemical reply about the anthropological status of a corpse. The removal of organs today, like anatomy lessons in the past, arouses either horror or militant enthusiasm. . . . Campaigns for the removal of organs encounter difficulties which show how strong is the social resistance to the idea that the human body is an empty shell, a mere reservoir of organs. . . . No one emerges unscathed from a debate in which there is a conflict of values, world views, and moral reasons, each having its own validity. The status of the corpse, especially that of a loved person, arouses in everyone the deepest sense of sacredness.[64]

As early as 1991, in his contribution to the Lenoir Report, Professor Carpentier had correctly observed the dangers of simplistic statements and a triumphalist tone when communicating with the general public:

> All too often, in a presentation where sensationalism outweighs rationality and high profile personalities outweigh team-work, the only impression the public retains is of a race to obtain organs, a lack of respect towards corpses, a risk of breaking the rule that organs should be given without payment, and "errors" in diagnosis of brain death. Thus, the many TV programs put out in recent years to encourage organ donations have had the opposite result: every time one of these programs was broadcast, cases where families refused to donate organs increased.[65]

MONETTE VACQUIN

Monette Vacquin's book, which is both confused and visionary, blends the expression of her hostility towards assisted procreation with a psychoanalytic analysis of Mary Shelley's *Frankenstein*.[66] As a psychoanalyst, she sees medical techniques for aiding procreation (e.g., test-tube fertilization, embryo transplant) as risking serious misuse and even a revival of Nazi eugenics. She accuses the biomedical profession of pursuing unlimited and unshared power, in a totalitarian spirit, and sees scientists as being in the

63

grip of hubris, the real though unacknowledged motive for the work they do on embryos.

This excess of scientific zeal, in her view, is equally manifest in attitudes towards the dying. Advances in resuscitation technique have led to the chronic vegetative state, and control of artificial respiration to numerous cases of prolonged coma. According to this author, "the positivist logic of the medical profession made them regard it as their duty to make profits from the dying." She writes that thanks to the Cavaillet Law of 1976, "the corpses of the dead were at the disposal of doctors, available for any removal of organs, without consulting the dead man's family, unless he had made it known while alive that he refused this." In December 1988, after what she says was intense lobbying by Professor Alain Milhaud at the National Ethics Committee, the law passed by the Assembly "would endorse the priority of experimentation over therapeutic treatment, and would hand over the weakest persons to a biomedicine in which one can no longer recognise real medicine."[67]

Monette Vacquin gives an entirely distorted account of the debates around the application of the Cavaillet Law and around the attitudes and experiments of Professor Milhaud, for, as we saw above, he was reproved and penalized by his professional body. As for the law passed in December 1988, she distorts this too; in fact, the only research techniques authorized by this law were those of therapeutic purpose, and it embodied the recommendations of the National Ethics Committee.[68]

JEAN ZIEGLER

Jean Ziegler's militancy is inspired by his opposition to capitalist commerce. His 1975 book *Les Vivants et la mort* (*Death and the Living*)[69] is chiefly important because of its date, for at that time organ transplants were not yet widespread, and the Cavaillet Law did not exist, but the concept of brain death had already been defined, seven years previously. Ziegler's approach is a radical critique of capitalism and of the denial of death in contemporary Western societies, caused, naturally, by the advance of capitalism:

> The society from which I come, which decrees that a taboo of silence must suppress any discussion of the death event, offered me no means of understanding my own certain death. . . . Like millions of others, when facing the problem of

death, I fell victim to a specific social strategy—the one set in motion by the dominant capitalist class to maintain its privileges. This class inflicts upon millions of people sufferings which turn our planet into a charnel house. I discovered that among all its weapons of exploitation the most effective, the most insidious, the least recognisable, was symbolic violence, that is to say the corpus of images and representations which this class produces for its own use and imposes on the dependant classes. This symbolic violence nowadays reduces man, both in his life and when facing death, to his simple function as a commercial entity.[70]

The first part of the book is devoted to black communities in Brazil, their conception of death, and their ways of handling it, of which the author draws an enthusiastic picture, having been initiated into the syncretic Nago-Yoruba cults; in contrast, the second part is utterly negative:

I had to explore, area by area, the death practices (*thanatopraxis*) of the commercial capitalist societies of the West, . . . [and analyse] the relationship between the socio-economic aims of commercial capitalism and the images of death it produces. In the heart of the hospitals of Europe and America there has arisen a class of thanatocrats, of men conducting human sacrifice. . . . This class enjoys power which is almost total and unchallenged over the dead, the aged, and those seriously ill.[71]

It will be sufficient to reproduce the most striking passages which Ziegler devotes to commercial cannibalism, the rise of the thanatocrats, and the reign of those who conduct human sacrifice:

From now on, man in the West is a commodity. . . . One might have thought that at least the body, last stronghold of concrete individuality, with its mysterious networks, its hidden organs, its secret life, would escape commercial cannibalism. Wrong! Kidneys, heart, lungs, have become commodities, and so too, soon, will the liver. Man's essential organs nowadays are bought and sold, transplanted, stockpiled, used in commerce. Illustrated catalogues of organs for sale circulate in the world of American hospitals. Organ banks and organ exchanges operate with increasing profits. . . .[72]

The Harvard Declaration inaugurates a *conceptual revolution*: the institutions of capitalist hegemony, namely medical associations, State legislatures, the ethical code of hospitals, have seized control of the thanatological problem now that the usual concept of death, that is to say the concept generally accepted by popular consensus, is crumbling under the impact of new biological discoveries. . . . From now on, the dying man is denied a role in the drama he is passing through; never again will his intimate needs (or those of his family and friends), his claims, his wishes, be taken into account. The only things that count are the technical limitations governing the acts of those whose mandate is to organize the deaths of others. The new medical imperialism establishes itself through violence. A class of thanatocrats is born, organizing the deaths of others according to technical standards which are defined and controlled by this class itself. . . .[73]

An accident victim or a sick man is brought into hospital. In the same hospital, a seriously ill man is waiting for a new organ which will cure him. This organ will be removed from the body of the accident victim and transplanted into the recipient's body. . . . Conflict arises between two forms of the passing of time: on the one hand, the time needed to get the necessary instruments in place, and on the other, the length of time the organ will keep its vitality. . . .[74]

When vital organs are to be removed, or when the cost of care becomes too great to be socially acceptable, the thanatocrats imitate the criteria of selection and decision-making found in commercial society, weighing the relative profits to be obtained from life or from death. . . . Hospital thanatocrats become, in the most literal sense of the term, *the executioners of the dominant class*. . . . The thanatopraxis of commercial societies brings legal assassination, as surely as clouds bring storms. . . . There is nothing, absolutely nothing, in the conceptual apparatus of contemporary thanatocrats to exclude the arrival of a thanatopraxis similar to that practiced by Nazi barbarity.[75]

Le Breton cited this book as the work of a predecessor. Reading it reveals the ideological nature of the charges brought by many contemporary intellectuals against the medical profession. They seem to see its advances as being the very essence of a social system which they reject.

TRADE IN HUMAN ORGANS AND TISSUES

In parallel with the technical advances in medical treatment and surgery which gave therapeutic value to elements of the human body, these elements became increasingly the objects of commercial trade—that is to say, "a trade which is always more or less secret, immoral, and unlawful."[76] As regards organs, two sources feed the market: the so-called "voluntary" sale of organs by the living, for which the chief evidence comes from India, and the use of organs from executed criminals, for which most evidence comes from China. As regards tissues, which are less fragile, it is admitted that there have been cases where corpses were illicitly used, in secret and without the knowledge of the kin, by professionals working in morgues and operating theaters where autopsies were carried out, and that they were paid for this.

"VOLUNTARY" SALE OF ORGANS BY THE LIVING BEFORE 1990

This is a subcategory of the situation where a living person donates one of a pair of organs, which happens between relatives and also between unrelated but medically compatible friends, and could theoretically occur through altruism towards strangers. It is worth noting that France has its own tradition on this point; very little use is made there of donations by the living (only 3 percent of kidney transplants in 1993), unlike Scandinavia (26 percent) and the United States (25 percent).[77]

"Voluntary" sale of organs from the living has developed into a system in non-Western countries, where technical obstacles and, even more, cultural objections prevent postmortem removal from developing. There are technical obstacles in all poor countries, where there are few services capable of reanimating victims of road accidents, and where road and rail networks are inadequate. But this hardly matters in comparison with the cultural objections typical of Asia and the Middle East, where people attribute great moral importance to keeping the body intact until the funeral rites are over, since these alone can bring a human life to its normal close. The overriding importance of cultural context shows itself in the legal solutions to the problems posed by the need for organs. Whereas every country in the Western tradition has developed postmortem removals (based on explicit consent in countries of Anglo-Saxon tradition, and on presumed consent in those of Latin tradition), no country in the Asiatic or Middle Eastern tradition has yet done so. Nevertheless, one can foresee that in the long run the postmortem solution will prevail, since the trade in live donations puts any national medical community which accepts or organizes it at risk of being ostracized by international professional bodies.

In the early 1980s, foreigners with kidney disease would fairly often arrive in the West from distant lands, together with a "relative" who was to be the donor, and get themselves operated on. However, transplant surgeons in our countries soon ceased to tolerate these devices. They were barred from legitimate medicine, but still continued for quite a while in London, in the private sector serving rich clients from abroad. In July 1985 a first scandal, arising from a quarrel over money between the "donor relative," who was Indian, and the "recipient relative," who was Pakistani, led to the Humana Wellington Foundation, a private London hospital funded from America, having its license withdrawn. Yet a second scandal was required, in 1989, before Parliament passed a law forbidding commercial trade in organs. This scandal resulted in the British Medical Association imposing penalties on the kidney specialist and surgeons concerned; one of the latter had already been involved in the 1985 affair.

Towards 1990 there were scandals in both France and Germany over people declaring publicly that they were prepared to act as intermediaries to bring together those who wished to sell kidneys and those who wished to buy, which in effect would mean organizing a kidney transplant trade. It seems these declarations were largely bluff. For instance, a Netherlands organization called ROGB (Reiner Oude Grote Bevernog) claimed in the autumn of 1989 to have arranged a commercial transaction between a Dutch woman who had sold her kidney for 260,000 francs and a girl from the Gulf States who had received it; ROGB stated that the operation had taken place "in a private clinic in the neighbourhood of Paris . . . by a team of surgeons that did not include any French doctors."[78] These claims caused the Council of the Order and of France-Transplant to issue statements of their disapproval, but were never followed by any penalties, since there was never any proof that the operation really took place.[79]

Again, in Germany in 1993, a Polish intermediary named Robert Konarski said he was organizing operations in cooperation with clinics in Baden-Württemberg and Bavaria, the "voluntary sellers" being Poles. The practice was not illegal at the time, but the law was later changed.[80]

"VOLUNTARY" SALE OF ORGANS BY THE LIVING IN INDIA

Western nations having rejected the practice, transplants by "voluntary" sale from the living became limited to countries in Asia or the Middle East which have good medical services: Egypt, Iraq, and, above all, India. There, such operations are not illegal. Information from the first two countries is scanty, since transplant surgeons there do not publish their results, and it is difficult for Western journalists to get any access to these countries, which is not the case in India. Therefore we will describe the situation in India, where the trade is considerable, since it is estimated (in 1997) that there are about two thousand kidney transplants per year in which the donors are paid. But this trade in organs became increasingly marginalized, because of mounting hostility from the Indian medical profession, from 1990 (date of the first protests) to 1995 (when a legal scandal erupted at the beginning of the year).

The year 1990 saw the publication of two important articles. A cover article in *India Today*, headed "The Organs Bazaar," described the situation in India, showing the dilemma of doctors who disagreed over what their conduct should be. Some rejected commercialization, others organized it, in order to make it more moral. The article reminded readers of the national data: 80,000 cases of kidney failure per year, 650 kidney dialysis units, allowing only one in five of the patients to be treated. Poor villages were living on the proceeds of "paid donations." It should be noted that to cover themselves against legal action, the surgeons would make the "donor" sign a declaration that he was acting out of the affection he felt for the recipient.[81] The other article, in *The Lancet*, signed by four surgeons from the United Arab Emirates and Oman, severely criticized 131 kidney transplants carried out in Bombay on patients from those countries. The treatment they received turned out to be unsatisfactory, and the surgeons considered that these patients had been exploited rather than cared for.[82]

It was not till 1995 that the world press mentioned the Indian organ trade again, and again it was because of a scandal. Almost a year previously, the Federal Indian Parliament had passed a law forbidding "paid donations," after three years of debate. In India's federal system, a law has to be adopted by the state parliaments to become effective, and so far only three out of the twenty-five states had done so: Goa, Himachal Pradesh, and Maharashtra, of which the capital is the large city of Bombay, which some years previously had been deeply involved in the organ trade. However, the organ trade was gradually driven away from major hospitals, which confined themselves to treating Indian nationals and to using organs from unpaid donors; it shifted to private establishments, which were concentrated in Madras (Tamil Nadu State) and Bangalore (Karnataka State).

The scandal which brought India back into the headlines of the world press in 1995 was virtually identical to a previous one concerning Ahmed Kroc in 1989, involving Turkey and Britain:

Bangalore, India/Middle East, 1995

In Bangalore in 1995, a certain Velu told the police that he had become a donor, but involuntarily. He declared that after being lured to the great city by recruiters promising him a job, he agreed to go into a clinic to sell his blood, as a way of paying the money he owed them.

He awoke heavily bandaged, but it was explained that he had had a fall while giving blood. When he later discovered that he had a kidney missing, he accepted five thousand rupees (according to his lawyer), or ten thousand rupees (his own account)—which is a great deal for a blood donation.

Turkey/London, Britain, 1989

Ahmed, an Anatolian peasant who had been lured to London by the promise of employment, went into a clinic to undergo (so he thought) blood tests and health examinations before signing a contract.

He then discovered that his kidney had been removed. He accepted twenty-five hundred pounds, and returned to Turkey. Having spent this money and been refused a second sum, he went to the editors of the widely circulating daily paper *Hurriyet*. He was prosecuted under Turkish law for the illicit sale of an organ, and received a suspended sentence of eighteen months in jail.

Velu's complaint was taken seriously by the Bangalore police, and led to a mass of other lawsuits. Nine complaints were accepted for prosecution, and there were four arrests of doctors and intermediaries. Journalists rushed, logically enough, to the villages and slums where the people who had sold their kidneys lived, and drew a pitiful picture of their situation: the money was all spent, and only their mutilation remained. There was a host of complaints from sellers alleging that they had been deceived; the police recorded fifty, but only kept five on their books, in addition to the earlier ones.

In the ensuing debates, it was noticeable how vigorous were the responses of those Indian surgeons who had chosen to accept commercialization in order to save the sick. The best known is Dr. K. C. Reddy, who as early as 1980 had defended his actions at international medical congresses by setting out his dilemma: "Buy, or let die." For scandals and complaints, as the surgeons knew perfectly well, would destabilize the system they had shared in creating.

There were other complaints of abuse besides those from Bangalore; for instance, a man in Bombay who was in debt (he owed 160 pounds on his credit card) went to the police because surgeons had approached him by telephone after his creditor advised him to clear his debt by selling a kidney.[83] The police, eager to prove their zeal, closed down a "clandestine" clinic near Bombay, the Kawshaha Clinic.[84] These clandestine networks were acting for foreign clients brought to Indian clinics by intermediaries. The doctors and recruiters arrested in Bangalore had already undergone an investigation by the Medical Council, launched at the request of the consul for Saudi Arabia; this led to nothing, having apparently been only slackly carried out. So the scandal revealed a situation where administrative neglect came close to wilful blindness, and showed how commercial excesses were linked to the unregulated acceptance of foreign patients paying heavy fees. Meanwhile, Indian patients whose lives had been saved by transplants defended their surgeons, marched in support of them at Bangalore,[85] and presented motions in the parliaments of Karnataka and Tamil Nadu demanding that the law should be only gradually applied and that the organ trade should continue, in a regulated and moral manner, so that lives would still be saved. Dr. Reddy gave journalists some solid arguments against the law forbidding organ trade, which he considered unrealistic:

> In the West, there is a system which takes charge of the health and the needs of citizens. The program for taking organs from corpses is an integral part of that system. One cannot take one element from the system and transfer it to another country if the rest of the infrastructure does not come too. In your countries, dialysis and hospital treatment are free. Moreover, one must take cultural traditions into account. In Japan, as you know, transplants taken from corpses are illegal; it goes against their culture.[86]

However, it seems logical to foresee that the trade will continue to be marginalized, but will persist for a long time, in increasing secrecy, and so without regulation. The following unconfirmed incident shows such marginalization, and may indicate that the trade is now worldwide in scale. It is said that a small group of people arriving at Delhi airport from Latin America towards the end of 1994 were X-rayed, for since they had no luggage they were suspected of being drug smugglers; they were not carrying any drugs, but each had a long, recent abdominal scar, and they admitted having gone abroad to sell a kidney.[87] No doubt Indian surgeons, who are indispensable to the systematic organ trade, will become more and more unwilling to take part in it. Nevertheless it is almost certain that the ending of this trade in India will be a long and gradual process.

CHINA: EXPLOITATION OF ORGANS FROM THOSE EXECUTED

The practice of taking organs from executed prisoners has existed in China since the early 1980s, and an official document from 1984 already regulates it.[88] In 1990, and again in 1991, this exploitative situation had been denounced, but the governmental authorities denied its existence.[89] In 1994, it hit the headlines of the world press. In August 1994 the organization Human Rights Watch (Asia) published a report speaking of two or three thousand transplants done every year with organs taken from executed prisoners. It denounced as "vivisection" cases where kidneys or liver had allegedly been taken from prisoners even before they were executed. In October 1994 the BBC broadcast an accusatory documentary entitled *The Organ Trade in China*, the coproducer being the dissident Harry Wu. Wu is Chinese but an American citizen. He runs the Laogai Foundation, the principal activity of which is to denounce all human rights violations in China, in particular the workings of the judicial and penal systems, where forced labor is a major feature. I have seen this film, which lasts less than a quarter of an hour, and it seemed to me to be far from solid. It consists of a succession of accusatory statements and powerful images of public executions, which are horrible to see but are no proof at all that organs are being taken on any large scale, the whole being accompanied by a commentary full of innuendos. The Chinese, furious, defended themselves vigorously. But their arguments were rather contradictory; on the one hand they asserted that the main source for transplant operations was brain-dead victims of traffic accidents, and on the other hand that they sought the consent of those about to be executed, or of their families, and that the latter received financial compensation. This last claim contradicts the proven custom of making the families of condemned men pay the costs of execution (bullets included), and seems very improbable.

It is very difficult to assess the plausibility of these accusations. Some highly fantastic incriminating incidents are related in a surprising way. For instance, Harry Wu's documentary presents an expatriate dissident doctor who explains how he removed both kidneys from a man condemned to death shortly before his execution. This doctor comments on the "operation," explaining that the kidneys were intended for high-ranking officials, while he is enjoying a hearty meal in a noisy restaurant, which, in my opinion, considerably diminishes the force of his evidence.

In these denunciations there is a mixture of different levels of practice, scientific and magical. Thus, the document which the Laogai Foundation issued soon after the BBC program came out, giving a commentary on it, begins with the description of a horrific incident which happened in 1970 and was witnessed by Harry Wu, who at that time was undergoing forced labor. After the execution of a prisoner "condemned to death for writing 'Down with President Mao' on his cigarette pack, this prisoner's brain was removed immediately for the use, so they said, of the eighty-year-old father of a Party official, who was hoping to regain his mental faculties by this means."[90] Yet even the most extreme accusations may be true, and are not improbable in a system which is simultaneously totalitarian and profit oriented, in a culture which accepts the sympathetic magic where like cures like. They are in any case widely believed, for with the pitiless Chinese authorities everything seems possible.

In April 1995 Harry Wu was arrested during a secret trip to China, and at the end of July the Chinese authorities broadcast the video of an interrogation during which Wu admitted having made seven inaccurate statements of fact in his reports, three of them being in the film about organ transplants.[91] As we know, this dissident, who because of his American nationality was an obstacle to the normalization of relations between the United States and China, was condemned to fifteen years in prison but then immediately expelled and sent back to the States at the end of August 1995, just before the United Nations Conference on Women, hosted by Beijing.

Are these denunciations aimed at the proper target? Should not the human rights organizations make it their priority to denounce the totalitarian nature of China's regime and the massive scale of capital punishment which it carries out? Though the exact figure for executions in Mainland China is not known, it is assessed at around 1,500 a year, which is high even for such a populous country. (We may recall that in the United States between 1976, when the death penalty was restored, and 1997, 330 people were executed; while human rights organizations estimate that there were 700 executions per year in the Soviet Union between 1960 and 1990.)

The idea that a criminal can pay his debt to society by agreeing to donate a kidney was put into practice in another Chinese country, Taiwan, in the mid-1980s. But these donations, which often involved setting up a plaque in memory of the condemned man, were discontinued after protests from the Western medical community.

ILLEGAL EXPLOITATION OF TISSUES FROM CORPSES

Cases where corpses are illicitly exploited do not form a coherent block, simply a succession of small, isolated scandals, generally marked by brief newspaper items of a few lines only, announcing that persons employed in some morgue have been found guilty. They are not a topic for press analysis.

At the same time, we may note an increasing tendency to present as irresponsible, or even criminal, actions which had hitherto been considered perfectly legitimate, when human body products (such as placentas, endocrine glands, brain tissue) are gathered by laboratories which extract medical or cosmetic substances from them. There are clearly some quite legitimate reasons for this change in attitude: the fear of contamination has been revived by certain dramatic examples of diseases appearing as a result of medical treatments.

For example, instances of a fatal type of encephalitis, Creutzfeldt-Jakob disease (CJD), occurred among children treated with a natural growth hormone made from endocrine glands taken from corpses. In 1983 in France a report from IGAS (the General Inspectorate of Social Affairs) condemned the high-risk procedures involved in collecting glands from corpses which, for reasons of convenience, had come from neurological departments; this report had no effect at the time, but was remembered in 1994 during the scandal over growth hormones which involved the Pasteur Institute, which had produced several contaminated batches of hormone in 1984 and 1985. These had affected twenty-seven families, whose children had in most cases died. In 1993, the state undertook to grant compensation to these families, who were also authorized to sue the people responsible for this negligence, but not to receive any further compensation.

The rise of diseases caused by prions was already causing anxiety before the mad cow scandal was revealed in April 1996. Thus, as early as November 1993, anxiety was expressed over blood products made from placentas at the Mérieux Institute.[92] The advent of AIDS has substantially increased the risks of contamination from products of the human body, as the contaminated-blood affair plainly showed. The era of almost blind trust in therapeutic novelties seems to be over.

Yet one can equally well see these dramatic ways of presenting the therapeutic or cosmetic uses of human body products as the result of an irrational, morbid sensitivity, and the pursuit of sensation at any price. The way militant antiabortionists create confusion by regularly accusing laboratories of making medicines and cosmetics out of fetuses, when in fact they are using placentas, is another instance of the same unhealthy rhetoric.

EVALUATION: EXPLOITATION AND FANTASIES

Earlier, I deliberately put the term "voluntary" in quotation marks, even though there is much data to show that many people in the world do indeed choose the option of selling one kidney. Living in harsh conditions which damage their health yet bring no benefits, those who are trapped in the infernal cycle of debt, or who face heavy expenses (such as the marriage of a daughter, in India), really do want to sell an organ in order to solve their problem. All over the world since the mid-1980s one could see small press advertisements making such offers, which generally lead to newspaper articles or interviews with the would-be donor. When I was doing research in France among those involved in organ transplants, both medical correspondents and doctors told me they often received letters from the Mahgreb or from Eastern Europe proposing the sale of a kidney, and often also offering to share the profits with them, if they would organize it. But these offers did not result in setting up an organized trade between those regions and Western Europe, where such operations are now illegal everywhere, even if the laws were sometimes formulated after some small-scale trade had been discovered. My use of quotation marks is therefore technically inaccurate.

However, I have decided to keep it because it corresponds to the emotional truth—the judgement that the seller has no real choice.

It is easy to see that even when states tolerate or encourage the trade in human organs and tissues, these practices involve situations where poverty and distress are exploited, or alternatively where the power of the authorities over prisoners is abused. The possibility of turning to criminal activity is never far away. In spite of their intentions of putting the trade on a more moral basis, it seems that the Indian surgeons who chose to relieve the sufferings of their patients by organizing the transactions themselves have lost their way in a blind alley. Nobody who takes part in this trade remains unharmed.

What is more, when organs are taken from the living, there is necessarily an irreversible mutilation of the donor. Mutilations which are morally acceptable in cases where the organ is donated for altruistic reasons, and generally because of ties of affection, arouse feelings of disgust and rejection when a commercial transaction is involved. How could one fail to think that the man in poverty is the victim in this unequal bargain, where he accepts irreversible damage to himself in exchange for a sum of money which will only relieve his troubles for a little while? One feels pity and anger on seeing the scars of the "paid donors" in the shantytowns—slums which the Indians themselves call *Kidneyvakkam* because so many of the people there have sold a kidney. In contrast, it is precisely because one never sees any photograph of anyone who has sold his own cornea that one is led to doubt that such a trade actually exists, even though there have been repeated allegations to that effect since 1990; would anyone resist printing a photo of a man who has "voluntarily" become half blind, if a proven case could be found?

Already in the nineteenth century, when there was a market for hair and teeth, some observers condemned the way the poor sold their bodies piecemeal, seeing in this a symbol of their exploitation.

VIOLENCE IN LATIN AMERICA

In Latin America in the mid-1990s, the situation as regards the trade in organs was very different from that in India. In the second half of the 1980s, every country in the region had passed laws organizing postmortem harvesting and based upon the presumption of consent, and the "voluntary" sale of organs by the living was illegal everywhere. Yet there was a very widespread belief throughout the continent that such a trade did exist, which had been publicly declared for almost a decade. This belief affected all classes and was expressed (as was shown above) through the recurrent dramatic stories about eye thefts. The belief was reinforced by a series of actual events—the crimes that occurred in 1992 in Barranquilla and Montes de Oca, namely murders of street children, marginalized individuals, and political opponents.

Allegations of the abuse of adoptions in order to steal organs surfaced again in 1992, as was noted above. Also in that year, two scandals in March reactivated the belief in large-scale organ thefts: the Barranquilla affair in Colombia, and the one at Montes de Oca in Argentina.

BARRANQUILLA, COLOMBIA

It was at the start of the Carnival season that scandal erupted in Barranquilla, a Colombian town with a population of two hundred thousand, on the Caribbean Sea.[93] On Saturday, February 29, a ragpicker named Oscar Rafael Hernandez arrived at the police station; he had been knocked out and riddled with bullets by the guards at the Free University for Medicine, who had enticed him there by promising that there were cardboard boxes to collect, but had recovered consciousness in the medical faculty's morgue, surrounded by dead bodies, and had managed to escape. This led to a police raid. One dying man and eleven corpses of recently murdered tramps and ragpickers were found in the university morgue. On Wednesday, March 4, once Carnival was over (this being an important event in the region), the number of arrests rose to fifteen: ten guards and various university administrators. Three judges, all women, were put in charge of this terrible affair. The head guard admitted to fifty murders, but said he was acting on the orders of the university director, since there was a shortage of corpses for the students' practical anatomy work. Later stages in the inquiry revealed that the murders had been going on for several months and that the guards used to sell the corpses to the university for dissection. There was also a trade in skeletons and anatomical fragments, which were sold to other medical faculties, but these actions did not constitute a crime and were not the subject of legal charges. This was quite logical, and not the result of a conspiracy, as some have suggested, for why should the judges bother to charge self-confessed murderers over minor irregularities?

As one can see, the Barranquilla affair is a relatively simple one where the criminals were arrested as soon as their crimes were discovered, and where (though one could hardly guess this from sensationalist descriptions of the crimes which were published) the type of injuries received by the wretched victims made it obviously impossible to suspect that the use of their organs could have been the motive. Of the eleven corpses found, five had died from blows on the head and six from bullet wounds.

The repercussions of this ghastly affair were important for two reasons. Firstly, it revealed the inhumane social conditions prevalent in Colombia; Barranquilla is one instance among several cases in Latin America where the homeless and marginalized have been systematically murdered, as will be further discussed below. After the revelation of these murders, people from these dispossessed groups demonstrated, marched, and held press conferences not only in Barranquilla but in Cartagena and Bogotá too. Secondly, these murders seemed to replicate the crimes of early nineteenth-century body snatchers in league with doctors, especially those of Burke and Hare mentioned above.

MONTES DE OCA, ARGENTINA

It was also in March 1992 that the world press covered the scandal of Montes de Oca, soon after a judicial inquiry opened into the running of Colonia, a psychiatric asylum located there (about two hundred kilometers from Buenos Aires). This housed about twelve hundred patients, and there had been ill treatment of the inmates, most of whom were severely mentally handicapped. But this case is very different from the one at Barranquilla. The committee of inquiry, reporting in 1993, laid no charge of murder; the alleged facts were so far in the past (beginning in 1976) that the truth will no doubt never be known. A further and more general factor impeding the discovery of the truth is the existence in Argentina at the end of the 1970s and in the early 1980s of a military dictatorship which arranged the "disappearances" of people who opposed it—a euphemism meaning that they had been assassinated by official forces. This might explain some anomalies revealed by the tribunal of inquiry in the way inmates were buried, since it seems probable that Montes de Oca was used for secret burials of those who had "disappeared."

My discussion makes use of a source that is virtually unknown in France, an Argentine TV program put out in the autumn of 1993 embodying a debate between parties who disagreed over this dossier.[94]

After Dr. Florencio Sanchez, who had been director of Colonia for over fifteen years, was arrested at the end of 1991 on suspicion of financial irregularities, the most fantastic accusations appeared in the press. People alleged that he was engaging in a trade in blood (he did in fact run a blood bank in his own private clinic), and a trade in babies; it was said that the mentally handicapped inmates were encouraged to live promiscuously, and that the resulting babies were taken from their mothers soon after birth and sold abroad for adoption.

The main accusation was of a trade in organs. It was said that Florencio Sanchez would murder the handicapped, whom the asylum then registered as "fugitives." It was said that 1,321 inmates had disappeared between 1976 and 1991, i.e., 88 per year; other sources reckoned the number at 1,100 between 1986 and 1991, i.e., the enormous figure of 275 per year, almost a quarter of the inmates. This accusation was supported by the fact that the body of one "fugitive," Marcello Ortiz, was found in the vicinity, lacking its eyes; his family complained, pointing out that he was paralyzed, which made it unlikely that he had run away.

Some families had laid complaints against the asylum, but without result; similarly a complaint laid by the family of Dr. Cecilia Giubileo after she disappeared in 1985 was judged not to be worth pursuing, which cleared Dr. Florencio Sanchez from the suspicion of having got rid of a new employee who was curious, and was preparing to denounce the illegal trafficking going on at Colonia.

None of these earlier family complaints were reexamined by the 1993 tribunal of inquiry, which only retained for consideration some two hundred or three hundred cases concerning the illegal postmortem removal of eyes, done without consulting the families, between 1978 and 1985. The eyes had been sent to the ophthalmic clinic of Lagleize and used for corneal grafts. When the legal hearing was opened at the end of 1991, one witness, a former male nurse, was presented to the press by Araoz, the minister for social affairs. He said he used to regularly remove eyes from bodies in the hospital morgue, using a small spoon. Controversy ensued between the doctors, who maintained that at that period there had been nothing illegal in taking organs without family consent and that in those days hospital directors were authorized to make such decisions for the sake of the common good, and the lawyers, who considered that such procedures were illegal.[95]

Dr. Florencio Sanchez died in prison in 1992, after writing a book to clear his name. He had not grown rich. One will never know the extent of the abuses at Montes de Oca. It seems certain that the handicapped inmates were ill treated, perhaps due to inadequate administration at Colonia and to the sadism of some who were employed there.

A few weeks after they occurred, these two affairs inspired a couple of short twenty-minute documentary programs on the German channel Spiegel TV; their titles, *Organmafia Kolumbia* and *Organraub*, indicate a serious distortion of the facts, at any rate as regards Barranquilla.[96] The following year there appeared accusatory documentaries asserting that organ theft really occurs, and making great use of these affairs.

MURDERS OF THE MARGINALIZED AND OF STREET CHILDREN IN LATIN AMERICA

The Barranquilla affair is one instance of those murders of marginalized groups—tramps, homeless ragpickers—which have recently occurred on a large scale in some Latin American countries, especially Colombia and Brazil. By organizing marches and demonstrations in several towns, other *desechables* showed nationwide solidarity with the Barranquilla victims. (Marginal groups in Colombia seem to have defiantly appropriated the contemptuous term *desechables*, literally meaning "what can be thrown away," a process like that by which Parisian gangs in nineteenth-century Paris adopted the insulting name "apaches" as their own.) But one should notice an important difference: the murderers at Barranquilla were arrested, whereas those who commit murders of marginal persons, being themselves members of the police or of private militias mainly recruited and organized by shopkeepers, are only arrested in exceptional circumstances. Indeed, these murderers enjoy active cooperation at many social levels, and their actions are regarded as useful by a large section of the public, who are delighted to be permanently rid of potential or actual delinquents whom it would be costly and ineffective to imprison. Yet the murders are not committed in broad daylight, for though they are widely tolerated they are not legal, and they do also arouse opposition—from human rights activists, and also from liberals and from left-wing opinion. The assassins know quite well that scandal would harm them, so they operate in a semisecrecy which encourages all kinds of rumors. The bodies of the victims are frequently mutilated, and these mutilations are then frequently interpreted as a proof that organs have been stolen. However, the practice of mutilation is an old one, recorded, for example, during the "violence" in Colombia in the 1950s and 1960s,[97] and one can easily see what a part it plays in establishing a reign of terror.[98]

It was the murders of street children, above all, which stirred worldwide public opinion, especially around 1990, when a report from the humanitarian organization Amnesty International informed the whole world about revelations made in the mid-1980s by a Brazilian association combating the rising violence (IBASE, "the Street Children Movement"). In France, books and television documentaries have often described these notorious facts; they stir public opinion, and sell very well. For instance, one can find one book about Brazil and one on the urchins of Bogotá in a series called "Children of the River," stating on the covers that it aims "to make readers aware of the suffering children and young people of our times." The writings of those who know the subject[99] make no connection between these heartbreaking facts and any organ trade whatever.

The film *Urchins of Bogota* broadcast on March 22, 1990, as part of the "Special Envoy" series on the TV channel A2 had as its main topic the murder of street children.[100] It stirred public opinion by briefly showing (for two minutes out of the twenty) a little girl who was supposed to have been a victim of eye thieves; it proved impossible ever to trace her.

MURDERS OF POLITICAL OPPONENTS

Ever since the sixties, periods of virtual civil war in countries of Latin America and Central America (Argentina, Guatemala, Nicaragua, Salvador, Colombia, Brazil) have been characterized by "disappearances" of political opponents or mere suspects, which sometimes affected whole sections of the population. However, it is not during the actual periods of terror but in their aftermath and during the return to normality that rumors of eye thefts arise, enabling people to speak indirectly about the past. As early as 1988, a group of Argentine psychologists proposed this as an interpretation.[101]

PRESSURES IN LATIN AMERICA

The poor of Latin America—afflicted by the "disappearances," enduring additional pressures from the rise of child trafficking (to be described below), and neglected by a medical system which, far from being egalitarian, gives high-quality treatment to the rich, but to them alone—saw their situation deteriorating in several countries at the beginning of the eighties. The anthropologist Nancy Scheper-Hughes considers that this deterioration explains the rise of the organ theft legend.[102] However, though this legend did first appear among the deprived, it spread to all classes, including the rich who do not experience the same difficult social conditions and insecurities as the poor. Also, it appeared more or less simultaneously in very diverse countries of Latin America—large and small, with and without a substantial Indian population. Conditions of civil war and the development of child trafficking seem to be the common factors for all these countries.

INTERNATIONAL ADOPTION, HUMAN TRAFFICKING, AND THE REIGN OF SUSPICION

INTERNATIONAL ADOPTION

International child adoption developed mainly after the end of the 1960s. Now firmly established, it constitutes the great majority of adoptions in France, where in 1990, and again in 1994, three thousand of the forty-five hundred adoptions made that year came from abroad. In Western Europe, Israel, Canada, and the United States there is a shortage of children for adoption, but they can supply their needs thanks to the existence in underdeveloped and heavily populated countries of numerous unwanted children among the poor (who do not choose for them to be born, but passively endure births, in countries where contraception is unknown or illegal).

Couples who are infertile need the children they cannot produce, and their demands create international adoptions—most of them normal, but some involving child trafficking. This situation can be compared with that created by drug takers in rich countries, who have created an international drug traffic flowing from producer countries to consumer countries. We must remember, however, that despite all the publicity they receive in the media, these cases of child trafficking are only a minority; most adoptions take place legally and do what they are supposed to do.

In rich countries, to adopt from abroad is regarded as a charitable deed, redressing injustice and putting an end to the material and above all the mental distress of abandoned children, while relieving the emotional lack in the life of the infertile couple. Child trafficking is deplored, but regarded as a secondary and relatively unimportant aspect of international adoption viewed as a whole, which is judged on balance to be a good thing. But there are many signs that in the countries from which the children come, the verdict is very different. There, international adoption is often regarded as plundering their human resources in a continuation of past colonial exploitation. From that point of view, child trafficking expresses the very essence of this unequal transaction, and the idea that international adoption opens the way to organ theft and murder appears logical and plausible to both rich and poor in the exploited countries.

CHILD TRAFFICKING IN LATIN AMERICA

In Latin America, belief in the reality of organ thefts appeared in association with the numerous cases of child trafficking which accompanied the development of international adoption.

This development gave real economic value to the abandoned children cared for in the charitable sector, since these children are of interest to people holding very strong cards. Moreover, it involved increasingly complex procedures, a process which made it necessary to have recourse to administrative and legal intermediaries. So one reads of lawyers whose fees have increased threefold in a few years in Brazil, or who "dominate an international adoption market estimated to be worth five million dollars"[103] in 1991 in Guatemala; likewise of notaries and judges (also in Guatemala) who take a profit at every stage of implementing the procedures, which they strip of all legality. At a

83

level closer to the poor, who supply the infant on whom all these benefits depend, one finds kidnappers, female recruiters who give information about suitable cases or who persuade the mothers, specialists providing forged birth certificates, petty officials who agree to falsify documents of civic identity so as to make the newborn baby into a perfectly adoptable individual.

In most cases, these intermediaries went astray after beginning with really humane actions, motivated by altruism. For example, among the intermediaries involved in illegality and arrested one finds a former priest, Lucca di Nuzzo, arrested in 1990 at Salvador de Bahia. It appears that in many cases the wish to relieve poverty and ease the distress of a mother unable to keep and rear her child only gradually gave way to the exploitation of poverty, where financial motives became dominant. Another reason why people go astray may be a wish to rectify administrative incompetence. It is a difficult profession:

> Those who act as intermediaries in adoption matters put themselves at risk: the risk of yielding to the feeling of power which comes from the ability to create ties of kinship; the risk of becoming "traffickers" if they make the least false step, for they walk a tightrope where any official can be corrupted, and where wealth is offered to any doctor, social worker, solicitor, notary or registrar who has few scruples.[104]

Accusations circulate, and become attached to various people in succession. For example, as I showed in the first chapter, the allegation made in 1990 that three thousand Brazilian babies adopted in Italy had disappeared, after passing through the charity run by Lucca di Nuzzo, was entirely baseless. We hear this same figure of three thousand once again from one of the accusers of the American lawyer Patrick Gagel, arrested in 1992: "In Peru, the American lawyer Patrick Gagel, arrested last February, sent a total of 3,000 children to the United States and to Italy. What has become of those children?"[105]

The accusations hurled at these intermediaries are very often highly exaggerated. That is because they often come from others who are their partners in crime, denouncing them because they themselves have not received what they consider to be their fair share of the cake.

Patrick Gagel was officially charged with having deceived a Peruvian mother who did not understand that she was giving consent to her child being adopted in the United States, but was released two years later because the mother's accusations turned out to be flimsy.[106] He declared in 1994, once he was back in the United States, that the main reason he was arrested was because he refused to pay a police officer in Lima, head of the bureau dealing with missing persons, the three hundred dollars he was demanding whenever he supplied the certificate necessary every time a child was adopted abroad, to prove that the child had not been reported missing.[107] Gagel also stated that he had arranged no more than fifty adoptions abroad.[108]

All the same, the fact remains that a recurrent trade in children does exist, accounting for a by no means negligible fraction of international adoptions. It mainly involves Guatemala and Brazil, but also Honduras and Salvador in Central America, and Argentina and Peru in the south.

Guatemala was one of the first countries where the baby parts accusation appeared, a scenario involving the misuse of adoptions. An inquiry conducted during the summer of 1988 by lawyers representing the International Federation for Human Rights had uncovered considerable child trafficking in that small country, which was undergoing large-scale political violence at the time, and had 110,000 orphans in its population; 750 children had been officially adopted abroad in 1987. Children were frequently kidnapped for adoption. So the military police, who were anxious to improve the disastrous image they had had since being implicated in the civil war of the early 1980s, showed great zeal in 1987 in closing down secret orphanages which supplied the traffic, and recovered 300 babies abducted that year. The international adoptions, although apparently legal, were often based upon illegal practices: false identity documents, forged birth certificates—a certain Anna-Maria Valdez had supposedly given birth to thirty-three children between 1965 and 1986! The largest of the trafficking networks was controlled by Ofelia Rosal de Gamez, sister-in-law of General Mejia Victores, who was head of state from 1984 till the beginning of 1986. His daughter was then secretary of state for social affairs, and his son-in-law director of the migration service, which supplied exit visas for adopted children.[109] Four years later, a French reporter found that Ofelia was still active.[110]

The attacks which took place in Guatemala in March 1994 against foreigners accused of stealing children (as described in chapter 1) can be partly explained by the fact that the traffic in children for adoption is not always suppressed in that small and very poor country, where it brings in a lot of money. Officials in charge of adoptions are always accused of pulling the strings of this trade. January and February 1994 had been notable for some furious public denunciations against those who trafficked in children for adoption, by the state prosecutor responsible for cases involving minors, and then for the discovery of the *casas de engorde* and the arrest of traffickers. In general, public opinion in the countries to which the children are taken knows nothing about this trade, with the notable exception of Italy, a country which is itself often accused of organizing the misuse of adoptions, and one where the press gives great publicity to arrests of child traffickers. By contrast, when there were accusations from El Salvador in 1992 that there were adopted children in France who had been kidnapped for the purpose, these accusations went no further than a couple of popular daily papers which gave them a brief mention.[111] It should, however, be noted that *Le Monde* had published an article on this subject the previous day, commenting on illegal international adoptions and some arrests of those organizing them.[112]

During the military dictatorship in Argentina, the young children of those who had "disappeared" were not killed, but adopted by military personnel—often the very ones who had murdered their parents—or by adopters who were acting in good faith. After the gradual return to normality, some of the natural families searched for these adopted children, establishing their relationship by genetic tests carried out by scientists in the United States. Of 200 children being sought, 60 were found.[113] Similar things happened in El Salvador during the civil war of the 1980s, except that in that country the children snatched from their natural parents were often sent abroad for adoption, their parents being peasants considered to have been accomplices of Marxist guerrillas. After peace was restored, in 1992, a committee was set up to search for missing children, and began looking for 280 of them. By the autumn of 1996, 29 had been found, some thanks to genetic analysis; some were in El Salvador itself, others in the United States, still others in France or Italy.[114] These violent deeds and kidnappings certainly reinforced the belief in organ thefts.

SUSPICIONS IN EASTERN EUROPE

In Eastern Europe, where international adoption developed with lightning speed when frontiers were opened after the fall of Communism, the suspicion that false adoptions occur is likewise very current. Albania expressed these suspicions officially in April 1992,[115] while Bulgaria demands that foreigners seeking to adopt must sign a document in front of a lawyer, stating that: "I shall not allow my child to be an organ donor, I shall not let him give an organ, nor shall I give my authority for him to be used in any medical experiment."[116] A rather pathetic procedure, for can one imagine that real child traffickers would feel bound by such a promise?

Romanian press cuttings show the response which allegations of this kind meet with in that country. The first reports the arrest of a sexual pervert residing in both the Netherlands and Switzerland, who had stated that he had bought children in Romania in order to torture and kill them.[117] In the popular French press, reports of this notorious trial concentrated upon the "ogre-like" character of the accused man.[118] Child trafficking does appear to be a real fact. For example, two other cuttings describe the arrest of traffickers suspected of selling Gypsy children in Cyprus for organ transplants (about a dozen of them) and their trial six months later at Jassy in Romania; eight were found guilty.[119]

FORCED LABOR AND PROSTITUTION

Corrupt middlemen who arrange adoptions make an illegal and exploitative profit from the children they place, but these children do generally find themselves with loving families in real homes, and the affair turns out well for them. This is not the case for the children who nowadays are victims of the age-old practices of forced labor and prostitution. Global communications have made their fate worse, as it is easy now to send the exploited children away to regions where they will bring in money, or to bring the exploiters to them. As regards forced labor, it was noted in 1989 that a trade in children was developing between the Indian subcontinent (Bangladesh, India, Pakistan) and countries in the Persian Gulf where they were employed as jockeys on racing camels.[120] In the course of a few months the authorities in the countries of origin arrested several traffickers and intercepted almost a hundred children.

As for child prostitution in Southeast Asia, everybody has heard tell of sexual tourism organized in Europe and the United States, which brings the exploiters to the scene of action in Thailand or the Philippines. This has been going on for a long time without any punishment for those who make use of it. World opinion is very aware of the misfortunes of these children, as was shown by the first world conference on the sexual exploitation of children held in Stockholm in August 1996.

BLUNDERS AT GENEVA

Nongovernmental organizations working in the fields of human rights and child protection and international bodies linked to the United Nations, such as the International Work Bureau, the World Health Organization, and UNICEF, are all struggling against these violations of human rights. At Geneva, following the precedent of the League of Nations in taking action against human trafficking in the 1920s and 1930s, the United Nations Human Rights Commission and its offshoot, the Working Party on Contemporary Forms of Slavery, offer a strategic setting and forum where denunciations of such violations can be heard by the media.

As soon as the allegations of pseudo adoptions of the "baby parts" type appeared in the world press at the end of 1987, they were brought before the United Nations Human Rights Commission, but did not convince it. Things changed at the end of 1990 when Vitit Muntarbhorn, a lawyer from Thailand, was appointed as special reporter to study the question of child trafficking. By following the reports he presented to the commission one can see this special reporter's increasing conviction that the sale of children for organ trafficking really does occur on a large scale—yet without any convincing proofs to support this conviction. One instance will be enough: the way the questionnaire sent by Vitit Muntarbhorn to various states was formulated. Already in June 1991 the question on sales of children was formulated in rather tendentious terms, putting together on the same level some proven facts and others that are merely allegations not supported by established facts: "The sale of children is done essentially for the following purposes: (a) adoption; (b) exploitation of child labor (including sexual exploitation); (c) organ transplants. To what extent and in what forms do these violations of children's rights occur in your country? Give details." But in 1992 one finds the categorical assertion: "The sale of children is done essentially for the purpose of organ transplants."[121]

At the end of 1994 Vitit Muntarbhorn resigned. He had not convinced his superiors, and one may suppose that diplomatic pressure was exerted by the rich countries indirectly accused. In 1995 the tone changed; the next special reporter, Ofelia Calcetas-Santos from the Philippines, showing herself to be cautious, declared in connection with the sale of children for organ transplants that "though this practice has sometimes been reported, one has never had formal proof of it."[122]

THE TRUTH OF THE SUSPICION

How can we account for the blunder of the special reporter and of many nongovernmental organizations which persuade themselves, without proof, that the worst is true?

Firstly, states do not always tell the truth. It is enlightening, in this respect, to read Vitit Muntarbhorn's reports. The 1993 report contains vigorous denials from Saudi Arabia and from the United Arab Emirates in reply to a question he posed at the end of 1992 "concerning the alleged practice of bringing into your country children who have been bought by middlemen in India, Pakistan, or Bangladesh, to ride dromedaries and take part in extremely dangerous races." According to the Saudi government, (a) dromedary races have no problem recruiting riders to take part, since this traditional sport is a source of pride; (b) slavery was abolished long ago in the country, and the accusation is inadmissible; (c) betting is illegal in the country. The denial sent by the government of the United Arab Emirates recalled that "the sale of children, together with all exploitation and ill-treatment of them" was explicitly forbidden by current legislation, but announced that the authorities were concerned "to complete the legislation, especially as regards dromedary racing." The 1994 report further announced the promulgation of "a law forbidding the use of children in these races and ordering all such children to return to their own countries."[123]

In 1995 China was called in question by the United Nations Human Rights Commission for its practices regarding organs removed from people executed, but "the Chinese observer replied that criminals condemned to death had the right to make voluntary donations of their organs, and that . . . removing the organs . . . was not possible without their consent and signature, or that of their next-of-kin, and the approval of the courts."[124]

In 1994, the observers from Mexico and Colombia reacted to Marie-Monique Robin's film[125] by denials:

> In the matter of organ transplants, Mexico had appropriate modern legislation forbidding the use of donors who were still minors, and laying down penalties should this occur. . . . Donation and distribution of organs was free. The Mexican Government was not unaware of the rumors concerning illegal organ transplants in that country, but such activities had never been proved. . . . The Colombian observer mentioned a case of organ trafficking where it was said a Colombian child was the victim. An enquiry led by the Defender of the People had concluded that this allegation was without foundation. . . . The conclusions of this enquiry had been submitted to the President of the Human Rights Committee on February 23 1994. . . . The Colombian Government deplored the irresponsibility of certain journalists whose one concern was to mislead public opinion.[126]

One can understand why these denials—though they do seem to me more convincing that those quoted in preceding paragraphs—can be greeted with scepticism.

Moreover, the subject of the disappearances and abductions of children is one of the most complex there is. Of course abductions do occur, but they can arise from the pathology of individuals (e.g., sexual crimes, or the abduction of babies by unstable women wanting children); or from social problems and family problems (separated parents of different nationalities, conflicts over custody rights); or sometimes from trafficking (for forced labor or prostitution). It is very hazardous to discuss disappearances and abductions of children on a worldwide scale, lumping together countries that are very different. Vitit Muntarbhorn seems sometimes to have been overwhelmed by the complexity of the facts. For instance, the paragraph about disappearances and abductions in the United States in his third report makes absolutely no distinction between these various levels:

> In the USA, recent news items tell of abductions of children from hospitals. In one of the cases reported in the *Los Angeles Times* on September 17 1992, it is said the kidnapper had worked as a male nurse. According to the same paper, in the issue of April 1 1992, some 3,000 children are said to have left the country

illegally. This network goes through Mexico, and in some cases the children are transferred to Canada.[127]

Quite apart from the case of the special reporter, this readiness to believe the worst corresponds well to our emotional impulses, to the rejection we feel when faced with the tragic reality of the traffic in human beings. In the first few moments, we think a person who exploits his fellow beings is capable of anything, that a person who commits one grave abuse may, or is even bound to, commit plenty of others. We spontaneously give our agreement, for example, to statements by François Lefort, an active supporter of a nongovernmental organization working for street children in the Third World, who says of the traffickers: "Myself, I am convinced those people sell anything and everything, it's a sort of horrific supermarket. That's to say, they sell for prostitution, they sell for adoption to people who have been refused permission to adopt because they are mentally unbalanced, and they certainly also sell for organs, and if there was anything else one could sell, they'd sell it."[128]

But then rationality resumes its sway when, rereading this statement, we understand how implausible are these allegations which transform the traffickers into demigods—when in most cases they are people who are hardly any better off than those they make their living from. This is the logic of the sensational novel, not an analysis of reality. Even so—and this is something we have to admit—the first impulse of anyone who has heard the description of the tragic facts of human trafficking will be to believe the stories.

WHY ORGAN THEFTS ARE IMPLAUSIBLE

General arguments demonstrating the implausibility of organ theft narratives, which have been developed in conjunction with the French Establishment for Transplants, will be briefly set out below. This section will be kept short, for it is obvious, alas, that it will in no way convince those who believe that organ thefts are common; conspiracy theories and rumors can answer any logical argument.

Organ theft narratives convince people in many milieus, but meet skepticism from those who understand the subject well, namely transplant specialists.

In March 1996, when the Spanish Premio Iberoamericano de Periodismo Rey de España (King of Spain's Prize for Latin-American Journalism) was awarded to a series of articles printed in December 1994 in the daily paper *Correio Braziliense* which repeated the stories and allegations about organ thefts, this scepticism was clearly expressed by Mario Scalamogna, a medical official of the North Italy Transplant Organization:

> These rumors have been going round in Italy, as they have everywhere. They are legends, which are then elaborated in pursuit of sensationalism. It is a blatant lie. A transplant cannot be done in conditions of secrecy. It involves sophisticated procedures, appropriate medication, and follow-up treatment which cannot be obtained in a clandestine organization.[129]

The chief arguments forming the basis for the skepticism of experts relate to technical limitations and to the persistent absence of proofs.

TECHNICAL LIMITATIONS

Technical limitations concerning the length of time organs can be preserved, the large amount of surgical equipment required, the follow-up of the transplants, and above all the indispensable human resources needed render utterly implausible the links which rumor makes between mutilated corpses[130] discovered in Latin American cities and these sophisticated operations. I will briefly expand on these points.

(1.) Preservation of organs. Though the possible delay has been extended now, it is still limiting. The period of cold ischemia (the period during which no blood circulates through the transplant) cannot exceed thirty-six to forty-eight hours for a kidney, ten to twelve hours for a liver, six hours for lungs, four hours for the heart. Therefore organs can only be taken from people who have died under very precise, and very rare, conditions, namely in reanimation units where the functions of breathing and blood circulation have been maintained even after brain death. In France, such deaths amount to about five per thousand of the deaths occurring in a hospital environment. (2.) The necessary surgical equipment. This is sophisticated and expensive; for instance, the equipment for external circulation of the blood is indispensable for heart transplants, and often necessary for liver or lung transplants. (3.) The follow-up. A transplant is not just a matter of one operation, for it presupposes numerous preliminary examinations and tests, together with a postoperative follow-up extending over several years. (4.) Human resources. Kidney transplant operations are the least demanding, yet even so they require the presence of more than fifteen people. This personnel is far too numerous for systematic secrecy to be possible. We are speaking, furthermore, of highly qualified personnel, the transplant surgeon having had over ten years of training and the nurses of such advanced operating theaters having had two years of specialization. Training of this standard makes it highly unlikely that they would systematically participate in a criminal enterprise which would lead to their being ostracized by their colleagues and disqualified from practice, and where the financial returns do not appear to make it worth their while.

Yet, some may say, though these technical limitations are valid in the case of organs, they are not valid for tissues: bones, skin, corneas, heart valves, blood vessels, which are not bound by such tight limits for their preservation, and in some cases need fewer human resources. However, the shortage of grafts is far from being as severe for these tissues, for some of which (bones for instance) other sources are available, and for which transplants are in fact rare—skin is needed for major burns, and heart valves for certain heart infections.

A high proportion of the narratives center upon one tissue, the cornea, of which there is indeed a real shortage in France, but the shortage is by no means general. For 90 percent of cornea transplants performed in France, the corneas are imported from neighboring countries. The imports are possible because the removal of corneas from people who die in hospital is often better organized in those countries.

With regard to the cornea, one should take note that there is total incompatibility between the technical realities and what emotional narratives and rumors say. The cornea is a tissue which is easily removed after death, but which, as specialists stress, it is impossible to remove from a living subject:

> The fragment of a cornea which is to be used in a possible transplant is a small disk between 7mm and 8mm in diameter and 5mm thick, which it is impossible to manipulate correctly except in a specialized operating theater under sterile conditions. Never has it happened, anywhere in the world, that a cornea alone

was removed from a living subject in order to be transplanted to another subject. . . . To remove a slice of sclera from a living subject is impossible without general anesthetic, and would inevitably lead to a very massive hemorrhage.[131]

In the language of emotion, the eye is the seat of the personality, or even of the soul (as the lasting shock caused by the Amiens affair in 1992 clearly shows), and the deeds most often denounced in rumor are the sinister activities of the eye thieves.

THE ABSENCE OF PROOF

Without excluding the possibility of occasional isolated crimes, one is forced to emphasize how implausible is the idea of a substantial criminal network that leaves no trace of its frequent and repeated crimes. To talk about an "implacable law of silence" is to adopt the seductive logic of sensational thrillers, not in any way the reality of the criminal world, which abounds in clues and informers. On the occasion of the Spanish film prize mentioned above, this was the main argument of the Spanish transplant coordinator Rafael Matesanz: "How is it possible that thousands of so-called secret transplants throughout the whole world have left no trace, and that no doctor ever questioned the origin of the organ?"[132]

Finally, one common-sense argument demands attention: if any undeniable facts about organ thefts were established, they would become a major news item. They would be treated as such, making the front page of the daily papers and the lead item on the TV news. But so far, organ thefts have only been taken up on documentaries produced for cable networks.

CHAPTER 3

EHPLOITATION OF THE LEGEND

The organ theft legend and the narratives expressing it are disseminated by various social groups, which exploit them to serve their own strategies. Members of the moral and political elites may be pursuing objectives that are very different from those of journalists and are similarly distinct from those of popular writers aiming at a mass market. In all these groups one can find many instances where organ theft narratives are exploited; then they are no longer the creation of folklore, but material which groups of professionals are using to promote the specific objectives they are pursuing.

Organ thefts may either be described in full, or simply alluded to. These two different modes correspond to a difference in the degree of acceptance. A full description expresses indignation and seeks to convince others, trying to prove that the alleged horrors really do exist. An allusion presupposes that the facts are well known and proven, and so can be used as an example or argument to reinforce the main theme of one's discourse. One is then using a datum on which everybody agrees.

The elite social groups whose attitudes will be discussed here have features in common; they are guardians of morality, active minorities who try to influence and change the public, to promote and defend the causes they support, to spread their own beliefs. It is in connection with these causes and beliefs that they discuss the horrors of organ theft. We shall survey the strategies of human rights organizations, militants, propagandists, politicians, moral authorities, and the so-called quality newspapers.

HUMAN RIGHTS ORGANIZATIONS

It cannot be said that there is one single opinion on this topic among non-governmental organizations (NGOs), for they are sharply divided over the truth of allegations of organ theft. Their diversity goes deeper too. They include both volunteers and professionals, and have frequent changes of personnel, so their attitudes sometimes change over time. They are international, so very diverse opinions may be found in them at the same time. Therefore within one and the same organization one may find important variations of opinion and behavior, in both time and space, as regards the reality of organ thefts.

The annual session of the United Nations Human Rights Commission in Geneva, and especially its Working Party on Contemporary Forms of Slavery, is an important forum for NGOs that have been granted consultative status by the commission (a status which is much sought after, and only obtained after investigation). Here the NGOs present reports, documentaries, and sometimes films condemning various violations of human rights. Using this platform, some of them acted as a driving force in spreading accusations of organ theft.

THOSE CONVINCED: IADL, SOS TORTURE

From 1988 onwards, the International Association of Democratic Lawyers (IADL), represented by Renée Bridel, presented accusatory reports and tried (in vain) to get the commission to pass resolutions condemning the horrifying acts she was denouncing. IADL, founded in 1946, had at one time been closely linked to the French Communist Party; it was expelled from France in 1950 and transferred its headquarters to Brussels. Mention was made in chapter 1 of its president, the barrister Joe Nordmann, and his letter to *Le Monde* in 1988. Nowadays the organization seems to have become marginalized, and one can justifiably wonder whether it corresponds to anything beyond the personal activity of Renée Bridel. Thanks to Professor Schwartzenberg, however, its accusations were taken up to a considerable extent from 1992 onwards, first in the media and then by politicians.

In June 1993 and in May 1994, SOS Torture presented two reports which gave credence to the allegations of a traffic in child organs. This body, founded in 1990, claims to coordinate a network of 190 NGOs, including the Association of Christians Against Torture, the Inter-Movement Committee for Evacuees (CIMADE), and the International Federation for Human Rights (IFHR). In 1993 it produced *Exactions et enfants* (*Children and Extortion*), written by Esther Bron and Eric Sottas for a United Nations conference on human rights held in Vienna in July 1993. *Trade in Organs and Torture* (1994) was a paper written by Eric Sottas, who presented it at the Eurosciences Media Workshop at Basel in March 1994 during a series of day conferences entitled "The Present State and Future Needs of Organ Transplantation," arranged by Sandoz Laboratories, which produce cyclosporine, the most widely used antirejection drug. This not very convincing document is carelessly written and contains no new element. Its method is to cite unsupported allegations pell-mell, and to conclude from this that proofs of organ trafficking are mounting up. When they were interviewed by the Swedish journalist Jonny Såganger (whose thorough work on the organ trade will be presented below), and by Barbara Hofstetter (author of a research paper on the activities of international organizations),[1] Esther Bron and Eric Sottas both independently confirmed that they had no proof that any trafficking of children's organs existed.

INCONSISTENCIES OVER TIME: IFHR IN 1988 AND 1992

The International Federation for Human Rights (IFHR), founded in France in 1922, has as its mandate to combat violations of human rights and to ensure that they are internationally investigated. The reader will recall that this organization sent the lawyer Alain Feder and the magistrate Antoine Garapon to conduct an inquiry in Guatemala in 1988. The conclusions of their report were negative as regards accusations of the baby parts type, and played an important part in discrediting these. On the other hand, their report did establish that there was a considerable trade in children intended for international adoption. Yet six years later, IFHR gave its backing to an accusatory TV documentary, *Voleurs d'organes* (*Organ Snatchers*), and presented it at Geneva. What had happened to make such a reversal possible?

In 1990, IFHR joined a collaborative investigation into the disappearances of children in Latin America, which had been set up by the human rights service of CIMADE. This organization works for refugees and migrant workers and is active in underdeveloped countries. The person in charge of the collaborative investigation was Maïté Albaguy. The organizations which were still collaborating on this project by 1992, that is to say the Association of Christians Against Torture, CIMADE, and IFHR, collaborated with Marie-Monique Robin, author of the program *Voleurs d'organes*. Sylvie Deplus, an ophthalmologist and a member of the executive board of IFHR, gave advice to Marie-Monique Robin and viewed the rushes of her film in the course of 1993. Nevertheless, IFHR did not give its full backing to the creator of *Voleurs d'organes* during the controversies of 1995—unlike CIMADE, which was deeply committed. The media have short memories, and there was no mention of the important report from 1988 until Rony Brauman (a human rights campaigner and a former director of Médecins sans Frontières, a medical charity operating in war zones and among refugees) mentioned it in terms of high praise in the course of his contribution to the program *Arrêt sur Images* in September 1995. How IFHR itself could be ignorant of this report is a mystery, but one which I am not able to solve.

REGIONAL INCONSISTENCIES: HEAD OFFICE AND DUTCH BRANCH OF DCI

The organization Defence for Children International (DCI) was formed in 1979 and centers its activity on child protection and the promotion of children's rights; in 1994, its head office was taking a cautious and subtly differentiated position on the question. At that central level, the organization stated that the search for information must continue, but that there are no proofs available of child trafficking linked to organ transplants, and that one cannot claim that there is a systematic and organized trade.

Things were different at the local level, however. Interviewed by Peter Burger at the beginning of 1995, the DCI's representative in the Netherlands said he was convinced that organ thefts were a reality. His line of argument is interesting, containing once again the idea that "suspicion is truth," which was analyzed above:

> Stan Meuwesse . . . is convinced that organ thefts are a reality. "The facts and figures about other abuses committed against children are so massive," he argues, "that this one too is certainly true. For instance, who would believe that six-year-old Pakistani boys are forced to work as camel jockeys in the Arab Emirates? Yet this is a fact acknowledged to be true." Meuwesse stresses that he has never seen a coherent, clear and reliable report of stolen corneas and kidneys. There are only stories, repeated indefinitely, but stories which all professional workers in the field of Child Rights find convincing.[2]

After publishing a cautious article in April 1987, DCI gave an interview which was exploited and distorted by *Izvestya*, and so became the target of fierce pressure from representatives of the United States at the United Nations, until it disowned the statements attributed to it. And—just for the record—it was a member of DCI in the Netherlands who had alerted them.

The humanitarian organizations (in the full sense of the term) did not take up any position on the question of organ thefts; similarly, the prestigious organization of Amnesty International showed itself to be very reserved on the subject. However, many of its active members, following the same process of thought as has already been illustrated in connection with DCI, are convinced of the reality of organ thefts, and occasionally make statements to this effect to the press. One example in France was Dr. Jean-Claude Alt, a member of Amnesty International who was convinced of the reality of organ thefts and made public statements to this effect during the controversy over the French documentary in 1995.

The capital of a nongovernmental organization is its reputation. IFHR and CIMADE took risks when they gave their backing to the documentary *Voleurs d'organes*, and it seems likely that they will be more cautious after the controversies of 1995, in which the most striking case publicized by the documentary was discredited.

CAMPAIGNERS, PROPAGANDISTS, AND POLITICIANS

Campaigners use the narratives of organ thefts as a perfect argument, because they are so dramatic. They present them as an illustration for whatever good cause they are devoted to, following their more or less exclusive concerns. We have already described Jean Ziegler's militant book, battling against his adversary, commercial capitalism, source of all the evils on earth.

THE STRUGGLE AGAINST VIVISECTION AND BIOMEDICINE

Thefts of children's organs became, for Swiss campaigners opposed to vivisection, the perfect example of the evil deeds of their enemy, biological medicine. The long article they published on the subject gave full details of the criminal cases at Barranquilla and Montes de Oca (discussed above, in chapter 2), adding, in the case of the Colonia, some unpublished and horrifying elements:

> Enrico Romero, who is shut away in a room two meters square in Pavilion 16, makes his accusations: . . . "I've been shut in this room because I know too much; for instance, I saw two male nurses throw a patient into the big swimming pool in the garden and drown him. I know what happened in the end to many *desparacidos*, and to sick people murdered by the nurses to sell their corneas and their kidneys, whose bodies were thrown into the swamps round this asylum."

The article contains several violent attacks against the medical profession: "such a trade would not exist without the complicity of surgeons, doctors, paramedical staff, and the government's health authorities. What is happening is a clear proof of vivisectionist madness." As for the petition accompanying the article, it completely assimilates animal vivisection (and the animal thefts which supposedly go with this practice) to the theft of children's organs:

> A cat is sunbathing on a windowsill, and disappears without trace; a dog tied by his lead at the entrance to a shopping mall is no longer there when one comes back for him (these are everyday occurrences in Switzerland); in South America people disappear as readily as animals. And monkeys captured in their natural habitat, where do they end up? There is only one answer, a terrible, nightmarish answer: vivisection! Children are stolen in the streets, their eyes are cut out by surgery, and they are returned to the street, completely blind. . . . The fate of these people is called "vivisection," exactly like the fate of the animals on whose behalf we are committed to fight. Humans and animals alike are victims of the same obtuse, criminal, hidebound mentality, which must be eradicated—the mentality which allows vivisection to be "regulated" rather than abolished. This proves that vivisection of animals inevitably leads to vivisection of humans.[3]

FEMINISM

In 1993, the Coalition against Women Trafficking presented a report in Geneva which gave considerable credence to allegations of organ theft. The author of the report was Janice Raymond, a lecturer on women's studies and medical ethics in an American university; she was also the expert who was later interviewed about transplants in the United States in the French TV documentary *Voleurs d'organes*, where she repeated her allegations. Thus her opinions received publicity in France, which is why we will here analyze her book, aggressively entitled *Women as Wombs: Reproductive Technologies and the Battle over Women's Freedom*.[4] In this book we enter an intellectual universe where the search for truth is of secondary importance, and where the author takes up a stance of hostile militancy even in the introduction:

> This book is a challenge to reproductive liberalism, including its feminist variety. It is positioned against the liberal consumer movement that supports new reproductive technologies and contracts. . . . The new reproductive technologies represent an appropriation made by scientific experts of the female body, depoliticising reproduction and motherhood by recasting these roles as fundamental instincts that must be satisfied.[5]

These premises having been posited, the consequences ensue. In Janice Raymond's view, the new reproductive technologies create an international traffic in women, children, fetuses and fetal tissues, to which she devotes an accusatory chapter of some fifty pages. She begins by asserting that the trafficking related to reproduction is a continuation of sexual trafficking of women and children, and that international adoption is simply a variant of reproductive trafficking. She does not hesitate to assert in shocking terms (and without any proof) that:

> As I investigated the international dimensions of surrogacy (what brokers call intrauterine adoption), it became clear that an established reproductive traffic— the international adoption trade—already prevailed that surrogacy would only enhance. . . . Surrogacy contracts have become part of the international trade in women, with middlemen linking international supply and demand. These middlemen who deal in surrogate mothers offer money abroad on behalf of buyers who cannot legally obtain surrogates in their own countries. . . .
>
> Unwanted pregnancies from rape by Guatemalan soldiers is one of the three major products of militaristic violence in the Guatemalan highlands. Soldiers are often paid for bringing babies and orphans back to the barracks and passing them on to illegal adoption networks. The outcrop of the U.S. involvement in

Central America—in Honduras, Guatemala, and El Salvador—has traditionally been exportable products such as coffee and fruit. Now women and children have become the most recent cash crops, for sexual and reproductive purposes.[6]

When this author turns to the allegations of theft of children's organs, it is with the same intention of making accusations and giving examples of the perverse evils of reproductive techniques. The question mark on her section heading "A new reproductive traffic: children for organ export?" is a pure formality. She then sets out the allegations of 1987 and 1988 (the baby parts stories), then those of 1990 (the children adopted in Italy, and the myth that three thousand of them disappeared), and of 1992 (Montes de Oca), largely supporting the most extreme accusations. When she talks of disinformation, it is the denials issued by the USIA which are the target of her onslaught.

Next, she attacks the analyses of the organ theft narratives which were made in 1990 and 1991 by American intellectuals of diverse backgrounds and approaches. The anthropologist Nancy Scheper-Hughes,[7] the feminist Louise Palmer, and the linguist and political protester Noam Chomsky[8] all agreed in thinking that organ theft narratives are rumors; they are not to be explained by the reality of such thefts, but by the poverty and violence of their social milieu: "homeless and starving children, death squads who kill abandoned and poor children in the streets of Brazil, and the general contempt in which the lives of the poor are held create the conditions in which these allegations—not these realities—flourish."[9] Janice Raymond argues that, on the contrary, it is logical to think that this social violence leads to real thefts of organs, since there is a demand for organs—a very considerable demand, in her view—in the world of the rich. But here her argument is faulty, for it omits the main element, namely that the allegations are not backed by any facts, and that this absence of facts is what led the intellectuals she cites to reach the conclusions they reached.

According to Janice Raymond, the same is true of the demand for fetal tissue (or for fetuses, for she seems to use the two terms interchangeably), supposedly much needed in medical research for transplants, and for treating Alzheimer's disease, Parkinson's disease, diabetes. Many other uses are cited, and the author claims that medical needs are unlimited.

Janice Raymond devotes the second half of her chapter to the traffic in fetal tissues. Here she takes up accusations made in a book by Rolande Girard, published in 1985,[10] which had also been taken up in 1988 by a clever and very partisan journalist, Michel Raffoul, at the time when the baby parts accusations appeared.[11] This work of pro-Communist and anti-American propaganda defended the not very credible thesis that the American military establishment was creating "ethnic weapons," that is, weapons that selectively attack one racial group only. In 1987 the same journalist published *Tristes chimères* (*Tragic Hybrids*), a work claiming that the AIDS virus had been accidentally created by the Americans in the course of biological weapons research being carried out at Fort Detrick. She produced two televised documentaries (broadcast in France on TF1) apparently corresponding to these two books. The facts presented as proof of research into ethnic weapons go back to the 1970s, and these facts are known to be true: kidneys taken from fetuses obtained in abortion clinics in Korea were imported into America between 1970 and 1976, at which date the imports were stopped because of protests from Japan, a country through which they passed in transit. The United States has admitted these imports (twelve thousand pairs of kidneys in six years), and has stated that this fetal material was used in research on spontaneous outbreaks of infectious diseases. Janice Raymond, heightening the accusations of Rolande Girard, paints an apocalyptic picture of these facts: "Between 1970 and 1980, Girard reported that about eighty thousand seven- to eight-month-old fetuses had been imported annually to the United States from around the world."[12] She follows this with the usual assertions that fetuses are used in the cosmetic industry—assertions which exploit the confusion between fetuses and placentas, and are a recurrent argument deployed by antiabortion militants. The final pages of this chapter are devoted to bold, and extremely speculative, extrapolations concerning changes in abortion techniques which are to be expected in order to satisfy the demand, and also about the approximately ninety thousand fetuses already available every year in the United States for medical research.

In conclusion, the author pleads for a complete ban on new reproductive technologies "that violate women's bodily integrity."[13] From a French point of view, there is one solid basis for her argument, namely that the United States does recognize commercial contracts for surrogate mothers and likewise for a whole network of commercial transactions concerning human tissues. But this does not justify her in reproducing documents that are sheer propaganda in a way quite incompatible with serious work.

IRANIAN PROPAGANDA

The Soviet propaganda machine has disappeared, but propaganda from Islamic extremists still gives much emphasis to accusations of organ theft, which enable them to discredit the Western world, which proclaims itself the protector of human rights. *Echo of Islam*, a review edited in Iran by the Islamic Thought Foundation, is a propagandist publication intended for export, and written in an approximation of English. The main article in August 1995 was "The international trade in human lives"; according to a fierce editorial headed "Decadence is consuming the protectors of human rights," the article is the work of an Iranian professor of social economics at the German university of Oldenburg. Covering "the trade in babies, children, women, human organs, blood, arms, pharmaceuticals, toxic waste, and nuclear waste," it is a thoroughgoing attack on the West as the exploiter of the Third World, responsible for all its misfortunes. Extremes touch one another; here, among supporters of Islamic theocracy, one finds the same theories as in the Marxist materialist Ziegler: "the market in human lives is part of the global capitalist market." The editorial opens with some horrifying stories from South America, not previously published—that children's mutilated bodies had been discovered in garbage bins in Honduras and Guatemala; that there were fake charities in Brazil which gathered street children, enticing them with the promise of a fine career in football, but actually wanting them as "suppliers of fresh, warm organs." This document is scarcely convincing, but one can easily understand why propagandists of every type will go on using these extreme accusations of child organ theft, for the scandal they create guarantees them an audience.[14]

THE EUROPEAN PARLIAMENT AND THE SCHWARTZENBERG REPORT IN 1993

In 1988, the European Parliament had passed a resolution on September 15 condemning child trafficking in Central America, presented by the Communist deputy Danielle de March and relying upon an accusatory report presented to the United Nations by the International Association of Democratic Lawyers. This resolution drew an official protest from the United States, which had been targeted in one of its sentences. In October, the main media rejected it.

Nevertheless, this resolution was cited as a precedent five years later (together with one about organ banks in 1979 and one about transplants in

1983) when a resolution "for a ban on the trade in organs for transplants" was proposed at the European Parliament in 1993, in a fifteen-page document presented by the rapporteur Léon Schwartzenberg.[15] The document includes a paragraph asserting the real existence of a criminal trade in organs: "Considering the acknowledged facts of the mutilation and murder of fetuses, children, and adults, in certain developing countries, in order to supply transplant organs for export to rich countries . . ."

The catalogue of information accompanying the proposed resolution gives no details about the alleged facts, but peremptorily asserts that they are beyond dispute:

> Illegal organized organ trafficking exists, in the same way as illegal drug trafficking, and is often run by the same people. This traffic is even more monstrous when it is based upon killing living persons in order to remove their organs, which are sold at a profit. To deny the existence of this monstrous trade is like denying the gas chambers and cremation ovens during the war.[16]

When presenting his resolution before a session of the Parliament, Léon Schwartzenberg set out seven paragraphs of specific accusations, all taken from the article in the August 1992 issue of *Le Monde Diplomatique* (to be described below). These sensational statements had a great impact, especially in Brazil and Italy, as they picked up again the allegation that three thousand children had disappeared there. The Italian press gave much publicity to the accusations, which were firmly denied by the authorities,[17] especially after the Brazilian state of Pernambuco temporarily withdrew permission for any children to be adopted by Italians.[18] In France, *Le Monde* published a report of Schwartzenberg's accusations from its correspondent at the European Parliament, accompanied by another article noting the denial from Italy.[19] There was no article discussing the accusations listed, but there was a letter from doctors protesting against them:

> The way the Schwartzenberg report amalgamates organ trafficking with international adoptions brings the latter into disrepute, causes public anxiety, leads to some countries suspending all possibilities of adoption, and, in short, harms the best interests of certain children who are being kept in institutions where the quality of life is . . . dubious.[20]

Schwartzenberg responded to the letter by saying that he trusted the information given in *Le Monde Diplomatique*, and rejecting the accusation that he wrongly amalgamated two different questions.[21]

Eager for publicity, the rapporteur of the European Parliament had recourse to sensational allegations, though one can presume that he believed them. He thus distorted the legitimate objective aimed at in his resolution, which was to prevent commercial abuses as regards organ transplants. One can contrast the attitude of the European Parliament with that of the Council of Europe. The latter organization entrusted to two specialist journalists (one an expert on European affairs, the other on questions of health) the task of drafting a commentary on a convention on the ethics of biomedicine which the Council was proposing to adopt. The chapter on organ transplants[22] is a model of sound treatment, restrained, but not concealing that there are difficulties in the way the system works. Naturally, the report from the Council of Europe got far less publicity than the sensational Schwartzenberg report.

MORAL AUTHORITIES

THE CATHOLIC CHURCH: PAUL BARRUEL

Religious leaders in Latin America, gravely concerned over the violence committed against marginalized people and trying to combat this, began to worry that even more serious violations of their rights might be occurring, and demanded investigations. These demands for further investigation were speedily transformed, by those convinced that the allegations were true, into categorical affirmations of truth.

It was shown above, in chapter 1, how Paul Barruel's allegations launched the idea that three thousand Brazilian children had disappeared in Italy. This Dominican, professor of theology at the University of São Paulo, also sent to the United Nations Human Rights Commission a report drawn up by the Bishops' Commission of Brazil. This report expressed anxiety about the acts of violence committed against street children, quoted alarming articles in the daily papers stating that the victims were often found mutilated (without eyes), and demanded that an inquiry be opened.

The Swede Jonny Sågänger conducted a thoroughgoing investigation into accusations of organ thefts, in the course of which he clearly demonstrates how a chain of attributions turns the expression of a suspicion into the affirmation of a certainty:

> When I met Professor Paul Barruel, his eyes popped as he read the article in *Monde Diplomatique* and saw the comments which Maïté Pinero had associated with his name. When I asked him to show me his documentation, in the form of photographs or other documents as evidence for his assertions, he replied: "But I never did assert that."
>
> It is possible that this Professor, this Dominican priest, lied to me, but it is more likely that he had previously expressed speculations about street children, without being able to prove them true. Paul Barruel did not tell me so on this occasion, but I later read in one of his reports that he was quoting from the daily paper *O Estado de Sao Paolo*, which had written that some street children had been found without eyeballs (June 5 1991). So it was information from a Brazilian newspaper (whose truthfulness is more than doubtful) that the *Monde Diplomatique* falsely ascribed to the Dominican priest, Professor Paul Barruel. To present it as coming from Paul Barruel gave it more credibility than referring to a Brazilian paper. This spectacular assertion made it easier for the free-lance journalist Maïté Pinero to sell her article to the *Monde Diplomatique*. . . . Unfortunately, thousands of readers were deceived.
>
> The Dominican priest told me that in his capacity of representative of the Brazilian Bishops' Conference he passed information to the United Nations on various social questions, including among other matters the suspicions about trafficking in children's organs. "I never said it was proved that such trafficking existed, but that it was possible that it might exist, and that society should take steps about it."
>
> The reports sent to the United Nations by the Brazilian Bishops' Conference (*Assassinatos de crianças. Trafico de bebes e de organos infantis.* Geneva, July/August 1991) consist mainly of articles taken from newspapers.[23]

THE CATHOLIC CHURCH: THE POPE

Pope John Paul's references to thefts of child organs take the form of allusions, as is normally the case among people whose conviction is well established. For him, the organ thefts to which children fall victim are only one instance of the innumerable evils imposed on them by a materialistic society. The pope is particularly indignant at the violence committed against street children, a topic which he boldly raised when visiting Brazil in 1992. Two years later, a mention of "the terrifying trade in organs" is a mere aside in a speech condemning violence against children, the chief subject being a condemnation of abortion:

> On Thursday John-Paul II indignantly condemned the massacres of children, the shameful purposes for which they are sometimes exploited, and the "terrifying" trade in their organs. . . . Referring to the "really terrifying facts" one hears about the fate of children in some countries, the Sovereign Pontiff denounced "the brutal massacres of street children, the prostitution they are made to endure, and the trafficking by organizations which sell organs for transplant."[24]
>
> One alarming example is the way little children are treated—street children murdered, as the Pope reminded his hearers; children forced into prostitution, used in organ trafficking, led into crime, and others "whom the rich nations, in their selfishness, prefer to kill before they are born". Pope John-Paul then turned to abortion, a major theme in his thought.[25]

ORGAN DONATION ASSOCIATIONS

In 1988, Professor Jean Dausset, at that time president of France-Transplant, being questioned by a journalist from *L'Humanité*, made an emotional statement amalgamating trade in organs and theft of organs. In replying to her, he stressed that thanks to the efficient way things are organized in France such horrors are impossible there, and the condemnation of foreign horrors seemed to reinforce the perception of the excellence of French ways.

The main topic of the article was a press conference set up by the Department of Public Assistance in Paris after a meeting of its ethical committee on, in particular, "problems posed by the taking and transplanting of organs." Jean Dausset, president of France-Transplant, declared: "There is a world trade in organs, which are seen as commercial products. This is especially so in Latin America, where there is no organization similar to France-Transplant in charge of collecting organs. There, patients themselves try to get hold of organs, in which case all methods are possible—the purchase of organs, but other horrors too. This has not reached France, and will never concern her."

Replying to a question from the paper, Professor Dausset added: "Personally, as early as 1971 [?] I saw kidneys bought and sold in Peru. I expressed my indignation, and was told the law forbade it. But I know it goes on." He was then asked about Guatemala (the article is framed within another article by Maïté Pinero entitled "The Fishpond of Organ Traffickers," commenting on the revelations in *El Grafico*); he replied: "I have heard it talked about, but I have no confirmation. It is more than horrible, it's abominable."[26]

Seven years later, we find the same approach and the same implied reasoning in a dossier prepared by the Association for Health Education and Donation through Solidarity in National Education (ADOSEN). This dossier, entitled *Organ Donation*, was created by two medical counsellors, with the cooperation of the French Establishment for Transplants. It is in question-and-answer format. Here is the answer to the question "Does organ trafficking exist?"

> In France, there is no organ trafficking. Thanks to the principle that no payment is made, that removal of organs is well organized and their distribution is regulated, and that centres for taking and transplanting organs are legally registered, the French system is free from any risk of trafficking. This, unfortunately, is not the case in certain countries where the trade in organs flourishes and there are even instances of vital organs being removed from living persons. One of the most intolerable instances is that eyes are taken from Latin American children.[27]

Admittedly, in the same publication, but a few pages earlier, Professor Didier Houssin had been more realistic. In answer to the question "How do you explain that people are still talking about organ trafficking in France, and that there are implausible yet persistent rumors about children who disappear and are found again 48 hours later minus a kidney?," he stressed two causes of confusion—first, that tissue banks are legally allowed to sell their products, since they are in fact selling the work done, not the tissue itself; second, that in some countries, India, for example, the sale of organs is legal. In conclusion, he said: "A whole web of fantasy has been woven round malfunctionings of international adoptions. It is true that stories about children adopted in dubious circumstances must have been associated to the demonised aspects of organ transplants to lead to these tales of kidnapped children."[28]

One may well ask oneself which message readers will remember: the one which supports a terrifying but unproven story, or the one which calls their certainties into question? It seems certain that it is the former which will be remembered. This example shows how widely diffused is the conviction that thefts of children's organs do really occur—a conviction which can even affect professionals. It is true that associations promoting donations of blood or organs have been in crisis ever since a scandal concerning contaminated blood in French hospitals undermined their dogma that if one excludes market forces and relies on altruism, there will never be any problems (the National Blood Transfusion Center was formed from associations based on altruistic blood donating).

THE QUALITY PRESS

Quality papers, though they may occasionally report allegations of organ theft, do not support them. However, they maintain a cautious reserve and will on the whole ignore the topic rather than actively trying to disprove it, since they are keen to condemn organ trafficking. Moreover, they refuse to enter into disputes with humanitarian bodies, whose values they share.

One opinion-forming journal, *Le Monde Diplomatique*, gave considerable and long-lasting publicity in August 1992 to Maïté Pinero's accusations.[29] Up till then, she had only reached the far more limited readership of *Viva* or *L'Humanité*, two publications linked to the Communist Party. Maïté Pinero's accusations were combined with those made by Renée Bridel at Geneva on behalf of the International Association of Democratic Lawyers. So although the IADL had failed to have its case accepted by the Human Rights Commission, it did manage to reach and persuade others, thanks to getting publicity in this way. The views of the *Monde Diplomatique* are pro–Third World and anticapitalist, which ensures it a considerable readership (its circulation at the end of 1995 was 125,000 copies per month), so its editors were inclined to be receptive to accusations of organ theft.

Sometimes papers devote just a few lines to rare and weird news items about organ thefts in distant lands, speaking of them in brief allusions which imply that their reality is perfectly well established, and treating them as typical "stories of our times" which tragically exemplify the horrors of the modern world. There were two examples of this in September 1995 in Delfeil de Ton's column in *Le Nouvel Observateur*, a Parisian weekly whose readers are mainly intellectuals:

> A woman has just been condemned to death in Bangladesh for killing her three-year-old daughter in order to sell her eyes and kidneys. In Egypt, a girl of twenty-two was forced by her father to sell a kidney, so that he could have a new car. He has been sent to prison, and meanwhile the car is standing at the roadside, deteriorating.[30]

The columnist found these two stories in dispatches from Reuters news agency (for Bangladesh) and from Agence France Presse (AFP) (for Egypt).[31] The Egyptian story refers to the facts of an organ trade whose existence is proven, and to pressure put upon a dependent relative, which is only too plausible. Moreover, the AFP dispatch indicates that the girl had refused to return to her father's house after the operation he forced her to undergo so that he could buy a car (it brought in the equivalent of thirty thousand francs), and had gone to live with some neighbors. The father had then complained to the police, saying his daughter had been kidnapped, but she was soon found, and told her story. The dispatch had not mentioned that the father was imprisoned. The story from Bangladesh, which was also given in the London *Times*, certainly corresponds to an accusation made during a trial for infanticide, but, in my view, could not prove that there really is a criminal trade in organs.

Macabre and crazy stories from the Indian subcontinent often seem to be accompanied by references to organ trafficking. Thus the following item, which appeared in an international magazine of good quality, is a sort of moral fable about the evils of the Indian dowry system, but organ trafficking plays a part too:

> New Delhi: Dead for a Dowry. In India, unmarried women are a source of social shame and a financial burden on their families. But without money or consumer goods to offer a husband, they have little chance of marrying. Last week, a young man committed suicide in order to provide dowries for his two unmarried sisters. Sunil Kumar, aged nineteen, unemployed, and with no prospects of finding work, took it into his head to sell his organs. Even though the sale of human kidneys is illegal, impoverished Indians do sell their kidneys. Reckoning that other organs

too could be taken if he was dead, Kumar hanged himself. But his plan did not succeed. As all suicides have to undergo an autopsy, none of his organs could be transplanted. His grief-stricken family declare that in any case they would never have sold Sunil's organs.[32]

In an illustration printed in 1992 in *Colors*, the house magazine of Benetton (a firm known for its deliberately shocking use of tragic social problems for its own publicity), one finds the same morbid notion as in the *Nouvel Observateur*'s columnist—that organ trafficking is a symbol of modern life. The trade is here implicitly represented as criminal, for the illustration lists extravagant prices for various vital organs which could only be obtained by murder. It shows a frail teenage boy, of Indian appearance, standing naked, with his hands hiding his penis. Around his head, in large letters, is the inscription "How much?," while a series of arrows point to various parts of his body, accompanied by sums in dollars ranging from three million dollars down to sixty cents. To the left of the photograph is a panel, of a few lines only, listing the prices of various objects, this time ranging from one hundred million dollars to eleven cents.[33]

ACCEPTANCE IN THE MASS MEDIA

> Tickle the public, make them grin,
> The more you tickle, the more you'll win;
> Teach the public, you'll never get rich,
> You'll live like a beggar and die in a ditch.
> —*Fleet Street journalists' rhyme, early twentieth century*

The mass media discuss organ transplants either from the angle of "a good story," or of controversy, or of a scandal.

GOOD STORIES

These are, on the whole, stories where the organ is donated to a particular person, or those where exceptional circumstances allow the rule of anonymity to be broken—a rule most untypical of the media. There was the extraordinary and disturbing case of the American with heart disease, operated on five times and on a transplant waiting list for four years, who received the heart of his own twenty-two-year-old daughter, killed in an accident,[34] and the one of a group of Italian patients who received the organs of little Nicholas Green, killed in November 1994 on a road in Calabria.[35] These cases were given star treatment in the press, and later in the French TV program on organ donation in June 1995.[36]

As for bone marrow transplants, the media were fascinated in 1991 by the cases of the Ayala family[37] and of the Bosze father.[38] The Ayala case really is alarming, since it concerned a little girl conceived and born in order to provide a bone marrow transplant for her elder sister, who had leukemia and whose marrow was incompatible with that of her parents and her brother. The father had had a vasectomy, which it proved possible to reverse by surgery. Apropos of this case, the director of the Center for Biomedical Ethics at the University of Minnesota declared that after questioning fifteen of the twenty-seven American centers doing marrow transplants, he reckoned that about four hundred births had occurred in the United States over the previous five years with the aim of finding compatible marrow donors.[39] As for the Bosze case, that concerned an American of Hungarian origin with a twelve-year-old son who had been suffering from leukemia since 1988, who in 1990 brought a lawsuit against his ex-mistress, by whom he had twin boys who were four years old at that time. Bosze wanted to force this woman to get the twins tested, so that they could give marrow to their half-brother, if this proved compatible. He lost his case, and the boy with leukemia died in 1991.

CONTROVERSIES

The stories of parents in Japan who died in giving their livers have remained, with the passing of years, simply that: just good stories.[40] However, the debates arising from requests to use organs from anencephalic babies[41] bring us into the field of controversies over organ transplants. In 1992, there was a case of a baby girl born anencephalically in Florida, whose parents wished to have her organs taken before she died (the Florida Supreme Court refused to allow this). This case did get publicized, especially in the Italian press, when an analogous case occurred in Palermo, bringing the parents and doctors into conflict with the judges, who refused to allow any removal.[42] The mass media, however, hardly ever discuss these controversies. The reports of IGAS, the General Inspectorate of Social Affairs on the way transplants are organized, or even on suspicions of corruption, are dismissed in a few lines, or completely ignored, being left to specialized journals and the quality press. Even the Amiens affair itself got hardly any publicity in the mass media,[43] which remain loyal to an idealized picture of the medical profession.

SCANDALS

Instinctively, and without setting out a reasoned argument, any journalist working for the mass media will see reports about stolen organs as "good stories." So small news items from distant countries are sure to get publicity through agency dispatches if they include shocking accusations about "organ snatchers" or "baby snatchers," and these dispatches from Associated Press, Agence France Presse, or Reuters become the basis for articles in the mass media. That is how accusations of the baby parts type obtained short-lived but worldwide publicity in 1988, and other cases have appeared sporadically since 1992. For scandals and denunciations of horrors constitute the main dish in the menu presented to us every day by the media which inform us about the wide world.

These distant news items, these scraps of international information which do not fit the specialized fields of politics, economics, or science, will only attract the "gate-keeper" who lets them cross the threshold of the press agencies whose dispatches go round the globe if they are spicy, shocking, sensational (or funny, but that is another matter). We receive them with all context stripped away; we accept them for their ability to amaze or horrify us, often without understanding them. The denials, explanations, and contextualizations which follow some days later in the press of the countries concerned, and which generally deflate the sensational assertions, have no chance of crossing this threshold, since their information, which is lengthy and expensive to transmit, would seem off-putting to the mass readership who are being targeted.

Here are two instances of the way in which the international media system functions (or rather, malfunctions). They do not directly concern organ theft, but situations that render accusations of organ theft plausible.

The first, the abduction in Rio, centers upon abductions and trafficking linked to international adoption. On March 28, 1992, a dispatch from Agence France Presse, which was taken up two days later in an article in *France-Soir*, reported an extraordinary piece of news coming from Rio de Janeiro. A woman of the poor classes who was shortly due to give birth was abducted by traffickers who forcibly induced labor and then stole her newborn baby: "Bandits abduct a pregnant woman, induce labor, and steal the baby" (AFP); "Baby thieves force her to give birth" (*France-Soir*, March 30, 1992).

In France, as no doubt in most countries of the world, there was no follow-up to the report of this news item, and I remained convinced that this dramatic and alarming abduction had really occurred, lending legitimate support to a good many accusations about unscrupulous traffickers, capable of anything. But now I do know the end of the story, which was treated in depth in the Italian press, always very sensitive to abuses concerning adoptions and to organ theft allegations.

On the twenty-ninth, *Unita* reported the news, with a headline virtually identical to the AFP despatch. On the thirtieth, *Unita* and *Stampa* elaborated on its various aspects in two or three articles apiece, the former stressing the mother's grief ("Give me back my son!"). But the true subject is the dramatic situation of Brazilian children in relation to international adoption (which *France-Soir* had already developed more fully than AFP). It is discussed under the headlines "Was the child bought by an American?" and "A child of the poor is just merchandise: bought, sold, eliminated" (both in *Unita*), and "The child business: a supermarket for the disappeared" (*Stampa*). Both papers also announced that the pope had launched an appeal for the street children of South America. Even though this appeal does not mention the dramatic news item, the papers made the link ("The Pope combats the horrors of Rio," *Stampa*; "Pope's appeal for South American children," *Unita*).

However, on March 31 the Brazilian police announced that the mother— a woman of forty-two, with two children already, who had concealed from her younger husband a spontaneous miscarriage which had happened four months earlier—had invented this abduction to cover up her lie. "She had invented it all" (*Nazione*); "The Brazilian woman confesses" (*Unita*). Women who have killed their babies or who are entangled in false announcements of pregnancy generally seize upon some danger which "everybody" knows about: in the United States, a black attacker; in Brazil, the baby-snatching trafficker.[44]

My second example, the murderous transplant surgeons of the Philippines, brings us back to accusations against the medical profession in matters of transplantation. It is presented by Todd Leventhal:

On August 24, 1994, both the Reuter and Kyodo wire services reported a sensational story from Manila: four surgeons who had performed the Philippines' first double organ transplant in 1988 had been charged with murdering the organ donor, Arnelito Logmao, [who was] admitted to a government hospital in Manila on March 1 1988, after falling from a pedestrian overpass. . . .

[Reuter reported that] "the court documents allege that while Logmao was still alive, doctors cross-matched his tissue with the recipient's and later pronounced him clinically dead. With intent to kill him in order to retrieve vital organs . . . for purposes of financial gain and glory [the respondents] surgically cut out his two kidneys and pancreas without the knowledge, consent and authority of his mother, thereby causing his untimely death, [special prosecutor] Apostol said in his report."

The Reuter account did note that "the four doctors denied the accusations and said that Logmao was brain-dead before the procedure began," but the bulk of the story and the attention-grabbing headline featured the accusation of murder for organ transplant.

On August 27, *The Manila Times* reported that in 1989 a Quezon city prosecutor had dismissed a murder complaint against the doctors in the Logmao case, a fact which the initial press accounts did not note. On September 8, several Philippine newspapers reported that the four doctors charged in the case had filed a 16-page supplemental motion to dismiss the case, in which they noted that the alleged murder victim had been pronounced "brain-dead" by [two other doctors, who performed a further electroencephalogram].

According to *The Philippine Star*, in response: "Government prosecutors justified the filing of murder charges by saying that a person, even if declared brain-dead, is still 'for practical [*sic*] and in a layman's point of view, alive.' "

On October 19, 1994, *The Manila Bulletin* reported other arguments by the four accused doctors in a 47-page reply to the charges against them [e.g., that Logmao was declared brain-dead several hours before the organs were taken; that attempts had been made to trace any relatives]. . . .

None of the Philippine press reports containing these additional facts was reported by any wire service.[45]

The poorly supported assertions of the Schwarzenberg Report were further distorted when relayed to the four corners of the earth; thus, in Sweden, his allusion to organ trafficking in India became transformed into a fantasy about South America (where there are "Indians" too!), as Jonny Såganger noted:

The credibility of the article in *Arbetet* is reinforced by the fact that Leon Schwarzenberg is there represented as being a professor and a cancer specialist. According to the article, in the course of his cancer research he was confronted by this "cruel traffic" (one wonders for what reason). He reported the following testimony about an Indian village in South America: "It is a very poor village, and today hardly any of its young people is still in possession of all his organs. They have almost all sold either a kidney or some other organ" (*Arbetet*, October 3, 1993). There is every reason to think that the "South American village" Leon Schwarzenberg is speaking of does not exist.[46]

There are also the extreme distortions produced by sensationalist journalism. In the West, papers such as the German *Bild*, the Swiss *Blick*, the American *Weekly World News* or *Sun*, are stuffed with exaggerated headlines about organ thefts, generally put together from a reading of sensational papers in Latin America. One example will suffice: a headline in the American *Sun* which announced in its inimitable style, on July 17, 1990, "Ruthless Gang Kidnaps Kids And Sells Their Bodies For Organ Transplants. Babies Are Cut Up For Parts While Still Alive." The text of the article referred to declarations by the police at Recife who had just broken up a gang trafficking in babies for adoption.

FILMED REPORTS

Accusations of organ theft have been submitted to skeptical analysis, but only rarely; I have only one televised documentary exemplifying this approach, namely about twenty minutes devoted to "child abductions for organ trafficking" in the program *Rumors* broadcast by Suisse Romande TV in December 1988. After relating the accusations of 1987–88, together with an account of the denials which soon followed, an opportunity to speak was given in turn to American information agencies, to Alain Feder (one of IFHR's investigators in Guatemala), to the historian Raoul Giradet, and to the sociologist Jean-Noël Kapferer, a specialist on rumors.[47]

There have been a certain number of TV reports condemning organ trafficking in India, China, or Russia, or exploiting the criminal affairs at Barranquilla and Montes de Oca. Besides the documentary films mentioned already is one by Jutta Rabe and Thomas Schaefer broadcast by Spiegel TV on December 14, 1993, condemning a trade in kidneys between Russia and Germany, and implicating Eurotransplant, a medical coordinating organization operating in the Benelux countries, Austria, and Germany. At the beginning of 1991, Eurotransplant had put a stop to current exchanges with Russia when a Russian surgeon, Dr. Shumakov, wanted to put organ transfers on a commercial basis. However, the film asserted that the exchanges were still going on. Eurotransplant complained, and Spiegel TV was found guilty of libel by a court in Düsseldorf.

Programs of this type, generally marked by their sensationalism, distort their subjects, creating nightmarish images without analyzing the situations which gave rise to these crimes or led to this trafficking. They fit into a category, very popular nowadays, which can be summed up under the heading "horrors in far-off lands." With a surprisingly clear conscience, authors writing within this genre will distort in order to denounce, feeling themselves entrusted with a real mission. In festivals of documentary films, the majority of subjects are of this kind.

I have already mentioned the documentary *Gamins de Bogotá* (*The Urchins of Bogotá*) broadcast by A2 in 1990, whose main topic was the tragic way of life of street urchins. In a twenty-minute program, two minutes were given to setting out an accusation of eye theft. This showed in close-up a little girl with empty eye sockets, pale and silent, on the knees of an equally silent woman, while a voice-over commented: "These children have no rights, no protection. They have become a commodity. This two-year-old girl was found again by her mother, forty-eight hours ago, with a bandage over her eyes and a note for five hundred pesos in her pocket. Her eye sockets are empty. Her eyes were torn out for sale to organ traffickers." This part of the documentary caused two viewers to write emotional letters, which were then published. "Tonight I am weeping for that little girl wandering in her darkness,"[48] wrote one, and the other:

> I saw a little girl of about four, reprieved from death. She had been stolen from her mother, then returned to her. But her eyes had been torn out for organ trafficking, her eyelids had been stitched up, a 500 peso note had been put in her pocket. As Easter approaches, I see in these children Christ tortured again, crucified again. . . . Could Colombia be expelled from the company of countries called civilised?[49]

Everything becomes entertainment. The lynching of June Weinstock in the marketplace of San Christóbal Verapaz in Guatemala in March 1994 was filmed, and this document sold well among amateurs both in Guatemala and in Miami. This video of violence served as basis for a documentary program broadcast in the United States by NBC on August 17, 1994.

HOSTILE DOCUMENTARIES

Some important publicity was given to the accusations by the production, in 1993, of several documentary films which were hostile, sensationalist, and tending to distort the material. There were three: a German one in 1992[50] which had little impact on the media even though it was broadcast in France on Arte TV on January 20, 1994 and an English-language Canadian one[51] and a French one,[52] both in 1993, which caused a great stir. They are accusatory films, as their titles show: *Organrauber, The Body Parts Business, Voleurs d'organes*. Their authors specialize in reporting on the Third World. The English commentator in the Canadian film had previously made a documentary on the murder of street children in Guatemala; its Canadian producer had made a documentary on the organ trade in India and the Middle East. The French producer had previously made a documentary on guerrillas in Columbia, and several others on Cuba.

Detailed scenarios of these three films will be found in the appendix; they exploit as fully as possible the disturbing facts given here in the previous chapter, in order to prove that a trade in organs does exist.

Of the three films, the French is the most talented, the German the best documented. The Canadian film is the only one to show Central America, source of the earliest baby parts accusations, and tries to extend its assertions by showing cases in Argentina and Russia where doctors came into conflict with the families of accident victims.

The German and French films present the crimes committed at Barranquilla. The Canadian and French films devote a long sequence to the Montes de Oca affair. As regards Argentina, the Canadian film lists numerous cases which were then before the courts in Córdoba; its presenter, Bruce Harris, mentions 160 complaints, 60 of which were thought worth investigating. However, only three of them were judged to warrant litigation. Such cases highlight the problems in the relationship between the urgent, pioneering work of the transplant services, and the families of accident victims who suspect that their injured relative has been badly cared for, or even finished off, in order that some rich man can get a transplant.

The Canadian film had an important impact in Argentina and Central America. Todd Leventhal of the USIA asserts that the presenter, Bruce Harris, played an important part in unleashing the anti-American riots in Guatemala at the beginning of 1994, because of his statements to the press of that country at the end of 1993. In lectures on this subject in 1995, Leventhal quotes articles in the Guatemalan press where Harris is interviewed (*Prensa Libre*, November 15, 1993), or giving details of the accusations in *The Body Parts Business* (*Prensa Libre*, November 20, 1993; *Repubblica*, November 20, 1993). However, as we saw above, the Guatemalan press had no need of any external stimulus to produce sensational reports supporting the claim that organs were being systematically stolen by foreigners.

The French film began as a limited diffusion on the cable chain Planète on December 8–12, 1993, without causing any emotion or controversy at the time, either in Argentina or Colombia. But before being broadcast in France, it had appeared on several European TV stations in Sweden, Germany, the Netherlands, and Switzerland. However, pressure from the US Information Agency dissuaded American stations from showing it.

Two of these accusatory films, the German and the French ones, were endorsed by certain associations, which showed them at sessions of the United Nations Human Rights Commission in Geneva. The countries thus accused replied with firm denials, which were quoted above. In addition, the French film was shown before the Council of Europe and the European Parliament by CIMADE.[53]

In France, Marie-Monique Robin's systematic use of a concealed camera in her *Voleurs d'organes* caused some controversy when the film was shown at the Festival of Scoops and Journalism at Angers in November 1993, but all the same it received the prize as best documentary.[54] In December 1993, its broadcast on Planète TV got a very critical reception from the medical correspondent of *Le Monde*: "With its hidden cameras, its assumptions, its implied comments and its ambiguous montages, this documentary plugged as being 'exceptional and exclusive' reveals nothing in depth, and offers hardly any new elements."[55] There was a favorable review in *Libération*.[56] But as yet, there was no great impact; a report which CAPA and Marie-Monique Robin had linked to the launch of the film was not published in a French magazine, only in a Belgian one.[57] In November 1994, however, the film was again shown on Planète TV as part of a series of its best documentaries, chosen by Catherine Deneuve. At the end of that year *Voleurs d'organes* was being spoken of again, since it was shown (though not as a competitor) during the Festival of Reportage on Current Affairs at Le Touquet; this time the reporter from *Le Monde* covering the festival gave it high praise: "Marie-Monique Robin could and did unearth numerous testimonies in Latin America and in Europe, on which she has built *Voleurs d'organes* . . . a remarkable investigation . . . notably highlighting the thefts of corneas to which Colombian children have fallen victim."[58] Also that December, Marie-Monique Robin had her report published in a French magazine.[59]

A shorter version of the documentary, retitled *Les Voleurs d'yeux*, running for forty minutes rather than sixty and omitting the Mexican and American episodes, was broadcast at the beginning of 1996 on the channel M6 in the *Zone Interdite* series, obtaining the highest audience rating for that series since it was launched, namely 3,200,000 viewers.[60] All the press interviewed the author, who presented the film emotionally and indignantly stressed the vicious campaign mounted against it by the USIA (often referred to as "agents of the Pentagon" or "CIA").[61] In May 1995 she was awarded the prestigious Albert Londres Prize for documentaries. When the public became aware, in August and September 1995, of the controversy surrounding the Jeison case, the ramifications of which will be set out below, Marie-Monique Robin was still very favorably treated by French journalists as a whole, who were impressed by her personality as a heroine threatened by a mafia of organ traffickers. In 1996 the CAPA and Marie-Monique Robin won their cases in the lower courts after several charges of libel were brought against them; these victories were later confirmed in the upper courts.

ALLEGED CASES OF ORGAN THEFT, AND DENIALS

Each alleged case where televised reports and accusatory documentaries have "shown" surviving "victims" of abduction and mutilation by eye thieves in Latin America has been the subject of investigations, which have always ended in denials. These are the cases, details of which follow below: anonymous little girl, blind, aged about three, in Colombia (*Gamins de Bogotá*, 1990); attempted abduction of Charlie Alvarado, aged about six, in Honduras (*Body Parts Business*, 1993); Pedro Reggi, mentally handicapped, blind, aged about twenty-five, in Argentina (*Body Parts Business*, 1993; *Voleurs d'organes*, 1993); Jenson (or Jeison), blind, aged about eleven, in Colombia (*Voleurs d'organes*, 1993).

ANONYMOUS LITTLE GIRL, COLOMBIA (*GAAMINS DE BOGOTÁ*)

The program broadcast on March 22, 1990, by the TV channel A2, *Gamins de Bogotá* (*The Urchins of Bogotá*), contained a typical version of the eye thieves story, with the characteristic but implausible feature that the child reappeared, mutilated but still alive.

On July 31, 1990, this case was brought before the United Nations Human Rights Commission in Geneva by the International Association of Democratic Lawyers (IADL), who handed over a copy of the film and offered to bring to Geneva the man who had reported this case to the team of TV reporters. This man (according to telephone conversations I had at the time, his name was René Foulquié) ran a Help Centre for street children; on July 26 he had sent a fax to the IADL in which he "asserted that there was trafficking between the hospitals of South and North Bogota" (an accusation taken up in Marie-Monique Robin's documentary in 1993), and "quoted three cases of children whose corneas had been taken."[62] An investigation was begun in Colombia, but it never led to any confirmation, as is shown by a letter from a Colombian diplomat at the beginning of 1991.

This letter, dated February 7, 1991, was addressed to Jan Martenson, general undersecretary to the Human Rights Commission, by Eduardo Mestre Sarmiento, Colombian delegate to the international organizations at Geneva. He declared that the inquiry had proved totally negative: the accusation was baseless, and the film was a montage. Newspapers had published nothing about the alleged events, and the child's home could not be found, nor could the witness who had signed the fax. The letter concluded by saying that the IADL had behaved irresponsibly, and that Colombia would support a request to the secretary general of the United Nations that the status of that organization be revised.

CHARLIE ALVARADO, HONDURAS (*BODY PARTS BUSINESS*)

The case of little Charlie Alvarado is discussed in Bruce Harris's film of 1993. Harris interviewed the child, who was about eight years old, and who had told the police that he had been kept prisoner for about three days in a van, from which he had been able to escape. He repeated his story on camera.

What the film does not say, but what Barbara Hofstetter was told orally by the attaché at the Swiss consulate in Tegucigalpa, is that the child had identified as his kidnappers two social workers, Klara Dilger (German) and Wolfgang Heinz (Swiss), and that they had been arrested. The child had also identified the vehicle, a blue pickup, in which he declared he had been kept for five days. There was an investigation, but "during the reconstruction, this key witness was unable to jump from the moving vehicle (onto a mattress!). The two social workers were released, no charges having been brought against them."[63]

PEDRO REGGI, ARGENTINA (*BODY PARTS BUSINESS* AND *VOLEURS D'YEUX*)

Pedro Reggi, a mentally handicapped man, hardly speaks, but shows his empty eye sockets. His brothers declare that his eyes were torn out at Montes de Oca, and he utters the name of Dr. Sculco (or Fulco). He appears in the Canadian and French accusatory documentaries of 1993, in the sequences concerning Montes de Oca.

What is known about the complex and long-past case of the abuses committed at Montes de Oca was set out in chapter 2. There is an impression of great confusion in the sequences concerning it in the two documentaries, which rely on statements from inmates at Montes de Oca, who are not niggardly with their horrifying declarations. For instance, in the Canadian film:

AN INMATE: "They died from pills, poison, injections, sheets."
HARRIS: "Sheets?"
THE INMATE: "Yes, children were punished."

In the French film:

THE INVESTIGATOR: "Did they kill people?"
SEVERAL INMATES: "Yes, yes."
INVESTIGATOR: "How?"
ONE INMATE: "I don't know. They would take the bodies to the morgue."

The sequences also included statements ascribed to Judge Heredia. In the Canadian film, Harris says: "The judge told me he thought the eyes of some of the patients had been removed while they were still alive." In the French film, Heredia is shown in close-up while the commentary says: "He is struggling alone against everyone, at the risk of his life." Then a view of anonymous graves in a cemetery, with the commentary: "The judge is convinced that patients were being killed."

The French film concentrates on the search for Pedro Reggi's medical records, which cannot be found at the Pedro Lagleize Clinic; the Canadian film interrogates the Dr. Sculco whom Pedro had denounced, but he, very relaxed, declares that he was not practicing at Montes de Oca at that date. We gather that Pedro Reggi had lost his sight long ago, that the events go back to 1989, and that though no legal complaint was currently being laid against the hospital, the local community holds the hospital responsible for his blindness.

The two documentaries were shot at the beginning of 1993, and both expressed thanks to the same person as advisor. This is Maria-Laura Avignolo, an independent journalist who, in December 1991, had written two articles on organ thefts into which she put some typical eye theft anecdotes alongside some disturbing statements from Julio Caesar Araoz, the health minister having opened investigations into Montes de Ora and Córdoba.

The Canadian film was shown in October 1993 in the *Everyman* series on the BBC, and aroused strong emotions in Argentina, a country that has close cultural ties with Great Britain, which supported its freedom in the nineteenth century. So a month later, the TV discussion program presented by Grondona, a well-known Argentine commentator on current affairs, was devoted to a debate on this film, while at the same time an inquiry was launched into the allegations made by Pedro Reggi's family.

The evidence of Mario Barretto, Pedro's twenty-two-year-old younger brother, was one of the key points in this program. Mario declared that he had just learnt something, that very day, after a thorough medical examination had been carried out on Pedro. His blindness had originated from an infection, and was not due to any operation; this blindness could not be remedied by a transplant, and Pedro would never see again. Mario added that up till then, "I had had the idea that they [the hospital] had taken his corneas." This explicit withdrawal of the allegations was completed on December 6, 1993, by a letter from an ophthalmologist, Dr. Patricia Rey, to the director of the Pedro Lagleize Clinic of Ophthalmology. In the course of the investigation, she declared that she had examined Pedro Rege (i.e., Reggi) in 1984 and 1985. In December 1984 she had concluded that a surgical operation on his left eye might perhaps improve its defective condition, and had requested that routine preliminary examinations be done. But in November 1985, in contrast, she judged that the patient's condition had become so bad that she could no longer recommend an operation.

So there had been no criminal operation to remove Pedro Reggi's eyes. But what was the origin of his blindness? In his evidence, Mario Barretto said that Pedro Reggi remained for five years in the hospital at Montes de Oca, having gone there in 1981. But he added that in 1982 his family, who had gone to visit him, found him "at the bottom of a well, where he had been for two days. He had broken a toe, and he came home till the toe was mended, after which we took him back." Mario (who, we should remember, was only eleven at the time) had a strong impression that it was for lack of care at the hospital that Pedro's eye infection developed and led to his blindness. A male nurse questioned by Dr. Rey stated that the patient "suffered a trauma, after which he complained that his sight was failing." On the other hand Pedro's mother (who was not present at the examination) mentioned "congenital cataract in both eyes, operated on when he was nine months old."[64]

These two pieces of evidence are complementary, but merit some comment, since it is through these laconic pieces of information that one can see how suspicions arose and a rumor developed. (1) The patient's name is mistakenly noted as "Rege" rather than "Reggi" on his medical records. (2) One must find it strange that an operation considered necessary on December 10 of one year is abandoned on November 4 of the following year because the patient's condition has worsened, and that apparently nothing has been done, medically, between these two dates. (3) The trauma of Pedro's fall in 1982 is regarded as dramatic by his family and is still strongly present in their account. At the medical level, it is noted, but without curiosity. (4) It is only because of the emotion roused by the documentary film that any inquiry is launched. A previous formal complaint made by Pedro Reggi's mother (which lapsed because of her death) seems to have brought no reaction from the authorities.

Here we find the elements which give rise to the suspicion, even the certainty, that malpractice has occurred—the indifference, even negligence, and lack of explanations offered to lower-class families by an elite medical corps who are no doubt overworked, and are psychologically light-years removed from these simple souls. When, on top of all this, there arrive journalists who want sensational stories and are willing to listen, the simple families take advantage of the chance to express the accusations in their minds.

JENSON (OR JEISON), COLOMBIA (*VOLEURS D'YEUX*)

The fame of the accusatory French film *Voleurs d'yeux* (*Eye Thieves*) is largely due to the pitiful image of the child Jenson (or Jeison) playing the flute in an institute for the blind in Bogatá. A "Jenson affair" had in any case erupted before the film was broadcast, when the prestigious magazine *Life* printed two photos of Jenson, under the heading "The Big Picture," accompanied by a poignant narrative:

> The boy's name: Jenson. He is ten years old and lives in a charitable institute in Bogota, Colombia. You see he is blind, yet he has learned to play the flute. But it's not a nice story. Jenson is blind, says his mother, because his eyes were stolen.

The mother's story: When Jenson was ten months old, he got acute diarrhoea. She took him from their village to the hospital in the next town. When she came back to fetch her baby *next day* [my italics; see the remarks on this point after the next quotation] his eyes were bandaged and he was covered in bloodstains. Horrified, she asked what was going on. "Can't you see he's dying?" answered the doctor coldly. In a panic she took Jenson to Bogota, four hours' journey from there, where a doctor examined his wounds and said, "They've stolen his eyes."[65]

The image of Jenson playing his flute and the pathetic evidence of his mother are the most powerful moments in the film *Voleurs d'yeux*. Four months after the article appeared in *Life*, Marie-Monique Robin, producer of that film, took up the accusations again in a written report taken from her film, and made them even more serious. She declared that she had found out about the case while visiting the institute for blind children in Bogotá, and had learned from Jenson's little friends there that "a doctor tore his eyes out in the hospital." The mother's story is identical to the one published in *Life*, but even more condemnatory:

When he was eight months old, Jenson suffered from diarrhea and vomiting. Luz takes him to the public hospital at Villeta, where a doctor asks her to leave the child there "for a transfusion." Next day, there is a bandage over the place of the eyes, which Jenson no longer has. The wound is bleeding heavily. When the mother protests, she is told that "in any case her child is dying." Luz then seizes Jenson, whom she takes to a hospital in Bogota, after a four-hour bus journey. There, they explain to her that "the baby can be cured, but he will never see again." "We could do nothing, we had no money to pay a lawyer," whispered Luz, her voice breaking. "When I went back to ask for Jenson's medical records, they told me they had been burnt."[66]

This written report increases the gravity of the mother's accusations. In the film she says she had been called by the hospital, but does not say exactly how long Jenson's first hospitalization had lasted. In her sworn statement to the investigator she stated: "He was kept in hospital for a fortnight and afterwards he was transferred by ambulance to the Lorencita Villegas Hospital in Bogota. The child had his eyes bandaged." But to state precisely that the wounds were seen "next day" makes the crime seem indisputable.

On February 4, 1994, a few days after Marie-Monique Robin's written report was published, there appeared the results of the investigation set up in Colombia into the Yeison case (his Christian name is thus spelled on his identity card). This "Report of the Defense Counsel for the Department of Health and Social Security," Alejandro Pinzon Rincon, summarizes in four pages the conclusions of the "Evaluatory Report" presented on December 27, 1993, by the investigator Fabio Delgado Sanchez—a report which itself had summarized a thick dossier of "matters investigated." This investigation had been set in motion by a formal complaint lodged on October 23, 1993, by Hector Torres, a Colombian human rights campaigner, who said he was acting at the request of Marie-Monique Robin.[67]

The investigation established that the child had been in hospital from January 23 to February 12, 1983, at the Salazar Hospital in Villeta, and then from February 12 to 24 at the Lorencita Villegas Hospital in Bogotá, a pediatric hospital. The transfer had been decided on because of the serious condition of the baby, who was presenting "a grave infection in both eyes, leading to perforation of the corneas and conjunctives, with drainage of purulent matter affecting both eyeballs."[68] The investigator notes with severe disapproval that the journalist had given the mother forty thousand Colombian pesos; this is no revelation, however, for Hector Torres had spoken spontaneously of having given this money "so that she can buy the child something," pointing out at the same time that it was no great sum (in 1993, forty thousand pesos was about three hundred French francs). In conclusion, the investigator found that the journalist had lacked professionalism because she did not try to check up with the medical authorities on Jenson's mother's evidence.

Ten years after the events, the mother's memories of the pitiful state of her child and the lack of medical information were still extremely vivid, as shown in the pathetic evidence she gave on oath to the investigator:

> They handed him back to me with his eyes bandaged and they took him off in the ambulance, and there was blood and water running from his eyes. . . . [She is given a very unpleasant reception at the second hospital.] I got to Lorencita Villegas with him, and there they told me he was blind. They did nothing for him there. . . . [The child was in a terrible state when he left hospital the second time.] That child was examined all over, they just tore him to bits. He had holes in him, his head was swollen, and from the waist down, when I wanted to change his

diapers, his skin was coming off in shreds. He was rotting. . . . [The bill at the second hospital is a big one, and the debt still not paid off, ten years later.] To get him out of there, we had to give three litres of blood; it was my husband gave the blood, because we had no money and we were in debt over another bill too. I didn't go back to pay it. . . . [She speaks again of the child's terrible state on leaving the second hospital, and how she turned to a folk healer for help.] They gave him back to me worse than ever. That's where they told me he was blind, swollen, rotten all over, his arms purple, his legs too, and there were holes in his head. . . . I took him home and I took him to M. Luis Huerras, who is a healer, and I gave him herb baths. . . . [There was no explanation from the doctors.] At Lorencita Villegas, I asked them to tell me the reason the child was in that state. They never answered me. They just told me he was blind—full stop, draw a line. . . . [The investigator asks if she wants to add anything.] No, sir. Or rather, yes. I want an investigation on the reason why he went blind.[69]

So here we are faced with a case analogous to the previous one, but much better documented. Blindness occurred for medical reasons which were clearly established, and the child received treatment. However, no information was given to the family. How important was this lack of information, which justified the family's suspicions, was rightly highlighted in the report of the inquiry set up in August 1995 by the ophthalmic department of the Hôtel-Dieu:

When the mother collected her child at the Salazar Hospital at Villeta to take him to the hospital in Bogota, a dressing had been put in place across both eyes, and blood and purulent secretions were leaking from under it. As the mother had been given no medical explanation, she could quite legitimately think that her child's eyes had been removed, since it was only subsequently that she learnt of the eye infection affecting both eyes, and the very bad prognosis this implied. This interpretation by the mother arose from a lack of medical information, but does not in any way mean that a so-called "theft" of corneas or eyeballs occurred, since the mother never personally verified the state of the child's eyes during this transfer, and since the presence of bloody and purulent secretions is in no way surprising, as there was deep ulceration of the corneas accompanied by perforation and a purulent endophthalmia. The mother's evidence therefore cannot be considered relevant to the problem.[70]

To clarify the origins of the investigation's report, we must go back a bit. During the period when the CAPA film was enjoying the successful career described above, Colombian diplomats in France were exhausting themselves in vain efforts to make known the results of their inquiries. Nobody would listen to them. The CAPA Agency and Marie-Monique Robin cleverly chose to effectively ignore the contents of that inquiry. They exploited Colombian contradictions—for instance, the Institute for the Blind at Bogotá where Jenson was pursuing his studies told Colombian journalists, shortly after the article in *Life* appeared, that the child had been born blind—presented themselves as victims of a plot, and hinted that the Colombian authorities were accomplices of the "organ thieves." This dramatic interpretation was very successful in the French press, as can be seen in the remarks introducing an article which Marie-Monique Robin published in the summer of 1995:

> The televising of this testimony roused the anger of the torturers—of the very people who were not afraid to kill poor children to steal their eyes. Marie-Monique Robin, who had the courage to make these revelations, is still under dangerous pressures today. She is physically threatened, and her life has become a hell. The traffickers leave her no peace. We have wanted to know all the details of this affair.

Robin encourages this view in her article, stating: "Everything happens in a most sinister way, in the form of counter-rumors circulating at the highest levels."[71]

The awarding of the Albert Londres Prize to this film in May 1995 was a real slap in the face for the Colombians. They decided that in order to respond and to be heard in the French media, they had to get confirmation of the contents of their report from prestigious French medical authorities, so they arranged for the child to be medically examined in Paris in August. His medical records were studied by Professor Gilles Renard, Ophthalmic Department, Hôtel-Dieu; Professor Alain Fischer, Department of Child Immunology, Necker Hospital; Professor Marc Gentilini, Infectious Diseases Department, Hospital Pitié-Salpêtrière. Examination of the child took place on August 3 in the Ophthalmic Department of the Hôtel-Dieu, in the presence of Professors Renard and Gentilini. The conclusions of the report of the French medical examination confirmed the contents of the Colombian report, while showing sympathetic understanding towards the mother's mistaken convictions. When they were announced (on August 12 by *France-Soir*, on August 17 by *Le Monde*) and then published on September 16, it looked as if the advantage now lay with the Colombian side. The Albert Londres Prize was suspended, and a commission of inquiry consisting of six members of its jury was set up. But Marie-Monique Robin and the CAPA did not surrender; they arranged press conferences and stressed the reservations of an ophthalmologist with links to the International Federation for Human Rights.[72] Robin asserts confidently that "in the opinion of several ophthalmologists, it is impossible to tell, more than ten years after the event, whether Jeison, the boy with the stolen eyes, had his eyes taken out."[73] She accuses the French doctors of preferring professional loyalty to the search for truth: "The ophthalmologists at the Hôtel-Dieu know their Colombian opposite numbers perfectly well. Colombia has worldwide status in that discipline, and mandarins do not pass adverse judgements on one another."[74] No dialogue seems possible between the two parties.

Paradoxically, it is the very clumsiness of the Colombian dossier and its numerous anomalies which seem to me to show its good faith. One cannot believe that the report is faked when one reads in it that it was difficult to find the child's records in the first hospital because his name had been transcribed as Averis Jieson Vargas Ruis instead of Cruz, or again when the investigator indicates that the assessment done on departure was faulty, because the fact of a transfer to a second hospital was not indicated.

No trumped-up report, designed to create a good impression, could ever include the exchange between the investigator and the employee in charge of compiling dossiers in the first hospital: "Why did you write 'E.D.A.' in the section of the medical dossier relating to diagnosis, but in the section labelled 'Standard' that the child left 'on account of amelioration'?"—"The diagnosis, because that's how it was put down on the medical admission dossier, and 'amelioration' because I had not read in the nurse's notes how the child left. Generally, if they are alive when they leave, we write down 'on account of amelioration.'"[75]

In the same way, it seems impossible that a faked document would show the many inconsistencies about the age and precise name of Jenson or Jeison, as the document that was examined does. Moreover, this dossier is very complex, and includes the doctors' names. Thus, it could be legally verified.

The authoritative medical advice of the French professors brought about a permanent reversal of authoritative opinion among thinking people, and did permanent damage to the credibility of the film *Voleurs d'yeux*. Accusations of conspiracy lose all plausibility by becoming too all-embracing.

Nevertheless, it appears that at the beginning of 1996 Marie-Monique Robin and the CAPA still held strong trump cards, if one considers that their victories in the law courts reflect the state of mind of the judges, who themselves were close to public opinion. In January 1996, in all three of the suits for libel which had been brought to court (CAPA against the lawyer of the Colombian Embassy, the Barraquer Institute against CAPA, the Salazar Hospital against CAPA), they won their cases in the lower courts, with very favorable summing-up from the judges.

On March 20, 1996, the jury of the Albert Londres Prize, having heard the report of the commission of inquiry they had set up the previous September, decided "to maintain their award of the 1995 audio-visual prize to Marie-Monique Robin for her film *Voleurs d'yeux*, though expressing some reservations." The summary of the work of their commission (comprising four pages, and published at the same time as the announcement of their decision) gives equal importance to the two theories on the origin of Jaison's blindness, and seems to disregard the medical dossier compiled by the Colombians, even though the commission mentions that this dossier had been sent to them in its entirety. So ophthalmologists who disputed this dossier found their views were given great weight, when they were simply based upon their own opinions. Here are the passages from the summary which illustrate this approach:

> In the case of the child Jaison, the assertion that his corneas were stolen seems to us too categorical. The Commission draws attention to the fact that the event, the loss or "theft" of his eyes, took place twelve years ago[76] in dramatic conditions. Without entering into a medical debate which is outside its competence, the Commission noted that a high proportion of ophthalmologists thought it was more probably a case of purulent ulceration in one or both eyes. Other specialists, less numerous, think it impossible to reach a conclusion twelve years after the event, and that it is conceivable that theft of corneas could occur at that period in Colombia. It is known that Marie-Monique Robin sought the views of doctors throughout her investigation, and that at her request the film was seen by an ophthalmologist even before it was broadcast. He declared to us that he had raised no

objections to what Jaison's mother had said, nor to the images in the film to which objections were subsequently made.[77]

Further on, the commission quotes an article as an argument in support of the theory that Jaison's blindness was due to organ theft:

The Colombian press, and the international press, regularly report rumors of organ theft. Only recently, on March 15 1996 in *Libération*, Gilles Baudin was writing that: "Official statistics [in Colombia] list 480 persons as being held captive by criminals or guerrillas—or twice as many, according to newspapers in the capital. Among these are children, who are sometimes sold abroad or returned to their families after an organ has been removed."[78]

Here we can see a perfect example of the attitude of the media, as analyzed above. The article has as its starting point certain social evils which are, alas, only too true: vile kidnappings for ransom which happen frequently in Colombia, some of them being the acts of guerrillas with political aims. Then it confirms them in a sentence which picks up the persistent rumors of eye thefts, a sentence which is accepted by groups of the French elite as "proof" of the reality of such thefts, although it provides no concrete, verifiable element.

The same confusion marks the preface written by Christian Lefort, president of ADOT, a French organization campaigning in favor of organ donation, for a book published in April 1996 by Marie-Monique Robin.[79] This text assimilates theft with sale, and demonizes the "laws of the market." The work itself is of course a polemic. The final chapter, describing the reactions of people who had just seen the film (from summer 1993 to spring 1996), is centered on the controversy over the Jaison case, showing us a brave heroine facing the wicked Todd Leventhal of the USIA, who is represented as incompetent and ridiculous. The heroine must also confront the Colombians, depicted as absolute gangsters. The medical profession is divided between lying mandarins (such as Dr. Barraquer of Bogotá and Professor Gilles Renard of the Hôtel-Dieu in whose department the examination of Jaison took place) and brave defenders of human rights, these being the militants who drew up the "Questions about the Assertions" which called into question Professor Renard's expert report.

FOLKLORE ORIGINS

WAGERS, JOKES, HEALING; TRANSPLANTS IN
FOLKTALES AND PIOUS LEGENDS

In the folktale world, transplants are a speciality of learned doctors who perform them for a wager, or as a joke; however, some accident forces them to have recourse to animal organs, which keep their former habits and powers, and so transform the person receiving them. This plot outline has remained remarkably stable.

In the Middle Ages, a folktale tells of two doctors who take it in turns to remove and replace their eyes; a crow steals one of the eyes; however, it is then replaced by a goat's eye, which persists in staring at trees in search of edible leaves.[80]

One of the tales collected by the Brothers Grimm at the beginning of the nineteenth century features three doctors who put their skills to the test by the first one removing his eye, the second his heart, the third one of his hands; they have to put them back next day, without leaving any sign of a wound. But the organs are eaten during the night, and replaced by a cat's eye, a thief's hand, and a pig's heart. From then on, one of the doctors sees best at night, the second always wants to steal things, and the third often longs to scrape the earth.[81]

A humorous anecdote heard in the American West in 1961 tells the story of a cowboy who was injured while rounding up cattle, and is examined by a medical student who happens to be passing that way. In order to replace the organs destroyed in the accident, the student asks the cowboy's companions to kill a wandering sheep; then he carries out the necessary transplant, and goes off. A year later the student, travelling along the same road, sees the same small group of cowboys and inquires after his patient. "Oh, he's fine now. He had some problems in the spring when he had his two lambs. And we did have to shear him—he gave us a good eight pounds of wool."[82]

Transplants also occur in pious legends. Saints Cosmas and Damian, who were martyred in Asia Minor under Diocletian, were themselves doctors and are now the patron saints of surgeons because they performed a miraculous transplant after their deaths, which is often shown in paintings. Here is the story, as given in the *Golden Legend*:

> Pope Felix had a large church built in Rome in honour of the two saints. This church had as its caretaker a man who had one leg all eaten away with cancer. Now, in his sleep this pious caretaker saw Saints Cosmas and Damian appear to him, bringing ointments. And one of the two saints said to the other, "Where shall we find sound flesh to replace the rotten flesh we will cut away?" The other saint replied, "A Moor was buried today in the cemetery of St Peter ad Vincula; let us take one of his legs and give it to our servant." And that is what the two saints did, after which they gave the Moor's leg to the caretaker, and took the sick man's leg away to the Moor's tomb. The caretaker, awaking and seeing that he was cured, told everybody about his vision and the miracle that had followed. Then people ran to the Moor's tomb, where they discovered that one of his legs was missing and that in its place was the diseased leg of the caretaker.[83]

A TRADITIONAL THEME IN FANTASY: THE HARMFUL TRANSPLANT

Transplants figured in popular culture long before they existed in reality. In the fantasy genre, one major figure is the mad scientist who violates nature's sacred laws with disastrous results, the Baron Frankenstein invented by Mary Shelley in 1817 being the prototype. Furthermore, the mad scientist is more and more often presented as being a member of an arrogant ruling clique who are in the grip of unbounded ambition and cherish sinister designs against normal human beings, whom they see as mere material for experiments. Here is introduced the theme of a conspiracy by a malevolent elite, echoing and elaborating that of the dangers of science. One of the evil activities of the mad scientist driven by unbounded ambitions and eager to break the chains of nature's laws is to carry out transplants, which, of course, always turn out badly.

There are well-known fantasy novels and short stories involving harmful transplants: the creature made up out of bits of corpses by Baron Frankenstein receives a brain which is stupid and criminal; the pianist in *Les Mains d'Orlac* (*Orlac's Hands*), hero of a novel by Maurice Renard in 1920, is given the hands of a murderer, endowed with a life of their own; in 1965 the coauthors Boileau and Narcejac, in *Et mon tout est un homme* (*My Whole Word Is "Man"*), describe a decapitated assassin who ensures his survival by a series of transplants performed by a criminal surgeon. In his review presenting this last work, the writer Alexandre Vialatte drew a fantastic picture of the progress of transplants, which is comic yet vaguely worrying:

> Surgery is making considerable progress. One transplants kidneys, implants teeth, cuts hair, replaces noses, sends essential organs off to be mended and then puts them back in like socks in a suitcase; one fixes the head of the femur in its socket by nailing it to a silver pivot; one plugs up Botal's Hole, one puts a new strap on the Turkish Saddle, one makes Malpighi's Pyramid balance on its point. There is nothing but bladders, appendixes, glands and sinews. One lengthens things, stretches them, cuts them, reshapes them. One cuts pieces away, eliminates things, changes things. One opens, closes, creates keyholes, rubs, scrapes, and polishes. In short, one opens the body like a wrist watch, and repairs it like an alarm clock. And, above all, one transplants. . . . One transplants everything. Does one transplant heads? Why not? But that's done in secret. . . ."[84]

In the cinema, following the same spirit of fantasy and featuring a scientist who wants to push back the boundaries of possibility and thus becomes a criminal, *Les yeux sans visage* (*Eyes Without a Face*), directed by George Franju in 1960, has become a classic; nowadays it is considered a "poetic fantasy" (in Franju's own words), and also "a perverse fable about creation and scientific hubris."[85] In this film Pierre Brasseur plays a doctor, a mad genius who sends his assistant (Alida Valli) to kidnap girls in Paris so that he can graft their faces onto that of his own daughter (Edith Scobb), disfigured in a car accident for which he was responsible. The story ends tragically; the girl kills herself, and the mad doctor is eaten by the German shepherd dogs he was using in experiments.

ORGAN THEFT IN FICTION: NOVELS AND FILMS

NOVELS

Several popular novels have been inspired by organ theft allegations of the baby parts type. For instance, as early as 1989 there appeared in the Netherlands

Donor, by Thomas Ross, a thriller writer well known in that country. Giving as his source a Dutch magazine article[86] describing the incident which occurred in Guatemala in February 1987, Ross describes how a Dutch couple adopt a little girl from Colombia. Shortly before she is due to arrive, they are told that she has died. But the reader follows the Colombian child to a German clinic where a young boy is waiting for a heart transplant.

In France we have François Salvaing's novel *Une vie de rechange* (*Exchange of Life*), published in 1991, reprinted in paperback in 1993, and still in print in 1996. It contrasts the life of an average young Frenchman whose life can only be saved by a liver transplant, and whose parents engage in a desperate hunt for an organ, with that of a little Peruvian boy whose mother gives him up for adoption so that he can have a better life, not knowing that she is sending him to his death. Salvaing describes clinics in Honduras, hidden in the jungle, where light aircraft land and carry away the poor child's precious organs (heart, lungs, kidneys, liver) to New York, where four children will receive transplants on the very day his life is sacrificed.

Two years later, in 1993, Gérard Delteil won the Quai des Orfèvres Prize with *Pièces détachées* (*Baby Parts*). His novel, dedicated to the journalist Maïté Pinero, whose silhouette appears in the book, is set in France as a first-person narration by a police inspector. A secret operation is planned to take place in a Paris clinic, namely a transplant to be given to a little girl from Kuwait, using organs from a Colombian boy whose life is to be sacrificed, and who is to be brought there by drug runners. But it does not take place; a young Algerian go-between hides the Colombian child instead of handing him over to his executioners, and is himself murdered because of this. The daughter of the corrupt surgeon kills him on discovering his criminal activities, but is not brought to justice, because Article 64 of the Law Code applies (mental responsibilities). The affair never comes to light, for lack of proof, and the inspector encounters many difficulties in truly adopting the little Colombian boy who escaped death.

By now the topic of organ theft is so banal that it can be merely alluded to; as everyone knows what is meant, there is no longer any need to explain. Marc Eisenchreter's novel *Le Rallye des Incas* (*Inca Rally*), published at the end of 1995, is a good example of that treatment. The discovery of a secret transplant clinic hidden in the depths of the Amazon jungle and supplied with organs from marginalized people murdered in the slums of the great cities forms only one minor episode in a plot about two heroic adventurers escaping from all dangers. Another example of allusive treatment of the organ theft theme (the last one, for listing more would be wearisome): a review in *Le Canard Enchaîné* of the novel *Game Over* (published in June 1993), which casually notes that the heroine's Australian father is "a king of transplants, having become a millionaire thanks to the trade in organs taken from the corpses of murdered children in Brazil."[87]

In the world of suspense novels and political thrillers, organ traffickers are fashionable villains, replacing the Soviet Secret Service agent, who is no longer credible. For instance, Paul-Loup Sulitzer announced in November 1995 in the gossip columns of *Paris-Match* that his next novel would be about organ traffickers. This was *Les Maîtres de la Vie* (*Masters of Life*), published by Stock at the beginning of 1996; it describes an international humanitarian organization which, under the cover of adoptions, organizes massacres of children for use in transplants. An extract from the blurb gives the tone: "What strange links unite these Canadian, Roman, and English surgeons who are accompanied by half-breed children, all trace of whom disappears in luxurious clinics where guard dogs keep watch behind the marble pillars?"

Popular authors of political thrillers like to represent themselves as commenting on social facts whose reality is well established. Thus, *Organ Hunters*, a novel which came out in England in 1994, ends with a postscript where the author, Gordon Thomas, states that the horrible "organ hunters" in his book (former members of the East German Stasi who commit killings all over the globe to supply the bosses of world crime with organs) do really and truly exist. Thomas divides his work between novels and investigative writing, the latter being much embellished. In 1989 he published *Journey into Madness: The True Story of Secret CIA Mind Control and Medical Abuse*. His starting point is the authentic facts about psychotropic experiments on nonconsenting human guinea pigs, which the CIA carried out in the 1950s—experiments which were abandoned because of their unsatisfactory results. But in the world of conspiracy theorists and accusers, these experiments are now represented as the first phase of an "Operation Monarch," an all-embracing plan for world control by the CIA, which is supposed to be either a devoted ally of extraterrestrials who are ready to establish their domination on earth, or of a "New World Order" which is generally said to be inspired by Russians, but sometimes is blamed on the United Nations. Also in 1994, Gordon Thomas published *Enslaved: The Chilling Modern-Day Story of Abduction and Abuse in the Global Trafficking of Men, Women and Children*, which gave an entirely distorted picture of some isolated facts about the abduction and trafficking of human beings. In this work, naturally, a small amount of space is devoted to accusations of the baby parts type.

Other popular novelists set organ theft plots in our own countries. But in such cases the villains are doctors who falsify operations and induce brain-death comas in order to get rich by selling organs. We are here dealing with the very widespread genre of the medical thriller, where organ theft is only one of the misdeeds committed by diabolical doctors. Robin Cook's novel *Coma*, published in 1977 but still available in public libraries, is the prototype of this genre, which still flourishes today. Moreover, a later novel by Robin Cook, a prolific specialist in medical horror stories, was published in 1993 and deals with organ trafficking run by doctors.[88] Paul Wilson's plot in *Clinical Deaths* (1994) takes up the same theme of a hospital inducing brain-death comas, specifying that the victims are medical students from the Third World.

In novels of better literary quality, often belonging to the contemporary fantasy genre, the theft and trading of organs may be alluded to as a symbol of modern life. This was the spirit in which René Belleto used a plot about criminal transplants in his novel *L'enfer* (*Hell*) in 1986. In an interview four years later Belleto stressed that he had been a prophet, for eye thefts were now proved to occur in Colombia.[89]

More recently, a fine short novel by Emmanuel Carrère, *La classe de neige* (*Class Trip*) features a young boy living in fear and anguish, whose fantasies "are filled with organ traffickers."[90] This short and talented tale is centered on the secret haunting the life of Nicholas, the young hero. Fascinated by the anatomical models brought home for him by his father, a commercial traveller who is always on the road, the boy knows that the family had recently had to move house in a hurry, and that there is something not quite normal about them. At the beginning of the book his father, who is driving him to school in the snow to spare him a supposedly dangerous bus journey, forgets the child's travelling bag, and then himself disappears. But Nicholas does not forget his father's frightening stories. During a visit to EuroDisney, his father had informed him that gangs of organ traffickers lurk in such places, kidnapping, mutilating, and killing children. When a child really does disappear in the neighborhood, Nicholas thinks he knows the truth, that it's the organ traffickers. And when he finds out the real truth, which is closer to him and more terrible, since the man who raped and murdered the boy is Nicholas's own father, he will know that he had known it all along. In this fine and harrowing story, the tales about organ theft are a metaphor for a real evil: the sadistic child killer, who for us represents absolute evil. Reading *La classe de neige*, I thought of the sadistic murderer Christian van Geloven, found guilty in 1994 of murdering two little girls in southwest France. He was the father of a family; he had had to move house because of previous murders; he was a travelling salesman.

FILMS

In 1972, well before organ thefts were being talked about, Alain Jessua's *Traitement de choc* (*Shock Treatment*) showed a clinic where rich patients were rejuvenated thanks to blood and organs taken from young employees in the clinic. The acclaim given to this film when it appeared all those years ago shows how powerful is the symbolism of such plots. For Catholics, the perverse exploitation of the bodies of the poor symbolizes the exploitation of the Third World by rich countries; for Marxists, that of the proletariat by capitalists. Both Catholic and Communist papers offered political interpretations of this film: "A philosophical tale about how the well-to-do profit from underdeveloped countries"[91]; "A parable: the people taking this cure represent the ruling classes in a developed society, whose very existence depends on the vampiric exploitation of the proletariat and sub-proletariat, whose perpetual renewal ensures their survival."[92]

Nowadays, the plots of fictional films closely follow those of the novels analyzed above. For instance, *L'enfant d'Arturo* (*Arturo's Child*) has a plot similar to Salvaing's. In order to save their child, who is going blind, a French couple pay traffickers in Honduras to obtain the necessary corneas by murder. The father of the murdered boy kills the wicked surgeon, and then kidnaps the French child who has his son's eyes, so as to see at least a part of him again. Touched, the policeman Rocca (played by Raymond Pellegrin) lets him go free in spite of the kidnapping. The film is serious and realistic in its treatment.[93]

Realistic too is *Sonata for Solo Organ*, a film by Joe Morgenstern which forms one episode in a TV police series set in New York,[94] describing a single criminal surgical operation. The plot features a criminal surgeon who, for the very large sum of two million dollars, finds a nonvoluntary kidney donor for a sick girl, daughter of a millionaire, who has already rejected two transplants; the "donor" is a homeless man whose blood test, undergone in order to prove his right to sickness benefit, has shown his blood to be fully compatible with that of the millionaire's daughter.

In contrast, an earlier film by Alfredo Zacharias, called *Sale Affaire* (*A Dirty Business*) is highly mythical, with the mafia kidnapping children in Los Angeles, organs being sold to the parents of sick children, a surgeon forced to cooperate because of his heroin addiction. The sexual pervert who does the kidnappings, played by the sinister Aldo Ray, lures little children with ice creams and then carries them off in his van, which has a huge ice cream cone on the roof, revolving slowly in the night. The plot is centered on a young illegal immigrant from Mexico, who is suspected of being the kidnapper. This low-budget film, apparently shot for a Spanish-speaking company in California in 1989, was shown twice in France, in 1990 and 1993.[95] One may also mention three Italian references in police serials showing networks of traffickers stealing organs from illegal African immigrants in Italy, or from children, or again showing a gang in Marseilles corrupting an ambitious surgeon;[96] also an American film picking up the typical "stolen kidney" plot.[97]

Morgenstern's film features a surgeon whose corruption was an exceptional one, because he was tempted by the huge reward offered by a millionaire father. But the film *Coma*, based on Robin Cook's plot and created in 1978 by the novelist and producer Michael Crichton, shows a regular, organized medical trade in organs, based on deliberately inducing comas through systematic "accidents" during surgery.[98] This film—or rather, extracts from its two great mythic moments, each lasting about fifteen minutes, which explain its success and its impact—was regularly referred to during the great discussions on cases of organ trafficking during the 1980s. The first is the scene where the heroine hides after a group visit to the futuristic garage where comatose patients are temporarily lodged, and so discovers the real business of that center: organs are auctioned there, with Zürich and Montevideo bidding against one another. The second is the great speech by Dr. Harris, organizer of the trade, about the future of medicine, which is that human beings will be exploited as merchandise. Not long after this another film, *Fleisch* (*Flesh*) by Rainer Erler, created a scandal in Germany; it features a network of murderous kidnappings for the sake of organ theft. The plot was quite crazy, and the villains were American army doctors.[99]

Highbrow cinema has occasionally used organ trafficking as a plot element. For instance in 1989 the Polish director Kryzstof Kieslowski in his *The Ten Commandments* illustrated "Thou shalt not covet thy neighbour's goods" by showing two brothers so obsessed with a stamp collection inherited from their dead father that one of them decides to sell one of his kidneys in order to be able to acquire a particularly rare stamp. But poetic justice strikes, for the collection is stolen while he is in hospital.[100]

In Pedro Almodóvar's film *La fleur de mon secret* (*The Flower of My Secret*) one of the heroines is a psychologist running a training session for doctors, using role play. We see two students talking with the mother of a young road accident victim, and trying to persuade her to agree that the young man's organs be taken for transplanting, and given "even to an Arab," which the supposed mother vehemently refuses. So in this case, it is the real issues involved in transplants which are being shown.[101] The list of acknowledgments thanks the Spanish transplant organization for its cooperation.

CHAPTER 4

ANALYSIS OF THE LEGEND

STUDIES BY THE UNITED STATES INFORMATION AGENCY

Rumors about organ theft accuse rich countries; Western Europe, Israel, and the United States are supposedly the places where pseudo adoptions and murderous surgery occur. On the whole, European and Israeli diplomatic services and information agencies have ignored these accusations, whereas American diplomats, and especially the United States Information Agency (USIA), which is attached to the State Department, have counterattacked vigorously. The name of Todd Leventhal is inseparably linked to this counterattack. From the time when the baby parts accusations first appeared until his transfer in 1996 to another agency of the department, he devoted considerable energy to denying "the baby parts myth."

The first widely circulating public document countering the baby parts accusations was a report in July 1988 signed by Charles Z. Wick, director of USIA, but prepared by Todd Leventhal who was at that time the "policy officer on Soviet disinformation and active measures." It is set in the context of the Cold War, as was quite normal at that period, and describes the "active measures," i.e., hostile propaganda and disinformation created "by specialists in Service A of the First Chief Directorate of the KGB."[1] Asserting that these "disinformation specialists can circulate and amplify existing misinformation,"[2] the report particularly denounces the role of the KGB in amplifying baby parts accusations. The other Soviet "active measures" he denounces are these allegations: (1) that AIDS was created in 1978, perhaps accidentally, in an American military laboratory at Fort Detrick, Maryland, which the accusers assert was specializing in research on new bacteriological weapons; the report indicates that Jakob Segal, an East German, had a role in spreading accusations against Fort Detrick, (2) that the United States, together with Israel and South Africa, was carrying out research aimed at creating an "ethnic weapon" which would only kill nonwhites, and (3) that the CIA organized the mass suicide of the followers of the Reverend Jim Jones in November 1978 at Jonestown in Guyana.

To reread this report of 1988 in 1996 brings out clearly an error of analysis which is typical of information agencies, namely crediting a political enemy with an exaggerated role in spreading stories unfavorable to one's own country, when actually there are many other factors involved. Certainly, the Soviet information services did frequently practice disinformation, slander, the creation of false news, and the creation of "experts," such as Jakob Segal, who actually were mere puppets repeating a lesson they had been taught. Yet even in early 1997, six years after the collapse of the Soviet Union, and with its disinformation services gravely weakened, the first two rumors were still strongly present, even if the accusations about Jonestown were forgotten (other more recent scandals involving religious sects having somewhat blurred the memory of that tragedy).

Information services seem not to know the classic idea in communications theory that a signal becomes distorted on reception because of the attitudes and prejudices of those receiving the message, so their only concern is to denounce whoever originated the emission of the message. Such analysis, centered upon the emitter of the message, totally neglects the way in which many social groups become convinced by stories which symbolically express the oppression of which they feel themselves to be victims.

For example, the idea that AIDS was deliberately created has been many times convincingly denied by scientists, yet it is still believed by millions of people, and not solely in the black countries of Africa. In 1996, activists and propagandists of many different backgrounds were still repeating theories asserting its deliberate creation. An information bulletin of 1993 picked up Jakob Segal's accusations (set out in 1986–87) as if they were quite fresh; its text did mention that the accusation was an old one, but totally ignored the denials it had called forth:

> Why have the revelations made more than four years ago [seven, in fact] by Prof. Jakob Segal, a biologist and epidemiologist at Humboldt University in Berlin, been concealed? What is the meaning of this conspiracy of silence? Like Irene Fuhrmann, we are convinced that in order to combat this scourge, we have to discover its origin.[3]

The analysis made by USIA similarly disregards the fact that Americans themselves are often convinced by such stories, a conviction which grew even greater after the national trauma of Kennedy's assassination in 1963 and has recently taken on dramatic proportions. Furthermore, the existence of the "ethnic weapon" and the deliberate creation of AIDS are accepted as true by a very large segment of the black population in the United States.

Todd Leventhal has written several reports on the allegations about the thefts of children's organs between 1989 and 1994. The strong points in his arguments are as follows.

Firstly, he makes a vigorous and still very relevant attack on the selectivity of the media filter: only the shocking item gets through, while the subsequent denial which puts the facts in context and explains them is ignored. His demonstration of this in connection with the accusations against surgeons in the Philippines has been given above (pp. 116–17). A similar passage concludes his demonstration of the weakness of allegations about the theft of infants' organs presented in 1993 by Rosario Godoy, a Honduran congresswoman:

[Her accusation] demonstrates once again how unfounded, sensationalist allegations can garner attention worldwide, while responsible questions and statements of fact debunking these allegations often go unreported. . . . As a result, news organizations and individuals worldwide know about the allegations, without being aware of the subsequent evidence calling them into question or repudiating them.[4]

Secondly, in his 1994 report given in response to requests from the special reporter of the United Nations Human Rights Commission in Geneva, Leventhal made some sound remarks on the deep irrationality of stories of the eye theft type. Noting that the film *Organ Thieves*, set in Mexico, quotes Hector Ramirez, a member of the Mexican Parliament, as claiming that he knows a child who was kidnapped, had one kidney removed, and was then sent home with two thousand dollars, he comments:

This story is a common form of the myth about the traffic in children's organs: the supposed kidnappers return the child to his family with a substantial sum of money. It is never explained why hard-hearted criminals, unscrupulous enough to steal organs from innocent children, would feel obliged to do this. Real criminals do not go in for such inexplicable actions. Yet even though this aspect of the myth cannot stand up to rational examination, it is often repeated, no doubt because it adds to the pathos of the myth.[5]

Thirdly, Todd Leventhal in his report also attacks the common allegation of the omnipotence of organ traffickers, who are said to pitilessly eliminate any witness who would be willing to talk. This assertion, which has more in common with the logic of thrillers than with real life, is nevertheless extremely frequent in accusations about organ theft.

The film *Organ Thieves* includes an interview with someone who presents himself as being a police investigator in Mexico, and who refuses to give his name because "to talk to anyone is to risk one's life." This allegation underlines another feature of the myth: that the trade in children's organs is run by an "organ mafia" so powerful and so omnipresent that it can destroy every person who might try to reveal its secret operations. In the classic manner of conspiracy theories, the supposed existence of this "organ mafia" offers a standing explanation for the lack of any evidence for the organ traffic: those who know about it are afraid to speak out, for then they would be killed. If this logic were sound, the world would not know of the existence of cartels of drug dealers and organizations of professional criminals in various countries. But numerous brave journalists, police officers, judges, and others have openly defied the cartels of drug dealers and other criminal organizations, and brought some of their members to justice. If these powerful groups of professional criminals, with their huge financial resources and numerous hired killers, were unable to prevent several of their operations being discovered and destroyed, then logically the supposed "organ mafia" would have to be far more powerful and efficient than all the known criminal organizations, in order to successfully suppress all information about its existence. There is no evidence that such an "organ mafia" exists. Instead, the less dramatic truth is that the supposed victims of organ thefts do not come forward for the simple reason that their stories are not real.[6]

However, although the contribution of the USIA is very useful because, thanks to its excellent information network, that organization convincingly established that the allegations of organ theft are not based on any tangible facts, and also highlighted the role of propaganda in spreading them, nevertheless Todd Leventhal's reports offer no analysis whatever of the reasons why people believe them.

A REPORTER'S INVESTIGATION: SÅGÄNGER

The independent Swedish journalist Jonny Sågänger spent several years carrying out investigations all over the world into the real facts of organ trafficking. Three chapters in his book *Organhandel* (*Organ Trafficking*), published in Swedish in 1993,[7] set out and analyze the belief in thefts of children's organs. His procedure and main conclusions are as follows.[8]

Sågänger begins by establishing one basic fact: in Latin America systematic murders of street children do occur, and such murderers would be morally quite capable of selling the organs of their victims. Then he asks, but is this true?

Sågänger has traveled all over the world and has met most of the chief actors in the controversy: Renée Bridel of the IADL (whom he describes as she was lobbying the UN Human Rights Conference in Vienna in June 1993); Esther Bron of SOS Torture; Paul Barruel, the Brazilian Dominican theologian whose statements launched the myth that three thousand Brazilian children had disappeared; American and Russian representatives of the USIA (Todd Leventhal) and of the former KGB (Yuri Kobaladze); Vitit Muntarbhorn, the special reporter at Geneva; and others.

The most original contribution of his inquiry derives from the many contacts he made in humanitarian and relief organizations. Unfailingly, every time he became aware of a statement or article asserting that thefts of children's organs really occurred, he would contact whoever had made the statement or written the article and ask him or her what had been the basis for it. So, listed in turn, we find:

Rosalie Bertell, holder of the Alternative Nobel Prize, a doctor, working on ethical questions in health systems for the International Institute of Concern for Public Health, based in Canada.[9]

The Inter-Press Service, a press agency for the Third World with offices in Amsterdam, Mexico City, Stockholm, and Washington.

Save the Children, a Swedish charity helping children in the Third World, which commissioned a report on the problem from a freelance American journalist, Lucy Hood—a report which Sågänger finds highly inconsistent. He notes that this journalist is thanked for her cooperation in the film *Organ Thieves.*

Björn Eriksson, chief of police in Sweden, who on returning from a meeting of Interpol in Uruguay in November 1991 issued an alarming communiqué to the press, entitled "Children are kidnapped and murdered for organ transplants." This communiqué also announced that he had been nominated as head of Interpol.

The results of Sågänger's procedure are instructive: all the thunderous declarations asserting that theft of children's organs is a reality are simply based on nothing, on a vacuum, on hypotheses. However, the personalities he contacted stressed that such declarations were of value in alerting and mobilizing opinion, and therefore they thought them justified by a kind of "duty of vigilance." A few more serious organizations (Sågänger mentions Amnesty International) were keeping the topic under observation, but considered that in the absence of proofs there was no need for any statement.

The general public, particularly in Sweden, is very vividly aware of statements which categorically assert the horrible reality of the theft of children's organs. People telephone to radio stations, write to newspapers, want to give money and take action. So for anyone who wants rapidly to acquire some celebrity in the world of humanitarian activity, making such statements is a first-class route towards notoriety, and that no doubt is a major reason why they are repeated without proof.

At the conclusion of this investigation, Sågänger unequivocally sums up his experience:

> Is it true that children are systematically murdered in pursuit of organs for transplant?
>
> It is impossible to prove that this has never happened. But even if it is theoretically possible, the likelihood is weak. The scenario, in such a case, would have to be as follows. A rich man has a sick son. A new kidney would improve his quality of life. A certain number of children are secretly kidnapped, secretly taken to a hospital which is also secret and has not been inspected by an uncorrupted hospital authority. One kidney, or both, is taken from the child who is

considered the best donor for the rich man's son. After this, all of the children are either released or murdered. Such an arrangement needs the collaboration of a transplant team of at least ten or a dozen people. Moreover, a further number of people must kidnap and possibly murder the potential donors.

That all this could go on systematically without any leakage of information occurring appears implausible.

After having studied the question for four years, to this day I have never found any solid evidence, in the form of photographic documentation or witness statements, to show that this form of transplant occurs.

However, this is not to say that such things have never happened or may not happen in future. Consequently, it is important to be on one's guard against abuses of this type committed against poor children in the Third World.[10]

Next, Sågänger examines the stories of the thefts of organs (especially kidneys) which run round the world. He stresses that the facts of the real voluntary trade in organs, which at first glance seem to make the rumors believable, actually, on analysis, show them to be implausible—for why should one steal what can so easily be bought?

The credibility of the rumors is increased by the way they mix real facts with sheer imagination. It is a fact that people buy and sell organs; but that they commit murder for this motive is doubtful. Poverty forces people to sell their blood, but is it true that it ever happened that someone was kidnapped for this purpose? It seems to me that this would involve a pointless effort, when so many people voluntarily sell their blood. The same is true for transplants. In India, for example, people wanting to sell are far more numerous than those wanting to buy. Nor does the pharmaceutical industry need to use direct violence in order to find people willing to risk their health for medical research. There are quite enough who will agree, for payment, to become human guinea pigs.[11]

In the conclusion to his work, Sågänger returns to his main subject, the real trade in human organs and tissues. He reminds his readers that to outlaw the trade in organs, though effective in many countries, is not enough to suppress it entirely "in so far as the fundamental conditions for its appearance persist, namely a shortage of organs, and an increasing inequality between the rich and the poor."[12]

ANTHROPOLOGISTS' ANALYSES

Among anthropologists, analyses are approached from another level. In particular, arguments which dismiss narratives about organ theft in the name of "truth," or which assert that inaccurate narratives do not merit analysis and can be dismissed as "mere rumors" are irrelevant here, since anthropologists know that discourses circulating through the fabric of society deserve to be analyzed, even when they are inaccurate. Anthropologists label all such things simply "rumors," for in their discipline the distinctions between "rumor," "narrative," and "legend" are not yet admitted as valid.

We have already mentioned in chapter 1 Nancy Scheper-Hughes's account of the rumors about organ thefts among the poor in northeastern Brazil.[13] In a substantial book which appeared in 1992 and is devoted to describing the general way of life of the poor in that region, she gives a chapter to the study of these rumors ("Everyday Violence: Bodies, Death, and Silence"). She starts by giving her thoughts on "the problem of 'the disappeared,' for the specter of missing, lost, disappeared or otherwise out-of-place bodies and body parts haunts these pages, even as it haunts the imaginations of the displaced people of the Alto de Cruziero, who understand that their bodies, their lives, and their deaths are generally thought of as dispensable, as hardly worth counting at all."[14]

The author lists the incidents of violence which marked the 1980s in this area of Brazil: the kidnapping of landowners' children for ransom, the appearance of death squadrons which kill young men (usually blacks) whom they see as suspects, and mutilate their corpses. These groups cause such terror that they are never spoken of in words, simply indicated in a complicated, rapid code of gestures. And all this is happening in an average town in the interior region, which sees itself as a peaceful zone, "far from the violence and chaos of the large cities on the coast."[15]

She stresses how facts and imagination are inextricably blended among the poor:

> The magical realism of Latin-American fiction has its counterpart in the mundane surrealism of ethnographic description, where it is also difficult to separate fact from fiction, rumor and fantasy from historical event, and the events of the imagination from events of the everyday political drama.[16]

And so the *moradores*'[17] feelings of vulnerability, of a profound sort of onto-logical insecurity, are manifested in a free-floating anxiety, and in rumors (that are never publicly squelched or denied) about the disposability, anonymity, and interchangeability of their bodies and body parts. They imagine that even their own chronically sick and wasted bodies may be viewed by those more powerful than themselves (by *os que mandam*, "those who give the orders"), as a reservoir of "spare parts."[18]

As a result of these organ theft rumors, there are a fascination and horror with autopsy, plastic surgery, and organ transplant operations, which are some-times understood quite fantastically. "So many of the rich are having plastic surgery and organ transplants," offered an older Alto woman, "that we really don't know whose body we are talking to any more." As the people in the Alto see it, the ring of organ exchange proceeds from the bodies of the young, the poor, and the beautiful to the bodies of the old, the rich, and the ugly; and from Brazilians in the Southern Hemisphere to North Americans, Germans, and Japanese. The people of the Alto can all too easily imagine that their bodies may be eyed long-ingly as a reservoir of spare parts by those with money.[19]

Next, she discusses the increasing hostility towards street children, which leads to murders:

The head of the Brazilian National Street Children's Movement reported the violent deaths of 1,397 street children between 1984 and 1989 alone. Many of these were victims of one version of "urban renewal," and similar to the death squad assassinations of adult marginals, the bodies of some of these "lost" street children were also mutilated. It is curious to note how the official public dis-course about street children has changed in Brazil (and more widely in Latin America as well) over the past two decades. In the 1960s, street children were accepted as a fairly permanent feature of the urban landscape, and were affec-tionately referred to as *moleques*, that is, "ragamuffins," "scamps," or "rascals." . . . Today, street children in Brazil tend to be viewed as both a public scandal and as a public nuisance. They are now referred to either as "abandoned" children or as marginals. The first connotes pity for the child (and blame for the neglectful mother), whereas the second connotes fear. But both labels justify radical inter-ventions and the removal of these all too public "pests" from the landscape of modern, congested cities in Brazil.[20]

Then she describes the practices of child trafficking which make the rumors plausible:

> One cannot suggest to Alto women that their fears of child snatching are fantastic and groundless in the light of the active domestic and international black market in Brazilian children. . . . In the absence of any formal child protective service, . . .child arrest, child stealing, and child saving are hopelessly muddled. When coercion, bribery, and trickery are involved in Brazilian child adoption, the humanitarian gesture is easily unmasked as little more than institutionalised reproductive theft that puts the bodies of poor women in the Third World at the disposal of affluent men and women in Brazil and elsewhere. But regardless of the form it takes, the trade in babies has contributed to the chronic state of panic I am describing and to Alto residents' perceptions of bodily destinies that are out of their control.[21]
>
> Each year many thousands of children change parents in Brazil. Some of this "circulation of children" is traditional and voluntary, as in the pattern of informal fosterage. . . . Some of it is formal and done under bureaucratic regulation, but much of the exchange, as we have seen, remains coerced, illegal, and covert. . . . Meanwhile, temporary and informal fosterage is problematic because of the ease with which any middle-class woman can go to a civil registry office and *limpar a certidão*—that is, be issued with a new birth certificate with her own name as the child's natural parent.[22]

Scheper-Hughes stresses that these practices have been made worse by the recent development of international adoption which, she says, has had very negative consequences in the lives of the poor in Brazil:

> Each year close to fifteen hundred children leave Brazil legally to live with adoptive parents in Europe (especially Italy, Scandinavia, and Germany), the United States, and Israel. But if one counts the more clandestine traffic that relies on the falsification of documents and political and bureaucratic corruption at the local, state, national and international levels, the number of children leaving Brazil has been estimated at three thousand per year, or about fifty children per week. The clandestine and black markets work through murky channels by relying especially on employers and *patroas* to put pressure on female workers and to exploit the ignorance of poor, rural women like Maria, whose children are living in a real state of poverty and neglect.[23]

She concludes by reminding readers that in circumstances such as these the poor have good reasons to think the worst and to believe in conspiracies against them:

> These incidents feed bizarre rumors, such as the organ theft stories, and the rumors feed a culture of fear and suspicion in which ambiguity contributes to the experience of uncertainty and powerlessness, which then present themselves as a kind of fatalism and despair. The privileging of rumor over reality, of the fear of what can happen over the reality of what has already come to pass, may be seen as a kind of collective delirium. Or by way of another analogy, it is not difficult to drive people crazy by telling them that their fears or beliefs are groundless or that they are "paranoid" when in fact everyone is actually talking about them behind their backs.[24]

The mechanisms which Nancy Scheper-Hughes describes likewise played a part in the countries of Central America where stories of pseudo adoptions of the baby parts type have appeared.

The panics about eye thefts which swept through the suburbs of Lima in November 1988 were described above, in chapter 1. As early as 1989 there appeared in Peru a little book, comprising several articles, entitled *Pishtacos: De verdugos a Sacaojos* (*The Pishtacos: From Cutthroats to Eye Thieves*).[25] These studies, assembled by Juan Ansion, analyze the phenomenon at Lima, and also discuss the panics that ran through the town of Ayacucho in 1987, when its inhabitants were taken hostage, trapped between guerrillas of the Shining Path and government forces. Its analysis of the vampire-like *pishtaco* figure will be discussed below.

Two of the contributors (Ansion himself and Eudosio Sifuentes) show that narratives about mythic cutthroats collected in 1986, before the panics, served to symbolize the violence which these poverty-stricken people encountered in great modern cities. In these tales, the inhabitants of the Andes become the unwilling providers of the wealth of the modern world, since the fat sucked out of them by *pishtacos* is exported and used to make medicines for the rich, or to grease machines and calculators. One can see how close this is to developing into an idea that children are carried off and mutilated in order to supply eyes for the rich. The *pishtaco* is also a secret butcher, supplying luxury restaurants in Lima with provisions of meat—the flesh of children from Ayacucho. Here, the authors note, one cannot exclude a European influence, coming from the Spanish tradition about cannibal fat-stealing ogres called *sacamantecas*. Interpreting the narratives from Lima in 1988, Ansion stresses that they correspond to a loss of trust in the possibilities of modernization, and asserts that the specific fears relating to eyes should be interpreted in relation to new strategies adopted by the poor in the pursuit of knowledge:

> The fact that the victims are children and that their eyes are torn out is a new feature, when compared with the classic versions of the *pishtaco*, but this is easy to understand in the new conditions of the country. For nowadays, much more than in the past, children are seen as hope for the future. One spends money on them, so that they will be able to study. In Quechua, . . . the phrase "able to have eyes" actually means "to go to school and learn to read and write." At the same time, access to education is one aspect of a general strategy to acquire the white man's knowledge. . . . The idea that someone from the external world comes to steal children's eyes reflects a retreat towards the internal world, not simply because in this way it is a foreigner who is suspected, but because it also means that the dominant world is defending itself against the possibility that others may acquire its knowledge. . . . The *pishtacos* take away the fat, a symbol of the life force in an agrarian society where the possibility of survival depends essentially on the ability to work. The *sacaojos* who appear at Lima take away the eyes, symbol of knowledge and of the acquisition of modern Western ways.[26]

Presenting further narratives about eye thieves which were collected in Lima at the end of 1988 and the beginning of 1989, Eudosio Sifuentes protests against the attitude of journalists who denounced the rumor without trying to understand its logic. To show that a narrative is not true has its own importance, but there remains the question "Why is this story going around?"

> At the end of 1988, the media set a challenge: if there were no complaints to the police, if the public was not shown at least one case of an eyeless child, then the whole thing was just a rumor, not a reality. Officialdom would only become interested in finding the truth if there were complaints—thus demonstrating once again the gulf between legal and political processes and popular culture.[27]

Three years later, the anthropologist Nathan Wachtel, comparing the outbreak of stories about these vampire-like figures in Lima with those he had noted at the same period among the Chipaya Indians in rural regions of Bolivia, stressed the ambiguous attitudes of populations where such fears flourish:

White coats, medical technology, foreigners, dollars—the urban cutthroat has abandoned his cutlass, his felt jacket, his little bell, his blowpipe, and his magic powders, but can we not find among the inhabitants of these miserable shanty-towns the same fascinated rejection of the power of the dominant classes and of some aspects of modernity? It is true that rumors about criminal organ trafficking, a theme in contemporary myth, recur in many other places; but why in this case are they aimed at children, and at eyes? . . . Here, a child's sight could represent the possibility of progress through education, a chance for the future, the frail hope of a better world. It is this hope that the cutthroat murders.[28]

A few years later, a reader's letter in *Le Monde* mentioned the Peruvian belief in the *pishtaco* as a possible source for the narratives collected in Colombia for the film *Eye Thieves:*

"Eye theft" is a very widespread phenomenon in countries of the Andean region of South America. It is an urban version of the *pishtacos*, imaginary demons of the post-Hispanic culture. . . . All these elements are linked, as will be easily seen, to the perceived symbolic violence created by the presence of the Western world in so-called traditional societies. Even more interestingly, from the 1980s onwards, these beliefs were transferred into the shantytowns with the exodus from the countryside, with new traits. All this shows that the trail the journalist followed was not a false one. What she did, quite simply but a bit naively, was to take the same road as the communal imagination. And if this imagination awakes and expresses itself in an archaic form, it does so in order to denounce the situation of poverty and neglect in which the deprived populations of much of Latin America now find themselves.[29]

These analyses, little known outside specialist circles, are interesting and merit spreading. However, one must not forget that rumors about organ thefts from children appeared simultaneously in regions of Latin America with very different cultural traditions: in Central America, in Brazil, in Colombia, the vampire-figure of the *pishtaco* is absent, but the tales about organ theft are certainly there. In spite of their differences, all these regions had to face the development of international adoptions, and a poverty which was seen as being aggravated by the peasants who had recently moved into the towns; it seems that these common factors were those which played a crucial part in the elaboration of organ theft stories.

FOLKLORISTS' ANALYSES

As soon as narratives of the stolen kidney (Kidney Heist) appeared, folk-lorists specializing in contemporary legends grasped the fact that they were different from vague rumors. In fact these narratives followed the character-istic mode of propagation of contemporary legends. They circulated in per-sonalized terms; they were adapted to the circumstances in which they were told in such a way as to provide convincing marks of truthfulness; they fea-tured that typical character in contemporary legends, the FOAF (friend of a friend), who is placed at the ideal distance—close enough to the narrator to seem convincing, and to make it embarrassing for the hearer to express doubts about the veracity of the story, yet far enough to make it difficult to ask for direct confirmation. Moreover, one was not dealing with brief state-ments that could be summed up in one sentence, but with properly con-structed narratives having an introduction setting the scene, the actual story, and a conclusion bringing a surprise.

The Italian narratives collected by Paolo Toselli, who conducts research on rumors and contemporary legends in a nonuniversity context, were cited above in chapter 1. They were taken up again in his book on contemporary legends published in 1994.[30] The central chapter, "The Kidney Heist," describes the narratives on this theme circulating in Italy and relates them to the South American context. Chapters entitled "The Supermarket Scare" and "The Ready-to-Wear Boutique" deal with allegations of kidnapping by Gypsies or white slave traffickers.

In an article published in 1991, the folklorist Bengt af Klintberg compared stolen kidney stories collected in Sweden with the baby parts allegations and the tales of eye thieves coming from South America. His folkloric analysis, which understands that when an untrue story is persistently retold it does require analysis, is an interesting one. In his view, the guilty uneasiness which a rich westerner feels when facing the exploited Third World generates narratives about aggression, such as the Kidney Heist Story in the versions involving a rash tourist. Furthermore, following the line of thought set out by Mary Douglas in her famous *Purity and Danger*,[31] he stresses how frequently bodily symbolism is a way of expressing conflicts between social groups. Finally, he points out that by a kind of mirror imagery it is the fear felt by the Third World when faced by the domination of the rich West that generates the accusations about baby parts and narratives about eye thieves in Latin America:

> The Kidney Heist story carries a symbolic message about the gap between rich and poor countries. It is a fact that ever since colonialism began the rich countries have stolen from the less favored countries not only their raw materials but also their labor force. Nowadays, the thousands of people willing to sell one of their kidneys are just one among the innumerable indications of this fundamental inequality.
>
> But there has been a change in the contemporary legends. The person whose kidney is stolen is generally the representative of a rich country, travelling in a poor one. The symbolic message emerging from this state of affairs is that the Third World threatens our security through its criminal activities, and other dangers. This same message is found again in certain contemporary legends which tell how venomous spiders and snakes surreptitiously entered our countries, hidden in consignments of bananas or yuccas.
>
> The anthropologist Mary Douglas has pointed out that social conflicts provoke the emergence of symbols relating to parts of the body. When one group feels itself threatened by another, this is symbolically expressed as a threat directed against its own body. In the past, little known populations were accused of cannibalism and other equivalent forms of physical violence. Nowadays, there are numerous rumors filled with symbolism, in which a hostile social group subjects bodies to scientific experiments, extraction of blood, or theft of organs.
>
> What, for instance, is the meaning of the persistent rumor that children in South America are kidnapped by organised gangs who send them to hospitals in the United States and Europe, where their bodies are used as organ banks for transplants? The anxiety giving rise to this rumor is different from that found at the origin of the Kidney Heist story. In fact, in this case it is a matter of the

anxiety which the people of South America feel when faced by the imperialism and domination of the rich countries.[32]

Bengt af Klintberg continued his research on the subject, and in 1994 he called his book, which presents and analyzes over one hundred contemporary legends, *Den Stjulna Njuren* (*The Stolen Kidney*).[33]

The stolen kidney stories reported by Rolf Brednich[34] and Jan Brunvand[35] in Germany and the United States were referred to above. Both authors offer little analysis, but transcribe vividly the numerous stories they received. Brednich and Brunvand are well-known authors who have written several anthologies of contemporary legends and receive a copious correspondence. So they are very well placed to spot the emergence and diffusion of contemporary legends.

Peter Burger, the author of two books collecting and analyzing contemporary legends in the Netherlands,[36] wrote an article in 1995 for a high-quality Dutch magazine summing up the controversy about the allegations of the theft of children's organs.[37] He subsequently published expanded versions of that article in Spanish[38] and in English.[39]

His starting point is the distress caused in Holland by the film *Organ Thieves*, which was transmitted there twice (on December 1, 1993, and January 7, 1995) on a Protestant TV channel, while an article by Marie-Monique Robin appeared in the Dutch magazine *Panorama*. Like Jonny Sågänger, Peter Bulger viewed the film in company with an ophthalmologist (something which none of the indignant French editorial writers commenting on that film seem to have thought of doing), and he tells of his negative reactions to the commentary on the Argentine case in the *Panorama* article. Pedro Reggi's eyes (which he displays to the camera) are impressive, but they are not "gaping holes," as is said in *Panorama*. The ophthalmologist, having viewed the film, suggested the presence of scar tissue rendering the corneas opaque. Then Burger sets out the documents and declarations which undermine the allegations that the blindness was caused by criminal acts, both in the case of Pedro Reggi in Argentina and that of Jeison in Colombia.

Recalling the history of these accusations, he stresses the extreme weakness of the evidence, but reminds his readers that many people do not need evidence and think they can make assertions on an approximate basis, considering that there are so many similar abuses of which Third World children are the victims. He quotes the statements of Stan Meuwesse, of the organization Défense des Enfants International. Solid proofs of the theft of organs were still lacking, despite the scandal in India at the beginning of 1995:

> Transplantation experts I meet do not deny that organ thefts might be possible. But they are not aware of any reliable cases, and too many disclosures are too fantastic to be true. They are not prepared to assume the existence of a large-scale mafia-controlled organ trade.[40]

Peter Burger's survey is thorough: he mentions the lynching of American tourists in Guatemala in 1994, and gives ample space to the statements of Guido Persijn, medical director of Eurotransplant, an organization coordinating transplants which is active in Benelux, Germany, and Austria. Persijn establishes a causal link between the spread of organ theft stories and the decline in consent from next of kin, noticeable in all the countries covered by Eurotransplant (except Belgium) since 1994. He points out the absurdity of certain sensationalist claims: "In September 1994 *Bild* announced on its front page that 3,000 children had been kidnapped in South America and were all supposedly taken to Italy. What is the use of having 6,000 kidneys? There isn't even any use for them." He refers too to the distress caused in Germany by recent declarations by Catholic and Protestant bishops on TV that "brain death is a mere alibi for transplant surgeons to do their work." The chairwoman of an association for the encouragement of organ donations mentioned how widespread were the reservations and anxieties felt by the public when faced with the possibility that they could be organ donors, as this forces one to think of one's own death. During a TV program discussing this subject, one man told her he had refused to carry a donor card "because they disconnect the plug when they need your organs."[41] She stressed that stories about organ theft give people an honorable excuse to reject the possibility of making a donation which frightens them.

Burger next deals with stories such as the Kidney Heist and the Euro-Disney kidnapping, stressing that they arise spontaneously by a collective, anonymous creation, a point not taken into account by theorists of propaganda and counterpropaganda. Burger also informs his readers about my own theories on the roots of the belief in the theft of children's organs: "According to Campion-Vincent, the rumor is the unreal synthesis of two real consequences of the poverty that afflicts Latin America: adoption, and organ traffic."[42]

The next two folklorists to be considered have not written about organ theft narratives, but have discussed closely similar topics and offered illuminating remarks.

A study by the folklorist Patricia Turner[43] concerns the rumors and contemporary legends circulating among the African American minority in the United States. In particular, she examines the rumors attributing a series of murders of children and adolescents which occurred in Atlanta in the early 1980s to a conspiracy with medical aims. If the CIA and the FBI had undertaken to kill these young African Americans (with the connivance of the Ku Klux Klan, it was sometimes said), this was in order to supply bodies to the Centers for Disease Control and Prevention in Atlanta, which was engaged in a program of research on interferon and could not proceed except by using substances which were present in the bodies of black people only. This series of murders was brought to an end by the arrest and condemnation of a single killer, himself an African American; however, the argument over his guilt was still continuing several years later. It is natural for Turner to compare this with the age-old tale of the slaughter of the innocents, and also to recall some remarks by Mary Douglas:

> [Mary Douglas] has stated that the symbols of conflicts between groups often take forms which stress the body. Body parts come to stand for the whole body, and the body comes to stand for the whole group. Thus attacks on Black individuals are perceived as affronts to the whole African American community. To protect their body parts, African Americans think they have to protect themselves at the same time both as individuals and as a people against the hostility of the whites. "When rituals express anxiety about bodily orifices," writes Douglas, "the sociological counterpart of this anxiety is a wish to protect the cultural and political unity of a minority group." By circulating these rumors, African Americans are trying to establish some degree of control in the face of the threats weighing on their presence and their status in a hostile environment."[44]

An article by the folklorist Bill Ellis[45] deals with the relationship between crime reports and legends in the case of allegations of "satanic" activity, which are common in the United States. He stresses how complex are the ties linking legend and action. Legends can be considered as descriptions of what is possible, as blueprints guiding the mind and permitting us to foresee the future. Bill Ellis describes three types of ostensive behavior used simultaneously by the public, in association with a corpus of narratives embodying a legend. These are: ostensions, actions where the legend serves as a model for deeds; quasi-ostensions, which are interpretations of ambiguous evidence to fit the scenario of a narrative; and pseudo-ostensions, which are actions loosely copying a narrative, in order to perpetrate a hoax. Legends, Bill Ellis concludes, may be about what really happened, but also about what might happen—not just expressions of fictional horror, but also paradigms which make the world more horrifying.

THE SLAUGHTER OF THE INNOCENTS: AN AGE-OLD TALE

The fundamental question is, why do we spontaneously, unthinkingly, accept the organ theft legend? We will approach this by way of a survey of the various forms taken by the age-old tale of the slaughter of the innocents, which in our time has become incarnate as narratives about organ thefts.

EMBLEMATIC THOUGHT

Horrific narratives about organ thefts arouse in us a painful but powerful emotion. They instantly command our acceptance, and we believe them without a second thought. This is because baby parts stories and eye theft stories tell of children whose lives we know to be a struggle, whose circumstances are full of danger. So many abominable things happen to unhappy children "over there" that it seems reasonable to accept the truth of this new horror.

Yet this first impulse towards unthinking acceptance has other, deeper roots. It is appropriate to look for them in the sphere of symbolic thought, where symbols and fables flourish, where our fears and wishes become incarnate in exemplary tales of horror. The names given to this sphere of thought vary from one author to another: for Claude Lévi-Strauss, it is "savage thought"[46]; for Michel-Louis Rouquette, "natural or social thought"[47]; for Nicole Belmont, "mythic thought"[48]; for Peter Leinhardt, "metaphorical or analogical thought."[49] In each of us, as is now understood, the mode of symbolic or emblematic thought alternates with that of thought which is rational and self-aware.

THE POWERS OF BODILY FLUIDS AND OF INNOCENCE

Notions widespread in all traditional cultures sustain and underpin the fable. Everywhere, including in Western society at the level of emblematic thought, we find the idea (the "prejudice," as Salomon Reinach called it in a more judgmental period) "according to which the bodies of human beings and animals, together with their secretions, possess extraordinary powers both for restoring health and for conferring some illusory invulnerability."[50]

To these powers of bodily secretions are added the powers attributed to innocence, which underpin universal concepts of sacrifice and exchange. To please the supernatural powers, a pure and stainless victim will be the most effective. This magical form of reasoning was applied to contagious diseases, which were thought to have a material basis, so it was believed that an "innocent" person could take your illness on himself or herself, and thus rid you of it. This terrifying concept of magical exchange explains some perfectly authentic cases of people deliberately infecting others with contagious diseases. In the past, it was smallpox:

> There remains to be discussed a magical form of reasoning whose long-lasting and sinister prestige might still have an influence on much popular behavior. If sickness was seen as a material element passing from one body into another, one could equally well imagine that the illness could be driven out if it was attracted by the sight of a healthy body. So by making a sick person and a healthy person have sex together, a horrible exchange was brought about; the former took the latter's health, the latter carried off the sickness. . . . In the sixteenth century, some people thought they could rid themselves of pox by taking a young girl's virginity, rather like ogres in fairy tales renew their strength by devouring the flesh of little children. This obscure logic supplies the context for the depressing anecdotes one finds here and there about jealous mothers who tried to cure their children of chickenpox by maliciously ensuring that they went near other children who were free of it. No doubt epidemics may have sometimes been prolonged through deliberate infection. Perhaps the fantasy about devilish people who helped to propagate the plague itself by smearing houses with substances carrying the

disease was not merely the effect of helpless terror in the face of the irresistible spread of infection. The contaminating action could have been the logical result of the ancient belief in the magical exchange of health and sickness.[51]

Or again, in connection with syphilis:

"Is it an accepted opinion that venereal diseases can be cured by sexual intercourse with a little girl?" It is sad to have to answer such a question, but I myself have so often been asked this in a court of law, and I have become certain that such a high number of attacks on little girls have no other motive, that it is impossible to ignore it, in spite of the contempt it deserves. . . . Indeed it is only too true that many men, whose very condition ought, it seems, to make them reject such shameful prejudices, have the notion that venereal diseases, and especially their discharges, will cease after contact with a little girl's virginity. A doctor, while vigorously condemning such an incredible and damaging error, cannot permit the law to remain unaware that it exists, and that depravity and ignorance still keep it in being in the lower classes.[52]

In our own time, sadly, cases involving AIDS prove that this concept of magical exchange has not disappeared. In South Africa, a pamphlet circulating in 1990 asserted that blacks could rid themselves of AIDS by sexual intercourse with an Indian woman, who would then transmit to the man the antibodies which all Indian women were supposed to possess. In neighboring Zimbabwe, cases of rape of little girls had increased towards 1990.[53] On an Internet folklore forum on April 1 (!), 1994, Brunvand and Goldstuck posted a dispatch printed in *The Star* of Harare stating that a man who was HIV positive had raped his eight-year-old cousin in order to be cured. One may note too a case of child rape in India in 1995, where the rapist explained after his arrest that he thought this would enable him to be rid of AIDS, from which he was suffering:

A policeman of the Railway Protection Force raped and murdered the nine-year-old daughter of one of his colleagues in Delhi. This policeman, who was suspected of having AIDS, was later arrested. He told the police he had committed this terrible crime because he thought sexual intercourse with a virgin would cure him of AIDS.[54]

Cases of this sort are also reported at second hand from Morocco: "Mme Warzazi indicated that there were cases of the rape of girls by men carrying the AIDS virus who were convinced that this action would cure this disease."[55]

Since most of the accusations of deliberate infection which were made during the major historical epidemics of plague have been rightly dismissed, there are many people who have mistakenly concluded that deliberate infection never did occur. Certainly most of these accusations were baseless fantasies, rumors which expressed prejudice against minorities by using them as scapegoats; however, one cannot deny the existence of instances of deliberate infection. Nor can one claim that such facts are horrors of past periods, associated with archaic ways of thought. Magical reasoning has certainly not disappeared from among us—indeed, it has probably gained ground over the past thirty years through the growing popularity of "alternative" ways of thought which reject science and rationality.

The powers of evil draw strength from the powers of innocence. It is a universal feature in traditional ideas about the powers of sorcerers to mention their cannibalism and child killing, thanks to which they increase their own strength. Everywhere, sorcerers are accused of "eating" souls, of killing and devouring very young children to acquire their vital force.

WESTERN TALES: LEPERS, HERETICS, JEWS

Narratives about organ theft, being centered on the victims, evoke the age-old legend of the slaughter of the innocents, which everyone more or less knows. The core of this tale, which has been embodied in numerous cycles of specific stories in various centuries and cultures, is that young children from the teller's social group are being abducted and murdered, or ritually slaughtered, by evildoers. The main outlines to be found in these various cycles can be summed up as follows.

A conspiracy is unmasked. An incomprehensible and meaningless chance is replaced by something which does at least make sense of the situation, although it is malevolent. The victims are the children of the group, its weakest elements, but also the embodiment of its future. Their extreme innocence makes them magically powerful, and hence precious to the evildoers. The evildoers are, most often, either hostile foreigners or members of culturally different minorities living in our midst. But they may equally be social deviants, e.g., heretics or sorcerers, who seem at first to be like ourselves. They can also be our own rulers, our elites. This extraordinarily adaptable story can express the fear of people towards deviants, minorities, and foreigners, but also the fears of the poor and the minorities towards the ruling elites. This has been especially true in situations of colonization or conquest, where the rulers were foreigners. The victims are eaten, emptied of their blood or their fat, and their vital forces are absorbed by the evildoers. The evildoers are sick or in some way defective, and the victims possess the precious and unique element which can cure them or supply what they lack.

Our own Christian culture developed certain specific narrative cycles embodying the fable of the slaughter of the innocents. These accusations, actively expanded by the clergy, were aimed at lepers, heretics, and Jews; in the last-named case they became lastingly entrenched. They became the fable of ritual murder (also called the "blood libel"), which claimed that Jews kidnapped and sacrificed Christian children, especially around Easter time, as part of their religious rites and also to cure themselves of various diseases of the skin and the blood. The fable of ritual murder existed already in ancient Rome; at that period, it was Christians who were accused of abducting and devouring babies in their secret rites.[56] It was important in medieval Europe, where it occasioned a blossoming of legends about young saints, children who were said to have been martyred by Jews and whose names are still remembered in folksong: Simon of Trent, Hugh of Lincoln, the Child of La Guardia. In modern Europe the pernicious fable of ritual murder by Jews was taken up again in the nineteenth century in a secularized form, encouraged by government authorities who were faced by opposition and who saw that rousing hatred against Jews was a way of turning popular discontent elsewhere. The fable of Jewish ritual murder has been food for demagogues, and has played an important part in the growth of modern anti-Semitism.

The accusations elaborated by the clergy found another long-lasting incarnation when the myth of witchcraft by satanic pact appeared. What was being asserted at that time was the existence of a real plot against society; society was seen as threatened by an alliance between sorcerers (especially witches) and the Evil One, creating a more serious form of witchcraft than that of the villages, and deserving more severe repression. Accusations of a slaughter of innocents during vast sabbats played a major role in the elaboration of that myth.

These historical facts have been studied by numerous specialists. As regards the ritual murder accusation, the entry entitled "Blood Libel" in the *Encyclopedia Judaica*[57] gives a clear and concise summary, while the fourteen articles assembled by the folklorist Alan Dundes[58] offer an analysis of the dynamics and symbolism of this pernicious fable, with the stress on its modern offshoots. One should also mention the penetrating analysis of its symbolism given by the anthropologist Claudine Fabre-Vassas.[59]

As regards accusations of devil-worshipping witchcraft, the bibliography is huge. Robert Moore's book has shown how the clergy in the Middle Ages stigmatized the figures of the leper, the heretic, and the Jew, and united them in a demonological theory which applied the broad outline of the fable to each equally, and which later developed into an obsession with satanic witchcraft.[60] In particular, Moore shows that allegations of an international plot arose as early as the first accusations against Jews and heretics in the twelfth century.[61]

WESTERN TALES: BLOOD, A REMEDY FOR THE POWERFUL

The age-old fable of the slaughter of the innocents is extraordinarily adaptable. It can express the fear the ruling classes feel in the face of minorities and deviants, but it can also turn itself inside out, like the interior of a mold, or like one of those optical illusions where the design reverses itself. Then it becomes the voice of the minorities, of the oppressed; it no longer accuses the marginalized, but those who are at the center and dominate society. Among Western tales, whereas the one about ritual murder accuses minorities, the tale about blood being used as an extraordinary medical remedy involves a plot by the elite against their subjects.

The idea of blood as an extraordinary remedy, which presents doctors as the allies of elites who prey like vampires on their own subjects, has been discussed above, in chapter 2. The theme, which exploits the notion that innocence has the power to be a weapon against evil, survived the fall of the monarchy, and two nineteenth-century texts testify to its vitality in two very different regions:

> In Antwerp, children who are naughty and refuse to come back indoors are told of the danger of the "bloody carriage." A finely dressed lady lures children who

play late in the streets into her carriage by tempting offers (she promises they will be allowed to play with her little daughter in the château), or snatches them by force. On reaching the château, the children have their big toe cut off and are bled to death. The blood is used to bathe a great king, who is sick. The children must be under seven years old.[62]

An English merchant living in Pernambuco (Brazil) in 1889 described a panic sweeping through the town. Some children had disappeared, and people were saying that it was because they were used as a cure for leprosy, which was endemic in the area at that time. "People suffering from it must eat the heart, liver and kidneys of a healthy young child, wash in his blood, and smear themselves with fat taken from his body."[63]

In Spain, among various ogres and werewolves, there appears the figure of the *sacamantecas*, who cuts the throats of children and extracts human fat for medical purposes. The horrible crimes of the *sacamantecas* played a large part in popular Spanish literature at the beginning of the twentieth century. As Nathan Wachtel wrote in 1992, citing earlier work by Julio Caro Baroja:

> In his study on this folk tradition, Julio Caro Baroja mentions as an example how "a twelve-year-old girl was dismembered in the Urdes de Placentia (Cacares)" by a certain José de la Inglesia, who extracts the fat from his victim to treat his sister, who suffers from tuberculosis. A further instance of the theme is "An account of the double murder and dismemberment of two children aged seven and nine, at Béjar in the province of Salamanca," perpetrated by Juan and Luisa Carricado, an incestuous brother and sister, who supplied the "child's blood" which a folk healer had recommended to a rich man who was also suffering from consumption.[64]

The parallelism in these horror stories from folk tradition is striking. In very different regions and cultures, the theme of blood as an extraordinary remedy for the benefit of the rich is tirelessly reborn.

TALES OF THE DOWNTRODDEN: THE *PISHTACO*, THE WESTERN OGRE

The less familiar complex of beliefs to be dealt with now concerns the tales told by downtrodden peoples subject to foreign domination of the colonial type. This will allow us to understand the roots from which developed the stories of organ thefts, whose first appearance is definitely placed in a continent formerly under colonial rule, Latin America.

The vampire-like *pishtaco* (also called *nakaq, kharisiri, lik'ichiri*) appeared in the region of the Andes as early as the second half of the sixteenth century. The chronicler Cristobal de Molina mentions a great panic which broke out in 1571 among the Indians, who refused to have any contact with the Spaniards, being convinced that the latter had come to Peru in search of human fat, which they used as medicine. This rumor, associated with a revolt of the Incas against the invaders, later turned into accusations against the mendicant friars of the Bethlemite Order, who tended the sick.

> Thus, at the beginning of the eighteenth century, the figure of the "cutthroat" takes on more specific features, some of which correspond to features of certain monks, the latter being themselves intermediaries between this world and the sacred powers, just like the native sorcerers.[65]

The *pishtaco* reappeared in the Andes regions in the early 1980s, and the studies inspired by his reappearance were mentioned earlier in this chapter. The continuity of this vampiric figure since the sixteenth century, through all the variety of its incarnations, is emphasized by Juan Ansion:

> What use the *pishtaco* makes of the fat varies according to the period and the circumstances (to make medicines, or grease bells, or lubricate sophisticated machines, or, most recently, to pay off the national debt), but it is certain that the *pishtaco* always represents the power of outsiders, dominating the Andean people by force and extracting the most precious thing they own, their vital force. This belief shows how deep is their fear of the social group which sends the *pishtacos* to sacrifice innocent children so cruelly. It reveals a radical distrust of the exterior world.[66]

In the nineteenth century, when Europeans arrived in Asia and Africa and seized control there, allegations that the new masters were cannibals and bloodsuckers became endemic. This is because the power of the Europeans is not thought of in political or military terms, but is interpreted as being of a magical or mystical nature.

In 1892, Salomon Reinach drew attention to the importance of such allegations in China and Madagascar, in an article analyzing the resurgence of anti-Semitic accusations of ritual murder in the nineteenth century: "Educated Chinese assert that Christian missionaries buy or steal native children in order to kill them and make talismans from their bodies; this fable was the sole pretext for the massacre at Tsientin [June 25, 1870]."[67]

In East Africa, during and after the colonial era, missionaries and anthropologists who lived for long periods among the indigenous populations were very often supposed to be guilty of various forms of cannibalism and vampirism. So far, these rumors have been mentioned, but not studied or analyzed.

Those researchers who have taken up such narratives as the focus of their studies have concluded by emphasizing that such allegations are linked to new types of employment imposed by colonial domination and regarded as alienating. The studies of Luise White, based both on archival documents and on oral narratives collected in the 1990s, offer a very penetrating analysis of stories accusing the White Fathers,[68] or targeting Africans who were thought to be their assistants—guards, and especially firemen and ambulance men.[69] These rumors did not vanish when independence came, but now they are aimed at the new rich, and at foreigners. Luise White collected some extraordinary rumors in Zimbabwe in 1995, presented as current facts. Certain traders who import lorries from neighboring South Africa were said to obtain them in exchange for the heads of children, kidnapped and murdered in Zimbabwe itself. These heads, smuggled into South Africa, would be used there as bait to catch large sea fish, which adore the fresh flesh of children, and are full of jewels.[70]

In an important article,[71] Richard Drake studied rumors about abductions, always presented as current facts, which recur frequently among the Dayaks of Borneo, who associate them with state building projects— projects run by the Dutch or English in the old days, now by Indonesians or Malaysians, but always by foreigners. These rumors circulate among tribal groups whose social organization was disrupted by the foreign domination which forced them to give up head-hunting. In his analysis, Drake emphasizes that these intermittent rumors, which have been appearing and disappearing for the past hundred years, have built the universal motif of foundation sacrifice into a legend which expresses a whole ideology of the relations between the local group and the state. A complementary article by Maribeth Erb shows that other populations, who were not head-hunters like the Dayaks of Borneo, do also use these rumors about abductions: "Construction sacrifice rumors are ideological weapons to express resentment, fear, and anxiety on the part of the powerless towards those perceived to be powerful."[72]

HORROR LEGENDS AND THEIR SYMBOLIC VALUE

Horror legends play an important part as a tool for alerting public opinion when a new social problem appears. Horror legends are exaggerations and elaborations which spring up around disturbing facts, situations of social conflict, mistrust between social groups. Often encouraged by propagandists, who find in these worrying and sensational stories a means of mobilizing the masses in support of their own objectives, horror legends appear, one after the other, adapting themselves to the diverse historical circumstances of the time. More often than not, it is the age-old fable of the slaughter of the innocents which is incarnated, more or less, in these terrifying narratives and demonic figures.

KIDNAPPING FOR THE WHITE SLAVE TRADE

To illuminate the legend of organ theft, we should compare it with another horror legend, that of the systematic abduction of women for the white slave trade.

It is well known that in France in the 1950s and 1960s there were public disturbances caused by accusations about abductions of women for forced prostitution, aimed against certain shopkeepers:

> In France, rumors accusing shopkeepers of abducting women for the white slave trade were already going round in the 1930s and 40s; in those days they concerned shops selling shoes, gloves, or lingerie, but over the past twenty years they have been about ready-to-wear boutiques. They sprang up again in several towns from the 50s onwards—in Paris as early as 1955; at Dinan, Rouen and Laval in

1966; at Le Mans in 1968; at Châtellerault, Poitiers and Orléans in 1969; at Amiens and Dinan in 1970; at Strasbourg in 1971; at Châlon-sur-Saône in 1974; at Dijon and La-Roche-sur-Yon in 1985. . . .

At Orléans in 1969 the rumors were directed against Jewish shopkeepers, and could be considered as a revival of anti-Semitism. This gave them considerable weight, making them far more important than an old wives' tale, and inspired a major sociological study by Edgar Morin and his team.[73]

Various circumstances, some of them still not known, acted as triggers for this floating rumor to become incarnate in French towns. At Laval in 1966, the rumors started after a lecture by a well-intentioned woman from the Society for the Protection of Young Girls, who had listed the dangers girls faced in big cities. She warned her audience against some real dangers—seducers with hidden agendas, false offers of employment—but also against the imaginary danger of arbitrary abductions. At Orléans in 1969, the rumor cycle started up shortly after the magazine *Noir et Blanc* printed an account of an attempted abduction in a lingerie shop in Grenoble which had been thwarted by the intervention of the victim's husband. This account had been taken from a book of pseudo-reports on *Sexual Slavery*, originating in England, which had just been published in France. At Amiens in 1970 a young woman really had disappeared; the case was solved ten years later by the discovery of her body—it was murder, and one of her family was found guilty. But such circumstances only faintly foreshadow the rumor into which the floating myth develops; the rumor itself is, primarily, something shaped and elaborated by the public on the basis of petty happenings which the narrative organizes and renders significant. Once launched in homogenous social groups which are shut in on themselves, the rationalizing interpretation snowballs, and reaches the whole city.[74]

Even so, little is known about the origins of this rumor, which goes back to the 1880s. It is found alongside the campaigns to control international prostitution at the end of the nineteenth century. It lasted into the 1970s, producing stereotyped narratives which regularly created small-scale urban panics, despite denials from the authorities.

The phrase "white slave trade" is an emotionally charged term, which arouses indignation but which covers several very different situations and hides the fact that prostitution is often voluntary. As for organ thefts, it is obvious that the average public opinion is similarly very emotional, and does not differentiate between buying organs and stealing them, both being included in the hostile term "organ trafficking."

Up to the 1880s, the term "white slave trade" had been used by reformers like Victor Hugo as a synonym for prostitution itself ("The slavery of black women is abolished in America, but the slavery of white women continues in Europe"[75]), but it then took on a more limited meaning, and became a synonym for enforced prostitution.

Admittedly, "involuntary prostitution is as old as the profession itself, and so is the correlation between entrapment and the youth of the victim," but it is also quite clear that forced prostitution works by means of pressure and deceit practised against girls or women personally known to the pimp, whom he has usually seduced or threatened, and not by means of haphazard kidnapping—a risky method to use. Moreover, it is a method which could prove very costly and indeed catastrophic to the kidnappers if they happen to pick on a woman from a powerful or influential family, or even on a vigorous and strong-willed girl whom it is difficult to control. Furthermore, enforced prostitution is hardly significant in comparison with the major causes leading to prostitution: "There is no doubt that there were cases of white slavery. But the force of circumstances, of abysmal ignorance and grinding poverty were much more important than the wiles of the white-slave trader in keeping the brothels filled."[76]

Towards the end of the nineteenth century, people found themselves in a new situation. The trade in women became international and worldwide, European expansion having opened up new markets in distant regions such as North and South America, Asia, and South Africa, where newly established European populations, consisting chiefly of men, demanded European prostitutes. At the same time, tastes were changing in Europe itself, with brothels being abandoned in favor of cabarets and beer halls, so the pimps turned to these distant markets to recoup their losses.

Agitation against this situation began in England in May 1885, when reformers who were finding it hard to get a bill against women traffickers through its second reading in Parliament hired a moral publicist, W. H. Stead, the creator and editor of the *Pall Mall Gazette*. Stead pretended to be a debauchee, and with the help of a reformed prostitute he became the owner of a little girl, aged twelve, whose virginity he got doctors to confirm twice over: once before and once after he had gone into her room in a sordid London lodging house. He then sent her to France, to a hostel run by the Salvation Army, who were taking part in this publicity operation for moral reasons.

Beginning on July 6, 1885, Stead published his adventure in issues of his *Pall Mall Gazette* with sensational titles ("Virgins Violated," "Confessions of a Brothel User," "Girls in Chains," "I Ordered Five Virgins," "The International Trade in Young Girls") which he then gathered together under the umbrella title *The Virgin Tribute of Modern Babylon.*[77] The impact was huge, and even more so because the daily papers virtuously ignored the topic and the news-agents refused to distribute the *Pall Mall Gazette*, so that every time an issue appeared there was a stampede outside the offices of the magazine. The reformers had achieved their purpose, and the law was passed. The emotional effect on the English public, however, was deep and long-lasting. More than four hundred public meetings on the topic were held in the following year, one of which, in Hyde Park, was attended by 250,000 people.

The parents of the little girl sued Stead, declaring that they had thought they were getting their child a job in honest domestic service, not selling her virginity; they won, since it was absolutely illegal to send her, as a minor, to France. Stead served a prison sentence and so became a martyr in the eyes of the leagues of virtue. He died tragically, years later, in the wreck of the *Titanic*.

Fifteen years after the Stead scandal, the struggle against the white slave traffic had become international, and had achieved considerable successes: several international conferences took place from 1899 on, and in 1902 and 1910 international conventions led most European countries to establish special bureaux for the suppression of human trafficking. There is still one in France. Nowadays organizations such as the United Nations Human Rights Commission in Geneva, and especially its Working Party on Contemporary Forms of Slavery, are the successors to the League of Nations and its commissions of inquiry into the traffic in women and children in the 1920s and 1930s.

It was partly for tactical reasons that the reformers, who were combating all prostitution, even if it was voluntary and officially supervised, adopted the emotional term "white slave traffic" in order to bolster a campaign for abolition which was losing impetus in the late 1870s. But once the campaign was launched it went beyond the intentions of its creators. "The image of the abduction and defilement of women was so laden with symbolism, so psychologically significant, that the reformers and the public were carried away by their own rhetoric. . . . There were traffickers lurking everywhere, ready to enslave gullible women." In films, plays, and novels, or in newspapers and magazines, in the form of fictional narratives and warnings, popular culture developed a whole mythology in which rape and haphazard kidnapping was the chief source for those who trafficked in women. This mythology remained powerful until the 1970s, when it grew weaker, in parallel with the liberalization of the moral code.

The historian Edward Bristow, my main source for this material, gives several examples of the literary exploitation of this theme, and of local panics which resulted from it in the early twentieth century. In 1910, The Canterbury, a London music hall, put on *The White Slaves of London*, while in Italy there was *The White Slave*, a five-act melodrama about a young Italian girl entrapped at Buenos Aires, with a verse prologue written by the son of the poet D'Annunzio. In 1911 there appeared a first film with the title *White Slave*, financed by Danish and Swiss national committees campaigning against the traffic in women. However, the same committees refused to back its sequels *White Slave 2* and *White Slave 3*, which they judged to have been primarily made for commercial reasons, and liable to arouse "vicious instincts."[78]

In the United States it was said that by 1914 there had been over a thousand million pages written about the dangers of the white slave trade. Tracts with such titles as *The Great War on White Slavery, Fighting for the Protection of Our Girls, Truthful and Chaste Account of the Hideous Trade of Buying and Selling Young Girls for Immoral Purposes* were circulating widely, and novels were selling like hotcakes. *The House of Bondage* had reached its fourteenth edition by 1912.[79]

Fear of the white slave trade reached epidemic proportions in England in 1912 and 1913. All sorts of sensational and utterly improbable stories about sudden disappearances, abductions, and attempts to seduce innocent girls and lure them away were circulating orally. "Fake nurses were said to be on the prowl in department stores, a Hampstead hairdresser's daughter was carried off in a motor car, and girls were being chloroformed in the streets."[80] Frederick Bullock, head of the new bureau on white slave trade at Scotland Yard, emphasized at the time that there was no justification or foundation for these expressions of anxiety about dangers to women and girls in the streets of London. Similarly in 1913, "The 5,000 girls of London's telephone exchanges were given official warnings to watch out for drugged chocolates and similar dangers."[81]

An analogous outbreak of panic was noted in the United States from 1912 to 1914, involving young women of every social class—students, shop attendants, telephonists. Their unjustified complaints were reinforced by the sensational treatment they were given in the popular press.

Other panics occurred in the 1920s and 1930s. There was a fresh wave of anxiety in England in 1929:

> It was impossible to stem the tide of reports about pinpricks and numb thighs on provincial transport systems and in cinemas. One widespread tale concerned the hag-like old lady who asked for help crossing the street, and then bagged her prey with the help of a "dope ring," a hollowed-out piece of jewellery fitted with a needle and filled with quick-acting curare poison.[82]

The white slave trade became a familiar topic which permitted the expression of repressed fears, reinforced by the reality of female emancipation. The accounts of attempted abductions were linked to social novelties which were exciting, but also frightening: darkened cinemas, powerful motorcars, mass transport which brought the newly arrived girl into contact with everyone in the city. Widespread anxieties about female emancipation, together with unresolved childhood fears of the threatening father figure, could all be expressed and overcome through stories about the white slave trade, which projected pain and hatred onto the ignoble, bestial figure of the trafficker, and fulfilled the same cathartic function for adults as horror stories do for young children.

Anti-Semitism in its modern secular form was largely fuelled by horror stories about the white slave trade. Newspapers, whether or not they were explicitly anti-Semitic, gave prominence to the Jewish names of traffickers, but did not mention that most of their victims were Jewish too. The existence of numerous Jews who trafficked in women was a genuine social problem which the educated Jewish classes tried to deal with, but the association of Jews with abductions had much deeper roots. Was not the Jew already the scapegoat?

> Indeed white slavery allegations were similar to the other notorious charges in the anti-Semite's arsenal: that Jews were by nature criminal, that they organized widespread conspiracies to corrupt and pollute the Christian world, and they ritually murdered Christian children. . . . The parallels between the blood libel

and white slavery are particularly striking. Each involves violence to a defence-less young person, and the projection of hate onto a symbolic substitute for the evil father. White slavery was the sexualization of the blood libel.[83]

One can see how inevitable is the parallelism between narratives about white slave trafficking and narratives about organ theft. In both cases, popular culture, by means of narratives which are often presented as fictions but nevertheless correspond to beliefs, embodies narratives which are frightening yet "good to tell," as are legends and fables, because they allow one to speak of other truths, more symbolic, which can only be indirectly expressed through a story. In both cases, these narratives are then manipulated by professional propagandists who think they can use their symbolic power to rouse public opinion and attain their objectives, but in both cases the narratives break free from the manipulators, and outlive them.

Why do these narratives persist? To understand this, we must explore their symbolic content more deeply.

LITERARY ELABORATIONS, IRONY AND SYMBOLISM: THE RICH FEED ON THE POOR

The piecemeal sale of the bodies of the poor was already being condemned when it was hair and teeth that were traded. The best known example of this condemnation is of course the description of the downfall of Fantine in *Les Misérables*, which Victor Hugo recounts as a progressive dismemberment. Forced to leave her little girl in the care of the cruel Thénardier couple, who demand more and more money from her, Fantine starts selling her body piece by piece to get the necessary funds.

> Fantine was earning too little. Her debts had increased. The Thénardiers, being badly paid, were constantly writing her letters which made her bitterly unhappy, and were bringing her to ruin. One day they wrote to her that little Cosette was quite naked in this cold weather, that she needed a woollen skirt, and that her mother must at least send ten francs for that. She received the letter, and all day she crumpled it in her hands. That evening, she went to see a barber who lived on the corner of her street, and took out her comb. Her wonderful fair hair hung down to her waist.

"What beautiful hair!" cried the barber.

"How much would you give me?" said she.

"Ten francs."

"Cut it off."

Fantine buys a woollen skirt and sends it to the Thénardiers. Furious, because they want money, not clothes, they give the skirt to one of their own daughters, and shortly afterwards write to say Cosette is suffering from a nervous fever, and they need forty francs to buy medicine. Fantine is in despair. Where can she find the money?

As she was crossing the square, she saw a crowd round an oddly shaped carriage, on which a man dressed all in red was standing and orating. It was a fairground dentist. Fantine joined the group, and began laughing with the rest at this harangue, which was a mixture of slang for the plebs and learned jargon for respectable folk. The tooth-drawer noticed the pretty girl laughing, and suddenly called out, "You've got pretty teeth, you, the girl laughing down there! If you'll sell me your two incisors, I'll give you a gold napoleon for each of them."

"My incisors—what's that?" asked Fantine.

"Incisors," said the dental professor, "are the two front teeth, the top ones."

"Oh, how horrible!" exclaimed Fantine.

"Think it over, my beauty. Two napoleons can come in useful. If you feel like it, come to the inn called the Silver Crow's Nest, you'll find me there."

So Fantine lets her teeth be pulled out, and sinks into despairing apathy. Her poverty increases.

Fantine threw her mirror out of the window. She had lost all shame, and now she lost all pride in her looks. It was the last sign. . . . Her creditors were more pitiless than ever. . . . At about this time, Thénardier wrote to tell her he had certainly been far too kind in letting her have time, and that now he needed a hundred francs at once. "A hundred francs," thought Fantine, "where is there a job that brings in a hundred francs in a day?"—"Oh, come on!" said she, "Let's sell the rest of me."

The wretched woman became a public whore.[84]

Over a hundred years earlier, in 1729, Jonathan Swift wrote his satirical tract *A Modest Proposal for Preventing the Children of Poor People in Ireland from being a Burden to their Parents or the Country, and for Making them Beneficial to the Public*; he suggests that one should sell Irish babies as food for the rich. It would be the most rational solution to put an end to the problems of overpopulation and poverty in that country, says Swift, whose intention is obviously social criticism, even if expressed ironically: "I have been assured by a very knowing American of my acquaintance in London, that a young healthy child well nursed is at a year old a most delicious, nourishing, and wholesome food, whether stewed, roasted, baked, or boiled; and I make no doubt that it will equally serve in a fricassee or ragout."

Jonathan Swift reckoned that his "modest proposal," which would be easy to put into practice, would bring down the price of food, besides having other social and economic advantages. Moreover, the poor would have something to sell: "The mother will have eight shillings net profit, and be fit for work till she produces another child. Those who are more thrifty (as I confess the times require) may flay the carcass; the skin of which artificially dressed will make admirable gloves for ladies, and summer boots for fine gentlemen."[85]

These great literary texts are modern, and secularist. It is poverty itself (and of course the social system that creates it) which they hold responsible for the assaults they describe on the bodies of the poor; they do not turn their indignation against any scapegoats, as is the case when the age-old fable is invoked. Swift by his irony and Victor Hugo by his emotion convey the same point: poverty dictates the dismemberment of the poor. Here we see the birth of a very modern frame of mind, in which the misfortunes of the poor are an emblem of the injustice of society. The dramatic slogans of contemporary propagandists who assert that "the implacable law of the marketplace" finds its supreme expression in the sale of organs relies implicitly on the dramatic force of this symbolism.

THE TRUTH OF THE SYMBOL

I mentioned earlier Richard Drake's analysis of the rumors in Borneo about abductions associated with foundation sacrifices in building projects. His comments when he considers that this rumor/legend does have some truth as a metaphorical expression of the group's relationship with a political power they perceive as aggressive and whose authority they reject can apply very well to the social conditions in numerous poor countries where there has developed the horror legend of the theft of children's organs, the latest avatar of the age-old fable of the slaughter of the innocents. Seen from this point of view, the legendary narratives about the theft of children's organs appear as a corpus of protest narratives from social classes who feel alienated.

> Another similarity between rumor and legend lies in their truth status. Although they may be false literally, they may be true figuratively, especially metaphorically. . . . Rumor and legend provide meaning for unaccustomed or uncategorizable predicaments, implicate them in the relationship of credence to credo. Under conditions of social stress and cultural dissonance, such concrete expressions of conventional wisdom may be employed in the construction of a new interpretation of the socio-cultural context, a reformulation of ideology. . . . Rumors are ideal vehicles for the expression of intense sentiments in circumstances of ideological conflict. Rumor can resolve situational ambiguity temporarily, as ideology does in a more extended manner. . . . Anti-authoritarian rumors are an extremely common form. . . . The kidnapping rumor of Borneo is a story good-to-tell because it expresses intense feelings about tribal-state relations and that it is an aspect of the formulation of a Dayaks anti-state ideology. . . . The rumor motif and its associated elements resonate stereotypes of suspicious outsiders and dreaded state policies. These are elements of a nativistically-flavored self-definition and a shoring-up of cultural identity.[86]

VARYING DEGREES OF ACCEPTANCE OF THE ORGAN THEFT LEGEND

The harsh social conditions in developing countries largely account for their acceptance of narratives which symbolize the extent to which their resources are being pillaged by rich countries. In Latin America, the eye theft stories seem justified both by the attitude of movements protesting against child-trafficking linked to the upsurge in international adoptions and by the poverty afflicting many levels of the population; the stories therefore win a considerable degree of acceptance. Moreover, the level of trust in the authorities is particularly low among the poor on that continent, which helps to explain why denials issued by government figures and the medical elite often have an opposite effect, reinforcing belief in the tales of organ theft.

Among the rich countries, the degree of acceptance varies. In Western Europe it would appear that narratives about organ thefts are taken more seriously than in the United States. I am aware that this statement is far too great a generalization; nevertheless, one can state that the attitude of the press is much more skeptical in the United States. A typical instance of this skeptical attitude is the way the Kidney Heist Story is mentioned in an editorial of an Oregon paper, under the heading "Urban Legends Myth the Truth" (punning on "myth" and "miss"). The main topic of the article is the classic horror story of the Canadian air pilot who unwittingly sucks underwater fishermen into his plane when transporting water from the sea to extinguish large forest fires. The journalist gives other examples of urban legends, including the "Stolen Grandmother" and the Kidney Heist:

> About a year ago, people started ringing me up, saying that a man from Eugene had gone to Las Vegas with friends, had let himself be picked up by a woman in a bar, had gone to her hotel room, and then had woken up three days later, his missing kidney having gone off to the organ transplant black market. But if anybody can show me the victim of this kidney-napping or the underwater fisherman who got burnt, I'll apologize in this paper, and promise never to be skeptical again.[87]

Even so, narratives about stolen kidneys still enjoy a lively circulation among the American public. The folklorists Pat Turner and Jan Brunvand received several indignant phone calls after they were quoted in the media in the course of skeptical discussions of the stories about kidneys stolen at Las Vegas early in 1996. The indignant correspondents promised they would shortly send them accounts whose truth was vouched for by the actual and authentic witnesses who had told them the story—but these authentic witnesses evidently turned out to be FOAFS, and nobody phoned a second time.[88]

The question of the validity of stolen organ stories arises chiefly in connection with narratives of the eye theft type, generally regarded in Europe as solidly based on facts, and not "just stories" like the Kidney Heist type. Western Europe is less isolationist in its outlook than the United States (it is well known that European media give more space to reporting international news, especially from Africa, Latin America, or Asia); it feels strong concern over the widening gulf between rich and poor countries, and it is this concern which explains the difference between the two regions in this matter.

In France, the organ theft legend received a particularly strong response among the elite, the intellectual and moral leaders. This is partly the result of the importance in our country of a whole ethical system based on the ideal of the free gift, which has led people to think, disregarding prudence, that anything freely given is ipso facto perfect. This ethic was upheld by crusades which combined left-wing attitudes, militant secularism, and vilification of private profit. These crusades fought successfully to get the monopoly of blood donations. The contaminated blood scandal showed what calamities could result from this arrogant state of mind, yet it remains strong in many circles, where people seem to have rigidly maintained their convictions even after the disaster.

This ethical system was very influential in organizing noisy and guilt-inducing campaigns in favor of free organ donation, relying on what was being said in the media without really checking up on its accuracy. The campaigners did not make the desirable distinction between true organ donation and donation of mere tissue (bones, skin, valves, blood vessels, and corneas). The former requires the death of someone who has been on a life-support machine, and only concerns a tiny proportion of hospital deaths, five per one thousand, or about two thousand people per year; the latter might concern almost all hospital deaths, say about four hundred thousand per year, or 70 percent of all deaths in France. Consequently, these campaigns proved in the end to generate much anxiety and to be counterproductive.

This gift ethic grew strong because people are hostile on principle to the "wicked" sector of private medicine, which is demonized, and is believed to be motivated exclusively by the wish to make a profit at any price. The arrogant gift ethic considers that the absence of financial transactions means that there is no need for any inquiry into the practices, and that transplants are an activity which can ignore economic constraints. It has been cleverly criticized by Michel Demaison:

> For my part, I would say that the appeal to the principle of free gift, as it is propounded in discussions and practiced in France, is a bit exaggerated. An insistence

so emphatic, so exclusive, and sometimes not without flamboyance, is it not trying to make us forget or forgive other aspects? . . . Everybody knows that such surgery is extremely expensive, and that what is costly for some will necessarily bring money to others, whether the individuals and organizations are in the private or the public sector. So it should be self-evident that the rule forbidding commercialisation ought to be accompanied by an equal insistence on transparency in every aspect of these practices, including the economic ones. . . .

One doesn't give just anything, and not just anyhow. Giving in the right way, as approved by the legal system and the ethics of the courts, does, as I have said, put a bit too much emphasis on what is expected from a free gift, which I would not formulate in terms of all or nothing. In itself, the act of giving something does not forbid the donor to receive some token of gratitude, nor the beneficiary to feel gratitude—quite the contrary. . . .

I would argue that the appeal to the principle of non-commerciality should be harmonised with other criteria and judged according to varying cultural contexts. . . . The absence of money does not guarantee the morality of a practice, any more than its presence destroys it *ipso facto*.[89]

Quite apart from the situation in France, it is noteworthy that in all rich countries some people who are active in humanitarian work believe strongly in the legend of organ theft. These propagandists, who constitute the main routes of transmission for the legend in rich countries, are for the most part speaking in good faith, but their naivete is inextricably entangled with a wish to attract attention (and donations) to their cause. This leads to a real distortion of humanitarian concerns. What these activists say is echoed by the general public, who feel a mixture of guilt and compassion when faced with the sufferings of distant lands.

The general public, traumatized by the unanalyzed images of suffering with which it is battered, is ready to believe literally anything about certain countries, completely demonized in public opinion. And this does not simply affect the general public. I described earlier what extreme difficulty the Colombian authorities had in obtaining a hearing for the results of their inquiry into the Jeison case. And though they were eventually listened to in medical circles, they have had hardly any impact on journalists and the media.

In a very amusing article, a Colombian journalist described the astonishment of Katia Kaupp, a member of the jury of the Albert Londres Prize and a journalist herself, when he told her who was really the Colombian ambassador in Paris:

> From her conversation, one could soon see that the name of Colombia is a magic word which makes every kind of shameful villainy seem possible.
>
> The threats which were supposed to have been made against the journalist Marie-Monique Robin in Paris weighed heavily in the final decision [to award her the prize], and this member of the jury showed great surprise to learn that the Colombian ambassador at the time, Gloria Pachon de Galan,[90] is a journalist and public figure with a very high reputation in Colombia, the widow of a political leader assassinated by the drug-dealing mafia, and a private advisor to Frederico Mayor, Director of UNESCO.
>
> Katia Kaupp questioned me about Pachon de Galan, and opened her eyes wide at each of my replies, since it seems that she and the rest of the jury imagined that the Colombian embassy was in the hands of some kind of Al Capone who had sent hit-men to threaten the vulnerable French journalist.[91]

This is a case of classic prejudice against foreigners, which one may well be surprised to find in intellectual and well-informed circles. But the attitude of many investigative journalists goes further. In 1995 and 1996, two prizes for journalism were awarded, one in France and one in Spain, to a TV program and to a series of articles which loudly proclaimed that systematic theft of organs really occurred.

The program was the French TV documentary *Voleurs d'organes* (*Organ Thieves*), which received the Albert Londres Prize in May 1995. The series of articles, the author of which was the Brazilian journalist Anna Beatrix Magno, had been published in the daily paper *Corriero Braziliense* from July 24 to July 31, 1994. Her main subject was the trade in children leaving Brazil to be adopted abroad, but the articles also claimed that abductions of children for organ theft were common occurrences in Brazil, and cited the most striking cases from the accusatory documentaries (namely Pedro Reggi and Jeison) as if they had never been denied. She received the King of Spain Prize for Latin American Journalism in March 1996.

These two prizes aroused controversy, but were maintained. One can see in these events the symptoms of a controversy in which elite groups are divided on the question of whether systematic organ theft is plausible. While scientific experts and medical professionals remain skeptical, and while some of the accused countries react actively by issuing emotional denials, investigative journalists see themselves as courageous white knights denouncing well-established criminal networks which would supposedly function with the active connivance of the authorities—the very authorities who implicate themselves by their denials. Obviously, the investigative journalists themselves are the first to build up this picture of white knights, but the popular media are impressed by these intrepid characters. Thus, Marie-Monique Robin, the journalist who produced the French TV film, built herself up as a persecuted heroine, victimized both by the demonic Colombians and by the USIA, which was more or less assimilated to the CIA, whose image is obviously even more evil. Examples of this approach were given earlier. Another is an article in a Catholic weekly aimed at an intellectual readership, showing clearly the success of this strategy in the French media, even those of better class:

> During recent months Marie-Monique Robin has been subjected to libellous attacks. She has been the victim of a campaign, notably emanating from Colombia and America, which was dirty, despicable, and going far beyond the limits of ethical debate. That her *sincerity* should be recognised is no more than simple justice.[92]

This white knight role, which constitutes an implicit subtext claiming to justify the sensationalist documentaries which flourish on television, can lead to all kinds of distortions. Recent scandals showed this in the case of some who inspired certain humanitarian movements whose virulent language denounced the misfortunes of children in the Third World (e.g., Marie-Claude Bott in Belgium) or in France (e.g., the organization Enfance et Partage, which ran conspicuous poster campaigns against child abuse); they seem to have spread inaccurate information exaggerating their own role, or again to have proved quite frivolous in using the money they collected. Distortions about these sensitive subjects are also tempting for journalists, fraudsters, and pathological liars. Two other recent scandals involving journalists are significant—one an important affair linked to TV reporting, and the other a tiny one linked to anxiety about children.

The first concerns the independent journalist Michel Born, who frequently supplied sensational but false reports to German TV stations and has recently been condemned to four years in prison for fraud.[93] One of the topics he treated was "Indian child martyrs weaving carpets for a large commercial group in Sweden. . . . These little Indian martyrs were the children of one of the directors of the factory, and acted the part of victims for pay."[94]

The second also concerns an independent journalist, Jan Haerynck, who on September 28, 1996, published in the Dutch daily *De Volkskrant* the moving account of the attempted abduction of a little girl at the beginning of January 1966 at Disneyland near Paris. The victim, Nadja Wepper, was ten years old, and the article contained interviews with her and her parents in the small town of Düren, near Cologne, where they lived. Nadja had got lost while visiting Disneyland. Her family had hunted for her, with the help of the staff. She was found next day in the service lift of the Magic Kingdom Hotel; her long blond hair had been cut and died black, her skin turned black. She remembered having been snatched away when on her way to the toilets, by a man with a moustache and dark complexion. She had not been raped (nor operated on to remove a kidney).

Folklorists are certainly familiar with this story about an abduction that fails, where the victim's hair is dyed, skin darkened, and his/her clothing often changed by attackers whose identity is only vaguely designated (Gypsies are frequently mentioned); it is generally set in some large department store, driving away many of its customers. It has been going around the United States and Europe for more than twenty years.[95] Some time later a Dutch television team rang Disney, and discovered that the Disney spokesman quoted in the article was unknown to the organization. Nor was there any family named Wepper in Düren. Haerynck, who protests his innocence, has been struck off the list of contributors to that paper, which printed a denial of the story on November 23, 1996. It appears that he had previously sent many other doubtful reports to *De Volkskrant*, and earlier to *Het Parool*.[96]

Certainly, one must neither judge a profession from the frauds among its members, nor excuse such actions. But can anyone fail to see that Born and Haerynck are not the only ones guilty? All they did was to supply what the ever-increasing demand for sensationalism demanded, and they were only able to continue because those responsible for buying their reports were lax in their control.

THE UNSPOKEN: RELUCTANCE CONCERNING TRANSPLANTS

The organ theft legend certainly plays some part in the increasing number of people who refuse to allow organs to be removed for transplants. But the legend is not so much a reason as an excuse, for reluctance in the face of such removal has other, more general roots. Although transplants save life, they break deeply sacred taboos, and removing an organ upsets our concepts about life and death, and the link of the personality to the body.

Donald Joralemon, an expert on medical ethics, recently emphasized the persistent cultural reluctance concerning transplants and the rejection of the idea of brain death, and pointed out that belief in the legend of organ thefts should be interpreted above all as a symptom of this reluctance:

> Today, some 26 years later [i.e., after the appearance of the Harvard committee's report on brain death in 1969], there is ample proof that a redefinition of death based on brain activity is still the subject of significant cultural ambivalence. . . . The proliferation of sensational stories of black markets in organs points to cross-cultural suspicions that transplantation may stimulate unacceptable violations of human rights.[97]

In the United States, there is public debate between those who support the free donation of organs (which is the rule in the United States, even though other elements of the human body can be commercially exploited, e.g., in the sale of sperm or the hiring out of wombs), and those who can accept that the law of the marketplace sets a monetary value on organs. However, both parties in this confrontation accept that the body and the personality are two different things and that transplants are justified; the debate centers on how best to extend the application of transplants. Yet, as Joralemon points out, to accept this runs contrary to a universal cultural model which treats the dead man as retaining some part of his personality, and refuses to separate the personality from the body, seeing the latter as an inalienable whole. In conclusion, Joralemon notes that "after all, as is made clear by even a cursory view of the process of rejection, the intuition of bodily integrity has a solid biological foundation."[98]

Anne-Marie Moulin, a philosopher and a writer on the history of science, emphasizes that reluctance about organ donation has an insidious effect, which is the basis for the crisis in transplants. She too sees the fact that some people consider the existence of criminal organ trafficking as quite credible as being a symptom of this disgraceful rejection, which is marked by a strong ambivalence towards the medical profession:

> The almost universal social acceptance of transplants coexists with a furtive avoidance which undermines their foundation, revealing an illogicality at the heart of the system. . . . Doctors have forgotten that there is a popular tradition which associates them with the breaking of taboos, and in which the surgeon, who is part demi-god and part executioner, is close to the figures of the sacrificing priest and the butcher, so ambivalent in many cultures. . . . In the medical profession there is a "knowledge of the right-hand" and "knowledge of the left-hand," just as one speaks of "right-hand" and "left-hand" Tantric teachings, which sets beneficent science in opposition to a magic which should be condemned. The latter implies proximity to an interloping world which reappears with the transplants. One piece of evidence is the way that the fantasy of organ trafficking exploded in the collective imagination, thanks to scandals over waiting lists and cases of corruption, as a result of rumors about organ trafficking and the discovery of an actual market for organs involving several Third World countries.[99]

Anne-Marie Moulin emphasizes that science and technical processes must become rooted again in their cultural environment if we are not to expose ourselves to a breakdown.[100] In conclusion, she urges that more positive steps should be taken in favor of transplants; one should try to make the procedure more official, obtain more active support for it, and have it officially recognized that transplants have a communal dimension, in which exchanges take place between the living and the dead.

These exchanges form the subject of a synthesyzing study by the paleontologist Jean-Pierre Mohen, who stresses the deep unity of the funeral rituals which have characterized the human species ever since the Paleolithic period. Funeral rituals, a favorite area for symbolic thought, restore order after the disruption of death by allowing the life of the spirit to be given back to the ancestors, so that it can return to earth with new births. The existence of human groups is legitimized by a dialogue with the dead, who have become ancestors. Mohen deplores the reluctance of scientific thought to take account of this heritage of symbolic thought, and wishes the two ways of thinking could draw closer together:

> The stake would be that scientific thought would reintegrate two dimensions which have been abandoned, despite their importance: the social dimension and the spiritual dimension. . . . Philosophers have rejected all metaphysical and ontological ways of thought, assimilating them to religious thought, and adopting a general agnosticism, although a spiritual approach is required in every domain of social or moral life. In the same way, the social dimension is treated in its sociological, ethnological, or economic aspects, but without the breadth it had in ancient societies. What is most lacking in scientific thought is to renew a real worldwide dialogue between the living and their ancestors . . . in order to establish an active dialectic which will transform the negativity of death into a contradicting yet progressive power.[101]

The organ theft legend incarnates in personalized forms a classic rumor, involving denunciation of crimes, revelation of frightful secrets, the unmasking of evils and conspiracies. One should note that it contains a strong element of protest and an antiauthoritarian attitude. Nevertheless, its meaning can vary, as it does among the elites of our own countries, for whom the organ theft legend has come to symbolize rejection of modernity, and to express an expectation of catastrophe which has greatly increased recently.

The organ theft legend contradicts the positive aspects of medical treatment by its expectation of the worst and its detailing of what horrors might possibly arise as a consequence of that progress. It carries a warning message, calling for vigilance.

The legend reveals changes in people's attitudes towards medical developments, which now create anxieties after having at first aroused enthusiasm. It is also a reaction to the vague but increasing feeling that one has lost control over one's own life, in view of the astonishing increase in the number of transplants.

Paradoxically, one can see this negative message as having social value by acting as a warning to make the authorities aware that their actions have other dimensions beyond the benefits they bring. For instance, the legend poses a problem of social justice: how should one share out that rare and valuable commodity, the transplant organs?

The legend challenges scientists and doctors, forcing them to justify themselves, to stop expecting automatic approval, to face up to different forms of logic and different points of view which lead people to refuse to let their organs be taken.

CONCLUSION

Let us briefly contrast two propositions which are reasonable, and one belief. It is reasonable to say (a) that children in the Third World are victims of all kinds of exploitation, and it is right to take action to limit this; (b) that, thanks to medical progress, many parts of the human body can be used for diagnosis or treatment, and that this might lead to the development of new uses which might be abuses. The belief is that Third World children are regularly abducted and massacred for secret organ transplants by a powerful mafia including numerous criminal surgeons. The two reasonable propositions do make vigilance legitimate, but do not in any way justify accepting the belief, i.e., the organ theft legends.

Legends are worth analysis, for their organizing role in the social field is by no means negligible, as the medieval historian Alain Boureau has stressed. He devoted two books to the study of legend cycles,[1] one on Pope Joan and one on what is variously called *droit de cuissage, droit de seigneur*, or *jus primae noctis*—the supposed legal right of a feudal lord to take the daughter of any of his vassals into his bed on the first night after her wedding, before her husband can enjoy her. This is how he concludes his study of the latter:

> A historian cannot limit himself to establishing whether the institution was or was not a real one (*droit de cuissage* never did exist). Legends concerning the institution constitute historical items in their own right, for they give rise to discourses and practices, they contribute to weaving the social and political network by inspiring or justifying strife or allegiances, by polarising the field of memory. It is this organizing role of "beliefs" (in the wide sense) which I wanted to demonstrate in my book on Pope Joan; in that case, as in the present one, the point is to account for the historical functions enabling legends to survive in an active form beyond the moment when they took shape, beyond the historical event of their

creation. . . . It is appropriate to bear in mind the pressing necessity to privilege the interaction between social history and the history of discourses. The worlds of belief impinge perpetually on the worlds of event and practice.[2]

Alain Boureau also stresses how permanent are the themes of an attack on the bodies of the innocents, either as rape or as a massacre perpetrated by those in power:

The fear, or the threat, of sexual abuse by a dominant party is a constant factor, both real and symbolic at once, in all cultures. After all, social tyranny can only be exercised over one's person or one's goods. In the category of attacks against the person, all the possibilities, which are limited in number, have been exhausted: Imprisonment, mutilation, beating up, assassination, the abduction or rape of one's wife, infanticide. The repetition of the theme of the slaughter of innocents perpetrated so that a tyrant may survive, from Herod to Ceaucescu by way of Louis XV, is a sign of this universality.[3]

Like everything bought and sold on the black market, rumor supplies a need on the black market of information: "The need is for an interpretation which will suddenly and magically link scattered hopes and fears, nostalgias and hatreds, into a unique pattern that makes sense."[4]

Let us now briefly recall the symbolic significances expressed in the scenarios of the organ theft legends, satisfying our need for global interpretations.

(1) The organ theft legends articulate anxieties felt in our societies in connection with modern medicine, which transgresses boundaries which had seemed immutable, and transforms our traditional conceptions about life and personality. These anxieties cannot be directly expressed in our societies, where science is officially considered to be a force for good.

(2) The organ theft legends reactivate folk memories of the fable of the massacre of the innocents, appealing to our symbolic mode of thought which functions at the emotional and symbolic levels.

(3) Certain social situations which really are dysfunctional, such as the increasing hardships of the poor in Latin America, have rendered plausible the exaggerated and more terrible version of the misfortunes of the poor which is expressed in the organ theft legends. Here we see again the mechanism whereby horror legends are created.

CONCLUSION

More "true" than truth itself, horror legends, which are elaborate fictions collectively maintained, permit us to express our reactions and emotions when faced with social problems. Complementing analytical thought, this mode of grasping a situation by the roundabout way of fiction brings the emotions into play—hence its persistence. However, horror legends bring with them many negative features: the demonizing of the Other, the reduction of complex situations to caricatures, etc.

In the contemporary world, propagandists do use them to mobilize support for their causes, but it is above all the media industry which exploits them, being conscious of the spontaneous interest horror legends arouse in the public; unlike the propagandists, they do not exploit them for specific purposes, but just to boost sales. When I speak of the "media industry," I am referring to that section of the world of the press (both written and in television) for whom what counts above all else is popular favor, and for whom therefore it is always more important to entertain than to inform—since accurate information always involves some dry and difficult passages, if one is to set news items in context and explain them, and not just pass them on by giving them a sensationalist twist.

And that is how the horror legends of organ thefts were created, and are still maintained, by three forces: by the collective creative power of the public, who listen to it, enrich it, and pass it on for its value as a symbol; by the exploitation of propagandists conscious of its value in mobilizing support for their own objectives; and by the exploitation of the media industry, conscious above all of its capacity for boosting sales.

ORGAN THEFT NARRATIVES
IN THE EARLY 2000s

While organ theft narratives still circulate, they are no longer the object of serious public debate. The idea that they might describe actual crimes seems totally discredited among political authorities and within the medical world. But the hypothesis that a mafia kidnaps and kills people to harvest their organs is still considered plausible by many of the lay public, even in First World countries.[1]

When discussion of the possibility of organ thefts reaches the media, it is as a hypothesis put forward by authorities on the occasion of a puzzling and violent event or series of events (such as the Guatemala 2000 lynching and the murders of Ciudad Juárez).

At the academic level, there is also a debate on the links between organ trafficking—the importance of which is growing—and organ theft narratives.

Finally, it is to be noted that the production of popular fictions staging organ thefts continues on a great scale, mainly as examples of elite plotting against the common good.

GUATEMALA 2000 LYNCHING

In the Central American countries where the baby parts stories originated, there is evidence that fears about child kidnapping are still vivid. There is probably good reason for this, as kidnapping (of adults and children) is not rare in these countries. Lynchings of suspected child kidnappers occur in Mexico or Guatemala; however, they are underreported when the victims are nationals.[2] A case in Guatemala that involved a foreign victim generated several press articles:[3] on April 30, 2000, a Japanese tourist visiting the colorful

Saturday market in the Mayan town of Todos Santos Cuchuman, in northern Guatemala, was killed when the tourists' bus was attacked by a mob branding the group as thieves of children. In this case, the organ theft motive was only briefly mentioned:

> A rumour that kidnappers were stealing children to use their hearts in satanic rituals was given prominence as an explanation by the town's mayor. [Mayor] Mendoza said many neighbours were feeling "nervous" that day after a local radio reported that a satanic cult had rented the town's municipal gymnasium over the weekend to carry out their bloody rites. "This is an illiterate community and people believe in rumours. Many schools remained closed for days and women stopped venturing out of their homes."[4]

This rumor-panic may reflect the influence of American fundamentalists, often themselves fearful of satanists, who have made numerous converts amongst Indian communities in Guatemala.[5] This panic was not that different in substance from the episodes described in American communities (Victor 1989, 1991); however, no lynchings were recorded in the American rumor-panics. This lynching needs to be placed in the general violent context of Guatemala, where "mob justice is frequent in outlying Guatemalan towns: last year there were 71 lynchings by vigilantes."[6]

MURDERS OF CIUDAD JUÁREZ

Since 1993, the murder rate in the border town of Ciudad Juárez (Mexico), close to El Paso (Texas), has grown considerably.

> One analysis based on death certificates and other data concluded that 249 men were killed between 1990–1993, while 942 men were killed between 1994–1997. 20 women were killed between 1990 and 1993, and 143 women were killed between 1994–1997.
>
> The *2002 annual report of the Inter-American Commission on Human Rights* asserts "1993 marked the first year of a notable increase in the killing of women in Ciudad Juárez. . . . While 37 women had been killed between 1985 and 1992, approximately 269 were killed between 1993 and 2001."[7]

Attention has been focused on the murders of women, of which two-thirds were attributed by observers to domestic violence but one-third to unknown murderers, the women having been "found in the desert after being murdered and raped by shadowy unknowns." Political activists and NGOs lumped all the murders of women together and denounced the authorities' indifference to them. These murders became an important part of Amnesty International's 2003 report.[8]

When the authorities began to consider that these murders had to be solved, they relayed in their declarations the rumors that had been circulating for years, as remarks journalist Debbie Nathan: "For years now, Juárez has been convulsed in speculation about whether these 80-some desert deaths are due to a serial killer, several serial killers, the police, bus drivers, satanists, pornography makers, body organ traffickers, and the list goes on, ever darker and weirder." However, these speculations are far from being proven. Discussing an emotional documentary presented in New York by political activist Lourdes Portillo, Nathan expressed her skepticism towards the film author's assertions:

> A "web" of murderers, she [Lourdes Portillo] said, are capturing and killing girls in order to make highly profitable "snuff films." As far as law enforcement authorities internationally, including the FBI, are aware, no films have ever been made in which people are killed that films of their murders can be distributed or sold. Stories claiming they exist pack a punch, but operate on the level of urban myth. Neither is anyone known to ever have been kidnapped or slaughtered by body organ traffickers, though this, too, is a common explanation in Juarez for the murders.[9]

We can see here operating the very same mechanisms that have sustained in the early 1990s the legend of organ theft. Today the Juarez murders are not solved, but the accusations of snuff films and organ trafficking accompanying them are passé, stale; they did not "catch," did not raise political emotion.

ORGAN TRADE AND ORGAN THEFT

Since the early 1990s organ trade has grown considerably, "to several thousand of transplants each year" and its "routes crisscross the world." It centers on the sale of kidneys. Medical ethicists insist that it "exploits poor and vulnerable people."[10] David Rothman, who created an international task force entitled Bellagio Task Force on Securing Bodily Integrity for the Socially Disadvantaged in Transplant Surgery, deplores the weak enforcement of the rules condemning commerce in organs by medical transplant societies and the World Medical Association.

Already in 1998, Rothman mentioned—and firmly dismissed—organ theft tales:

> The international trade in organs has convinced many of the poor, particularly in South America, that they or their children are at risk of being mutilated and murdered. . . .
>
> Medical realities make such kidnapping and murder highly unlikely. . . . However rapacious health care workers may seem, highly trained and medically sophisticated teams of surgeons, operating nurses, anesthesiologists, technicians and blood transfusers are not likely to conspire to murder for organs or accept them off the street. Had they done so, at least one incident would have come to light during the past fifteen years.[11]

His arguments are convincing. To infer the existence of organ theft from the existence of organ trade is a misdirected approach.

Anthropologist Nancy Scheper-Hughes,[12] associated with David Rothman and founder of Organ Watch, rejects the legitimacy of the folklorists' approach towards organ theft narratives. Ignoring the nefarious aspects of the organ trade, folklorists are dismissive of the creators of the tales they study. They do not understand their symbolic value and consider themselves as superior to the poor who create and circulate the legends of organ thefts.

This irritation towards folklorists seems linked to the trivializing approach to urban legends held by counterpropagandists such as Todd Leventhal, who compares "baby parts stories" to "exploding pets in oven" lore. But folklore scholars do not identify with counterpropagandists and reject that trivializing approach. This essay, in parallel with Scheper-Hughes's analyses, has endeavored to show that the horror legends of organ theft are metaphorically true and are serious and significant.

Organ theft narratives are not limited to countries experiencing abuses and poverty. The First World variants, strongly linked to the evil science and evil doctor themes developed in popular culture through the genre of the medical thriller, present stories of abuses against the privileged perpetrated by the feared poor—and a motley bunch of villains in which crooked elites play a prominent role.[13]

Like the snuff films accusations, organ theft narratives are strongly represented in popular fiction through medical thrillers, which focus on the evil medical establishment, and political thrillers, which focus on the victims and whose authors often present themselves as social commentators. Through this new medium, they express medical and social critique.[14]

They comment on, first, our malaise regarding transplants that redraw the boundaries between life and death, self and other; second, our unease concerning the new powers granted to the medical establishment by the developments of modern medicine; and, third, our consciousness of the deep inequalities separating First World and Third World, especially in access to medical care.

APPENDIX

DESCRIPTION OF THE ACCUSATORY DOCUMENTARIES

(1) *The Body Parts Business*, by Bruce Harris (author and commentator) and Judy Jackson (producer). Alma, CBS, and NFB in Canada; BBC in Great Britain. Shown by the BBC in October 1993 as part of the *Everyman* series, and on cable in the United States in December 1994. No doubt also in Canada. Sixty minutes.

It opens with some general shots of street children against an unfocussed grey background, with the commentary: "For them, growing up is a struggle to survive hunger and poverty. Now a new and more terrifying danger threatens them," and the title of the program appears. We see Bruce Harris (tall, bald, fairly young, with a moustache) who will take on the role of investigator throughout the film. He is introduced as belonging to Covenant House, an American Catholic child-care organization. He had written and directed another film shown on *Everyman* two years earlier (1991), which had had a great impact, called *They Shoot Children, Don't They?*, about the murder of street children in Guatemala.

We are in Guatemala, and BH has gathered a small group of children around the grave of Joel (1976–1993). As a result of sniffing glue to forget his hardships, Joel had lost the use of his kidneys, and BH had tried in vain to obtain one for a transplant for him. In the course of his fruitless search, he had come across horrible stories about an illegal trade in children's organs—hence this film, which seeks to know whether it is or is not true. Shots of street children appear, with the commentary: "One fact to start from is that street children often disappear without trace in Central America." Then BH says, in close-up, "It's easy to win the trust of street children" (a montage of city scenes). "According to the papers, baby trafficking is part of an expanding business. A child for international adoption is worth twenty thousand dollars. There was an investigation in Guatemala in 1986, but the investigator was assassinated in a bus on his way home from work. It was Elena Ponse who launched that investigation, but she resigned after the murder." BH then interviews EP, who says she resigned because she was afraid of being killed.

We pass on to Honduras, where BH is also working, and where false documents are on sale in the main square of Tegucigalpa; we see BH ask the price of a birth certificate to get a child out of the country under a new identity. He is told he can have one in two hours, for ten dollars (!). Sending children for adoption abroad had been forbidden in 1992 because of corruption at high levels, but since that date eight hundred children had disappeared without trace at Tegucigalpa. "Some reports indicate a more sinister hypothesis: that these children were used for their organs."

The camera then shows a woman and two children climbing a hill, and the commentary says: "Eight-year-old Charlie Alvardo is lucky to be alive. He was kidnapped last April. His abductors carried revolvers; they put a cloth over his mouth to put him to sleep, and carried him off in a pickup. Five days later he threw himself out of the pickup and escaped. His abductors were talking about selling children and organs." Close-up of Charlie, seated and wearing a rather smart shirt. Charlie says, "They took me to the town center, where they met a woman. She had some money, but the man said it wasn't enough, and they were going to kill me. They were going to go to Cholotecas [?] to sell organs, and they were going to sell me, either me or a little girl of five." BH: "Are you frightened?" Charlie's mother: "Yes, very frightened, because I think they could try to take my child again and kill him. This is organized by the mafia, and many children disappear."

The camera shows a marketplace, then a small group of children crossing some waste ground, then tracks into the small courtyard of a stone house. Commentary: "One woman, Tonia X [surname inaudible], decided to give up her children for adoption, thinking she was too poor to raise them. They were kept, along with other children, in various houses where they were beaten and ill-treated. She got them back with the help of the police and brought them home, after they had sent her alarming messages about what they'd heard was going to happen to them." A little girl of about ten, sitting in the courtyard, says, "My neighbor told me, 'My poor thing, they're going to send you abroad to put you in a brothel, and your brother will be opened up and his organs will be used for transplants for rich children.'" The brother is beside her as she speaks, watching.

BH then interviews Rafael Callejas, president of Honduras, who, a voice-over declares, has appointed a commission of inquiry into the problem. BH: "What is the truth about these allegations of organ theft?" Callejas: "The commission we appointed has already shown that this is medically impossible in Honduras. We don't have the technology, or the hospitals." The denial is quite explicit, and BH seems satisfied. The commentary resumes: "However, one policeman, Gustavo Dominguez, has a different story." A man with a moustache, shown in a head-and-shoulders shot, says, "A doctor in Puerto Cortez has admitted removing children's organs, because it weighed on his conscience. But he spoke to the press, not to the police, and he has had to flee the country because of the threats of the drug-dealing mafia against children." There follows a sweeping conspiracy theory: "There's a lot of money in it. Very important people. Everything is hushed up. They can call a halt to investigations anywhere in the world." (This Gustavo Dominguez is the source cited on April 23, 1993, by Rosario Godoy, a Honduran member of Congress, whom Leventhal states to be untrustworthy and suspended for corruption in 1993.) BH is seen sitting alone, thinking and writing, in a park: "Who should one believe, with such completely contradictory stories?" What he does know is that there is a worldwide shortage of organs, since transplants are becoming more common. "Let us pass to the world of legitimate transplant surgery."

The scene changes to Holland and to Eurotransplant, stated to be a non-profit-making organization. There, Dr. Cohen says there is a decrease in the number of organs donated freely, and an increase in commercial transactions, which have an unsavory reputation. One can foresee that some will try to make profits from this shortage: "It's a simple economic law that if demand is too high and supply is low, somebody will try to make a profit from it." Technical shots of organs being transported, with the commentary: "It was hoped that organs would be available free, but a trade is developing. Events occurring in Argentina show that those organizing this trade have no respect for human life."

Twenty-five minutes. The scene shifts to Argentina, with the commentary: "In the time of the dirty war and the dictatorship, tens of thousands of people disappeared. Even though democracy has returned, I'm told the disappearances continue." The Montes de Oca case follows. Marcelo Ortiz, who was said to have run away from the hospital/asylum in 1990, could not walk. His grandmother shows the letter from the hospital. She learnt from the papers that his body had been found (horrible close-up of his mutilated head). There are statements from Horacio Esber (Secretary General of the Department of Health, in charge of the inquiry into Montes de Oca) about a trade in corneas removed from dead patients whose families lived far off and distressing shots of Montes de Oca, "a dumping ground for handicapped children rejected by their families." Then: "An investigation in January 1992 into the embezzlement of funds discovered something far worse: a network of trafficking in babies, blood, corneas. Many deaths and disappearances: 20 percent per year of the 1,200 patients (i.e., 240 per year). Discrepancies between the death certificates and the patients' case notes as to causes of death [BH is seen leafing through documents]. Those who disappeared later found dead nearby, in the marshes or the drains, as happened with Marcelo Ortiz, hence the mutilated head. It is hard to get the patients to talk: 'They died because of the pills, the poison, the injections, the sheets.' 'The sheets?' 'Yes, children were punished.'" Sanchez died in prison, taking his secrets with him. Judge Heredia considered it true that Sanchez would remove corneas, with the help of the male nurse Zavarttini. BH reads out the latter's witness statement: "The extractions were skillfully done, with a little spoon. They never spoiled a cornea." BH continues: "Judge Heredia told me he thought the eyes of some patients were removed while they were still alive. At least one patient survived this atrocity." We then see Pedro Reggi, "recovered by his brothers after his corneas had been torn out. He was barely sixteen at the time." Who had operated on him? "Dr. Fulco." The camera turns to Dr. Fulco, who denies the story with a big grin, saying, "But I wasn't here six or seven years ago." We return to Horacio Esber, who declares, "There are groups of unscrupulous people among transplant surgeons. These people are dangerous."

Now we come to the Córdoba affair, which concerned complaints made by relatives of sick people who died in the emergency hospital. BH says there were 160 complaints, of which 60 were legally upheld. There follows an emotional presentation of cases involving children. The parents are poor, but by no means from shantytowns. One set of parents found that the corpse of their little girl had been emptied of its organs; they had asked for an autopsy, she having died in hospital of appendicitis, aged thirteen, in 1991. A mother declared that her nine-year-old son had been "unplugged" while still alive (he breathed for three days without a respirator), because she had refused permission for his organs to be taken out, yet they were taken all the same. The doctor on the case, Dr. Lacombe, asserts that the child was brain-dead. A woman technician asserts that the machines recording EEG are fixed so as to produce a flatline. Judge Rueda says he investigated more than twenty-two doctors, and discovered serious irregularities in the methods of establishing brain death. BH leafs through dossiers. However, it is now said that only three cases will be taken to court, only one EEG having been taken instead of two, and on only two points instead of eight. Dr. Lacombe, who had been charged but left at liberty and still practising his profession, used his connections to prevent the judges from finding out how the organs he had removed were distributed in Argentina; many were sent to the lucrative sector of private medicine.

Forty-five minutes. Moscow. Very impressive images of emergency services, and a morgue. Joint ventures of export of tissues and organs, long lists of declarations. One man declares he narrowly escaped kidnapping. However, all this trafficking seems to depend on making use of accidental deaths and of people who go into coma while in the emergency services. None of the organs are for the Russians themselves; all are exported. Dr. Shumakov is still exporting tissues and organs, even though he no longer has a contract with Eurotransplant, the latter having repudiated it in 1991 when it received proof of his commercial activities (confirmed on screen by Dr. Cohen); he has permission from the Russian customs officials, who consider the Eurotransplant contract still valid.

Fifty-two minutes. Latin America. Children and ragpickers on a huge garbage tip. Final statement: "Having set out to discover whether there really was a trade in bodies and organs, I found a great deal of disturbing information. Everybody involved in international organizations should control this trade before it is too late, and rouse international indignation. One can't set a price on human life—it's as simple as that." A final written panel reminds viewers that in Great Britain organ donor cards are attached to driving licences. Research is credited to Maria Laura Avignolo and Alexander Vlasov. Thanks are expressed to David Halwoeth, Michaela Ravana, Heather Mansfield, and Richard Robinson.

(2) Marie-Monique Robin and Jihan El Tahri, author and producer MMR, research JET. *Voleurs d'organes* (*Organ Thieves*). France: CAPA Agency,

September 1993. Sixty minutes (forty minutes for *Voleurs d'yeux*). Broadcast on Planète (cable) in September 1993, then in a shortened version (omitting Mexico) on M6 in January 1995. Deals with Argentina, Mexico, Colombia.

Argentina. A lawsuit is being heard in a court at Lima (one hundred kilometers from Buenos Aires). "It's the first such case in the world. According to the Minister for Justice, they [i.e., patients at Montes de Oca] were made to disappear so that their corneas could be stolen." Pedro Reggi is seen, swaying backwards and forwards, in a miserable hovel. He is twenty-six, was confined in a hospital for five years, lost his sight at the end of a year. He answers questions, mentioning the name of Dr. Sculco. His mother's legal complaint lapsed when she died. Views of Montes de Oca, "the only public psychiatric hospital in Argentina." The patients are cunningly questioned: "Used they to kill people?" "Yes, yes." "How?" "I don't know. They would take the bodies to the morgue." Next, a close-up of Judge Heredia: "He is fighting alone against them all, at the risk of his life." Some views of the cemetery, numerous anonymous graves; excavations have shown that some of those buried there died by bullet wounds. The judge is convinced that patients were being killed. The Marcelo Ortiz affair, brief but frightening shot of his head (mouth and chin split open, eye sockets empty). The family weeping. An elder brother, the mother and the grandmother, rereading the telegram sent from the hospital on October 27, 1990, to say he had run away—but he was unable to walk. He had been damaged by meningitis when six months old, was confined to the hospital at six years old, disappeared at sixteen.

The film returns now to Pedro Reggi. We see a paper signed by Dr. Sculco requesting that he be operated on at the Lagleize Hospital for double cataract in 1985. We go to Lagleize to look for Pedro's dossier, and to ask some general questions from the director, who had been there since 1985. She shows dossiers which speak of removal of corneas from four to six dead bodies every week, so about two hundred fifty per year. Where is the dossier of Pedro Reggi? With the judge, says the director. But the judge says it has disappeared. Next, some interviews with the team currently running Montes de Oca. The director, filmed without his knowledge, uses the term "mafia" in speaking of his predecessors. The commentary states that "an implacable law of silence reigns at the asylum." Zavarttini, the male nurse who had given the statement about corpses having their corneas taken out "with a little spoon," now refuses to see them. Enrique Sdrech, a journalist on *Clarin* and author of a book on Montes de Oca, had a bomb go off near his home as he was leaving the house in September 1992. He is interviewed in his office, in a modern setting, with computers. Marie-Monique Robin asks, "Who was pulling the strings of this trafficking, the doctors? The politicians?" "No, all sorts of circles were implicated. Doctors, surgeons, sellers, buyers, politicians, bureaucrats. There are lots of pressures. Argentina, like all poor countries, has re-created itself as a supplier for rich countries. Recently, people were talking of a 'red mafia' which extracted blood. In a world which is looking for organs, which needs organs, the poor are ready-made victims."

Mexico. A view of the wall separating Tijuana from the paradise of San Diego. Notice boards of clinics, with the commentary stressing their renal specializations, nephrology, urology. One of the investigators gives a false medical case history over the telephone, explaining that her brother urgently needs a kidney transplant. Both investigators are then given an appointment with Dr. Ramirez, who says he is qualified, and can find a kidney within a few days. All the other surgeons practicing at Tijuana also carry out illegal transplants. But in Mexico City, at the National Transplant Headquarters of the Ministry of Health, a smartly dressed administrative doctor explains that there are no qualified establishments in Tijuana, and goes on to say, rather irritably, that there have been numerous denials supported by irreproachable persons such as the president of the Supreme Court, but they are not believed. His statements are cut short.

Still in Mexico City, there follows an interview with the mother of a little girl who was kidnapped in 1990 when she was seven; she tells the story with emotion and tears. She has set up a Fundacion de niños robados (Foundation for the Robbed Children), but says the authorities refuse to help her. We see rapid glimpses of a small gathering of parents and of a tiny demonstration in the Zocalo, the main square of Mexico City. This is followed by an interview with Hector Ramirez Cuellar, who had made a report on the kidnappings to Parliament. (Does this mean the national Parliament, or a regional one? No precise details are given, nor is the date of the report.) He tells us a fine kidney theft story: a child abducted in the middle of the town, found again two months later, with a scar, lacking one kidney, and with two thousand dollars in his pocket; the mother had not laid a complaint because she did not have enough money, and anyway they had had some payment. Cuellar then put the investigators in touch with a police officer. The latter, speaking anonymously and in shadow, says that when he and his American colleagues patrol the frontier they often find unidentified bodies bearing suspicious-looking scars which make him think of operations, "but the Americans deny that such things are possible."

Returning to Tijuana, there follows a hostile, caricatured interview with the American consul, who claims that the story was created by the KGB and that no evidence has ever been found to support it. Commentary: "Yes, the US Information Agency of the president of the United States is still accusing the KGB, two years after the Soviet Union has ceased to exist." We are briefly shown the 1988 pamphlet *Soviet Active Measures in the Era of Glasnost*, signed by Charles Wick, and the building where the USIA is housed. Then we pass to Janice Raymond, a professor at Georgetown, introduced as "the author of a recent book on human trafficking, one chapter of which is devoted to the traffic in organs." There are twenty thousand people waiting for a transplant, according to the United Network for Organ Sharing, which, she says, records four thousand transplants a year, "but everybody knows there are more than that." This forces people to turn to private clinics, which rely on "other sources of organs."

Colombia. A travelling shot over Bogotá, world capital for ophthalmology, thanks to the Barraquer Clinic, a powerful institution which refuses to give any interviews, "to protect the secrets of the dynasty." A false medical dossier is used to obtain an interview with a surgeon who says, in order to explain how it is that he can promise a cornea transplant so quickly, that "in Colombia there are fewer legal problems." Barranquilla. "The victims are ragpickers, the poorest of the poor." The garbage tip; Oscar, who escaped and is now living in a military base for protection (he has grown much thinner since the picture in *Der Spiegel* in 1992). His narrative; the eleven bodies in the morgue of the faculty. Interview with Vincente, the other man who escaped; "they had already injected him with formol." With his family around him, he comments upon the article telling of his discovery in the morgue. Then we return to Oscar, whose family lives in fear after receiving threats. An interview with the judge at the preliminary hearing, who says he regrets the fact (indignantly announced in the commentary) that organ trafficking will not be an issue in the forthcoming trial: "It is not a crime, I am sorry to say." An interview with Vincente's lawyer: "Who will get us to believe that this whole organization has been set up simply to provide for the needs of students? It makes no sense."

He holds forth eloquently on the way those responsible for organ trafficking are immune to punishment: "Those really responsible are not in court. The authorities do not have the will to bring the matter to light." A cunning question: "The judge said the trafficking has not been proved. What is your opinion?" (We did not hear him say this.) We return to Bogotá, where a doctor representing a human rights organization discusses the matter in the light of the contrast between poor regions of the south and rich regions of the north. Children talk about red vans which drive around and carry children away. Their mothers forbid them to go out. Returning to the false medical dossier, together with shots of the wretchedly poor clinics of the south, while the pseudo patient waiting for a corneal graft insists by telephone that her operation absolutely must take place in the north. Dr. Jimenez, unaware that he is being filmed, gives the pseudo patient who phoned him an appointment, promising her that he can find her a cornea "within a fortnight." We then visit the Bogotá Institute for Blind Children, affiliated with the Barraquer Foundation, where 150 blind children receive some education. The children talk to the investigators about Jenson, who shows them his empty eye sockets (in close-up), and says, "*Los medicos son muy malos*" ("The doctors are very wicked"). But the staff, noticing that the investigators are interested in Jenson, refuse to show them the dossier on him, and show them the door. Then a Colombian doctor, recorded as a voice-off, talks of corneas being exported from Colombia and mentions a colleague in Paris whose name is scrambled. The scene shifts rapidly to Paris (general view of the Champs Elysées), where the Parisian ophthalmologist is interviewed, with his face blurred. He says that many horrible things happen in Colombia, and people are killed there for their eyes. He would be able to do the operation, but only in Israel. We return to the Jenson case, since the investigators have now traced his mother, who talks with them in a taxi. Her story is a disturbing one. She had taken her child to hospital suffering from digestive troubles and diarrhea; when she returned, he was almost dying; she took him to a different hospital, where she was told his eyes had been torn out. The case notes had been burnt by the doctor. She did not lodge a complaint because they did not have enough money. The final image is of Jenson playing his flute.

The final credits list Jihan el Tahri as coordinator, Maria Laura Avignolo, Lucy Hood, Anne-Marie Mercier, Hector Torres. Acknowledgments to the Association of Christians Against Torture, the Inter-Movement Committee for Evacuees (CIMADE), the International Association of Democratic Lawyers (IADL), and Victor Clark Alfaro.

(3) *Organrauber: Menschen als Ersatzteillanger* (*Organ Thieves: Human Beings Used as Spare Parts*), by Jurgen Roth (producer) and Martina Fuhr (script). Germany, ZDF TV, 1992, ninety minutes. It was broadcast in Germany and France on January 20, 1994, on the channel Arte, as part of an evening on the theme of organ transplants. This included several German documentaries on transplants and those who had received them, extracts from the fictional film *Fleisch* (1979) about evil organ robbers, and *Britannia Hospital.*

The opening shows the huge garbage tip at Barranquilla (Colombia), accompanied by a dramatic commentary:

> The district of Punte de la Maria is the final refuge for these pariahs, these people who live on refuse. It's only when they are dead and cut to pieces that such people appear to have any value. That's what the organ thieves seem to have thought when they murdered several dozens of them and sold their corpses to the medical faculty at Barranquilla. Bodies were found in the streets and sewers. Nobody tried to find out who had killed them. The important thing was to have enough corpses for the anatomy courses. But early this year, the university began to run short of corpses. A solution had to be found. What has been happening in this university goes against all moral standards. More than forty human beings have been killed there, to get the material needed for anatomy courses. The trade in corpses brings in more than fifteen hundred francs per body to the organ thieves.

The documentary then shows records of the sales. Santander Torres, the new director of the private medical university at Barranquilla, estimates that forty people were killed, and says there have been fifteen arrests. In the ensuing discussion, the terms "organs" and "corpses" are used interchangeably. Showing homeless people in Bogotá, the commentary says: "For these people who live in the streets, the night is far more dangerous than the day. In the dark, the organ thieves can act in still greater safety. By taking part in organ trafficking, these criminals reach the ultimate in horror: they murder human beings, empty out their bodies, and sell the organs separately."

Then at Bogotá, Procurator General Gustavo de Greit says, "Are there organ thieves? It's possible, but unlikely." He is followed by a doctor from the eye bank, which is shown as useless. Then Diego Perez, a representative of a Colombian human rights organization supported by Danielle Mitterrand, chiefly discusses the murder of street children. We visit the morgue at Bogotá, where there are twenty autopsies every day, and where there were five thousand murders in the city in 1991 (whereas in 1977 Jacques Meunier had estimated only five hundred). We are told how in 1989 Edgar Arturo Velasquez, aged sixteen, was killed by persons unknown, by two bullets; his body was given back to his widow, without its eyes. She replies, "Yes," when asked whether she thinks he was killed for his organs, but does not sound very convinced.

There follows a German case rather like that at Amiens. The hospital at Winterberg in Saarbrücken did not ask permission from the family before taking the eyes of a young man who died in 1991. The woman director of the hospital at first denies that this happened, but later writes to the producers of the documentary that the eyes were indeed removed, because of an emergency. Another scene in Germany shows middlemen going around dialysis units and suggesting to patients that they could travel to Moscow or Bombay to get a kidney. The patients who were interviewed had refused. A Dutch middleman, masked, declares that it is Americans who control the criminal organ traffic; we are told that this man represents the International Dialysis Foundation. The documentary ends with a visit to the institution for blind children in Bogotá, where we can recognize Jenson.

NOTES

INTRODUCTION

1. Véronique Campion-Vincent, "The Baby Parts Story: A New Latin-American Legend," *Western Folklore* 49 (special issue, *Contemporary Legends in Emergence*, 1991): 9–25 and 134–41; quotation on p. 13.
2. Véronique Campion-Vincent, "Bébés en pièces détachées" ("Baby parts"), *Cahiers internationaux de sociologie* (1992): 299–319; quotation on pp. 316–17.

CHAPTER 1

1. "Les dépeceurs d'enfants" (Those who cut up babies), *L'Humanité*, April 23, 1987.
2. "Des enfants en pièces détachées" (Babies cut up), *Témoignage Chrétien*, June 22–28, 1987.
3. "Nouveau trafic de bébés pour une banque d'organes aux USA découvert au Paraguay. Des enfants vendus, tués, et dépecés" (New trade in babies for an organ bank in USA discovered in Paraguay. Children sold, killed, cut to pieces), *L'Humanité*, August 10, 1988.
4. "Paraguay: démenti par l'ambassade Americaine. Un juge dénonce un trafic de nouveau-nés pour les banques d'organes aux Etats-Unis" (Paraguay: denial by American embassy. A judge condemns the trade in newborn babies for organ banks in USA), *Le Monde*, August 11, 1988.
5. Jean-Michel Cordier, "La baby connection. Résolution du Parlement européen sur les trafics d'organes d'enfants" (The baby connection. Resolution of the European Parliament on the trade in child organs), *L'Humanité*, October 21, 1988.
6. *Izvestia*, July 25, 1987.
7. Vincent Jauvert, "La rumeur du KGB" (Rumor from the KGB), *Nouvel Observateur*, June 11–17, 1992.
8. The Ministry of Justice, the FBI, Food and Drug Administration, National Institutes of Health, Department of Health and Social Services, Immigration and Naturalization Service, United Network for Organ Sharing, and the Transplant Department of the Public Health Service.

9. Charles Z. Wick, *Soviet Active Measures in the Era of Glasnost*. Washington, D.C.: US Information Agency, 1988, 35–50. Vincent Jauvert, "La Rumeur du KGB" (Rumor from the KGB), *Nouvel Observateur*, June 11–17, 1992.

10. Alain Feder and Antoine Garapon, *Enquête sur un éventuel trafic d'organes d'enfants* (Investigation into a possible trade in child organs). Paris: Féderation internationale des droits de l'homme, 1988.

11. "US says Resolution on Baby Trafficking Results from Lies," *New York Times* (October 21, 1988). Jean-Pierre Cordier, "Les accusations de trafic d'organes de bébés latino-americains. Quand les parlementaires européens accréditent une rumeur" (Accusations of trade in organs from Latin-American babies; when European members of Parliament give credit to a rumor), *Le Monde* (October 23–24, 1988). "The endless legend," *Die Zeit* (October 28, 1988).

12. "Correspondance: les prétendus trafics d'organes de bébés" (Correspondence: alleged trade in baby organs), *Le Monde* (November 1 and 24, 1988).

13. Franco Scottono, "Il giro delle adozioni illegali dal Brasile sino alla Campania" (Illegal adoptions from Brazil aimed at Campagna), *Repubblica* (September 18, 1990).

14. *The Sun* (September 19, 1990), quoted by Paolo Toselli, "Bambini, carne da trapianto! La leggenda esplode" (Children as flesh for transplants! The legend explodes), *Tutte Storie* (July 1991).

15. Paul Barruel, "Enfants brésiliens disparus" (Brazilian children disappear), *EFE* (July 31, 1991), quoted by Todd Leventhal, "The Child Organ Trafficking Rumor: A Modern Urban Legend," Washington, D.C.: US Information Agency, 1994.

16. Todd Leventhal, "The Child Organ Trafficking Rumor: A Modern Urban Legend," Washington, D.C.: US Information Agency, 1994, 18.

17. "Rapiscono bambini per rubar gli organi" (Children kidnapped to steal their organs), *Corriere della Sera* (July 13, 1987), pointed out by Giuseppe Stilo and Paolo Toselli, "Gli acchiappa-bambini e l'ambulanza nera" (Child-stealers and the black ambulance), *Tutte Storie* (March 1991).

18. "El robo de organos es un mito que recrea las desapariciones" (Organ theft is a myth recreating the disappearances), *Pagina 12*, August 19, 1988, Psychology.

19. Maria-Laura Avignolo, "Children Robbed of Their Kidneys in Argentina," *Sunday Times*, December 8, 1991. Maria-Laura Avignolo, "La mafia des organes écume les bidonvilles" (The organ-mafia causes panic in shanty towns), *Libération*, December 12, 1991.

20. Nancy Scheper-Hughes, *Death without Weeping: The Violence of Everyday Life in Brazil*. Berkeley and Los Angeles: University of California Press, 1992, 233.

21. Scheper-Hughes, 1992, 234.

22. Scheper-Hughes, 1992, 234–5.

23. Scheper-Hughes, 1992, 232–3.

24. Mario Vargas Llosa, *Lituma dans les Andes* (Lituma in the Andes). Paris: Gallimard, 1996 (1993), 190.

25. Nathan Wachtel, *Dieux et vampires: Retour à Chipaya* (Gods and vampires: the return to Chipaya). Paris: Seuil (*Librairie du xxᵉ siècle*), 1992, 110.

26. Juan Ansion, ed. *Pishtacos: De verdugos a sacaojos* (Pishtacos: from cutthroats to eye-thieves). Lima: Tarea, 1989. A collection of papers, including: Juan Ansion and Eudosio Sifuentes, "La imagen popular de la violencia a travers de los relatos de degolladores" (The popular image of violence through tales of cutthroats), 61–105; Carlos Ivan Degregori, "Enter los fuegos de Sendero y el Ejercito: Regreso de los 'Pishtacos'" (Between the fires of the Shining Path and the Army: the return of the Pishtacos), 109–14; Emilio Rojas Rimachi, "Los 'sacaojos': el miedo y la colera" (The eye thieves: fear and anger), 141–7; Eudosio Sifuentes, "La continuidad de la historia de los pishtacos on los 'robaojos' de de hoy" (Continuity from tales of the pishtacos to the eye thieves of today), 149–54.

27. John A. Shonder, "Organ Theft Rumors in Guatemala," *Foaftale News* (October 1994), 1–3; quotation on p. 1.

28. Shonder, 1994, 1.

29. Shonder, 1994, 2.

30. Shonder, 1994, 2.

31. Paul Sieveking, "Panic in Guatemala," *Fortean Times* (August–September 1994), 48.

32. Mark Frankel and David Schrieberg, "Too Good to be True," *Newsweek*, June 26, 1995.

33. "Clowns protest," *The Times*, November 3, 1995; "Child-snatchers send in the clowns," *The Independent on Sunday*, November 5, 1995.

34. *Vestkysten* (a regional paper from Jutland, Denmark), February 15, 1990; cited in Bengt af Klintberg, *Den Stjulna Njuren: Sagner og rykten i var tid* (The stolen kidney: legends in our time). Stockholm: Norstedts, 1994, 15.

35. Rolf Wilhelm Brednich, "Unfreiwillige Organspende" (Involuntary organ donation), 77–80 in his *Die Maus im Jumbo-Jet* (The mouse in the jumbo jet). Munich: C. H. Beck, 1991. Belkis Kiliçkaya, "Alman 'kuyrukluyalan'" ("Thefts of German kidneys"), *Milliyet*, September 10, 1990.

36. Mark Moravec, "Organ Kidnap Legends," *Australian Folklore* (August 1993).

37. Personal communication (letter) from Bengt af Klintberg, 1992.

38. John Collee, "Cowboys in India. A Cautionary Tale of an Operation Overseas," *The Observer*, December 4, 1994.

39. Russell Braun, "The Kidney Heist," 154 in *The Big Book of Urban Legends*. New York: Paradise Press, 1994.

40. Jan Harold Brunvand, *The Vanishing Hitchhiker: American Urban Legends and Their Meanings*. New York: Norton, 1981.

41. Jan Harold Brunvand, "The Kidney Heist," 149–54 in *The Baby Train and Other Lusty Urban Legends*. New York: Norton, 1993. Quotation on pp. 149–50.

42. The scenario of this episode, *Sonata for Solo Organ* by Joe Morgenstern, will be given below, in chapter 3.

43. Brunvand, 1993, 151.

44. *Salzburger Nachrichten*, July 25, 1992, cited by Brednich (see next note).

45. Rolf Wilhelm Brednich, "Auf Nimmerwiedersehen" (Goodbye to the kidney), 53–56 in *Das Huhn mit dem Gipsbein* (The chicken and toothpaste). Munich: C. H. Beck, 1993.

46. Michel Bouffioux, "Des disparitions sans disparus" (Disappearances where no one disappears), *Télémoustique*, January 1996.

47. Paolo Toselli, "Bambini, carne da trapianto! La leggenda explode" (Children, flesh for transplants! The legend explodes), *Tutte Storie* July 1991.

48. Paolo Toselli, *La famosa invasione delle vipere volante* (The famous invasion of flying vipers). Milan: Sonzogno, 1994. The boutique story is discussed on pp. 139–48; quotations from pp. 141, 139, 142.

49. Giuseppe Stilo and Paolo Toselli, "Gli acchiappabambini e l'ambulanza nera" (Child thieves and the black ambulance), *Tutte Storie* (March 1991). Toselli, 1994, 165–73 (panic in the supermarket).

50. Toselli, 1994. The stolen kidney is discussed on pp. 155–64; quotations on pp. 156–8.

CHAPTER 2

1. "Report of the Ad Hoc Committee of the Harvard Medical School to Examine the Definition of Brain Death," *Journal of the American Medical Association* 205:6 (August 5, 1968).

2. Christiane Hennau-Hublet and Didier Moulin, "Les enjeux éthiques et juridiques de la transplantation d'organes" (Ethical and legal stakes in organ transplantation), *Louvain: Revue mensuelle de l'Université catholique de Louvain* 71 (September 1996), 15–21; quotation on p. 17.

3. *Le Monde*, May 17–19, 1992.

4. *Le Canard Enchaîné*, May 20, 1992.

5. *L'Express*, May 28, 1992.

6. Rocher editions.

7. Alain Tesnière, "Où est l'éthique?" (Where are the ethics?), *Etudes*, November 1996 (issue on organ donations), 482–4; quotations on pp. 483, 484.

8. *Observer*, July 23, 1995.

9. David Le Breton, *La chair à vif. Usages médicaux et mondains du corps humain* (Raw flesh: medical and secular uses of the human body). Paris: Métailié (Traversées), 1993. Quotation on pp. 113–14.

10. Maurice Garden, *Lyon et les Lyonnais au XVIIIe siècle* (*Lyon and its people in the 18th century*). Paris: Les Belles Letters, 1970, 585–6.

11. Jean Delumeau, *La peur en Occident (XIVe–XVIIIe siècles). Une Cité assiégée* (Fear in the West, 14th to 18th centuries: A city under siege). Paris: Fayard, 1978. Arlette Farge and Jaques Revel, *Logiques de la Foule. L'affaire des enlèvements d'enfants, Paris 1750* (The logic of the crowd: The child abduction affair in Paris, 1750). Paris: Hachette, 1988.

12. Departmental Archives of the Rhône District, 1 C 12; hereafter cited as Archives. Morel de Voleine, "Petite chronique lyonnaise comprenant une partie du XVIIIe siècle. Tirée de la correspondance d'un magistrat avec un gentilhomme du Beaujolais" (A brief chronicle of Lyon covering part of the 18th century, drawn from the correspondence of

a magistrate with a nobleman in Beaujolais), *Revue du Lyonnais* 2 (1851), 181–201, 274–86.

13. Archives, item 34 of November 28, 1768.

14. Morel de Voleine, 1851, 274.

15. Item 46 of the archival dossier gives a casualty list of thirty-seven persons: five women and twenty-five men injured, one woman and six men killed.

16. Archives, item 34 of November 28, 1768.

17. Archives, item 39 of December 2, 1768.

18. Archives, item 39 of December 2, 1768.

19. Archives, item 41 of December 5, 1768.

20. Archives, item 42 of December 10, 1768.

21. Archives, item 45 of December 24, 1768; a copy of the indictment.

22. Archives, item 48 of January 14, 1769.

23. Morel de Voleine, 1851, 181–2.

24. Morel de Voleine, 1851, 274, 276.

25. Arlette Farge and Jaques Revel, *Logiques de la Foule. L'affaire des enlèvements d'enfants, Paris 1750* (The logic of the crowd: The child abduction affair in Paris, 1750). Paris: Hachette, 1988.

26. Farge and Revel, 1988, 118.

27. Cited by Farge and Revel, 1988, 111–12. Sources: Barbier, *Chronique de la régence et du règne de Louis XV* (Chronicle of the regency and reign of Louis XV); d'Argenson, *Mémoires* (Memories); *Correspondance de la Marquise de Pompadour* (The correspondence of the Marquise de Pompadour); Ménétra, *Journal de ma vie* (The journal of my life).

28. John Knott, "Popular Attitudes to Death and Dissection in Early Nineteenth Century Britain: The Anatomy Act and the Poor," *Labour History* 9 (November 1985), 1–18; information given on p. 3, taken from the report of the Parliamentary Committee on the 1828 Anatomy Act.

29. Ruth Richardson, *Death, Dissection and the Destitute*. London: Routledge & Kegan Paul, 1987. Quotation on p. 145.

30. Thomas Laqueur, "Bodies, Death and Pauper Funerals," *Representations* 1:1 (February 1983), 109–31.

31. Roy Palmer, *The Sound of History: Songs and Social Comment*. Oxford: Oxford University Press, 1988. He mentions over twenty ballads or laments and twenty-three printed burlesques.

32. Sheila Douglas, "The Hoodoo of the Hanging Tree," in *The Questing Beast: Perspectives on Contemporary Legend, Vol. IV*, ed. Gillian Bennett and Paul Smith. Sheffield: Sheffield Academic Press, 1989, 133–43.

33. *Harraps New Standard French and English Dictionary*, 1991, vol. 3, B:74.

34. Willard Gaylin, "Harvesting the Dead: The Potential for Recycling Human Bodies," *Harper's* 249, no. 1492 (September 1974), 23–32.

35. Jean-Yves Nau, "Les comateux sont-ils des cobayes?" (Are those in a coma guinea-pigs?), *Le Monde*, January 28, 1987, 17, 19.

36. Frank Nouchi and Dr. Escoffier-Lambiotte, "L'affair du coma dépassé d'Amiens entre dans sa phase judiciaire. Une expérience utile, mais condamnable" (The coma affair at Amiens is about to come up in court. A useful experiment, but to be condemned), *Le Monde*, March 1, 1988, 12, 46.

37. Jean-Yves Nau, "Le respect dû par les médecins à la personne humaine continue de s'imposer après la mort" (The respect doctors owe to a human being is still binding after death), *Le Monde*, July 5, 1995, 5, 18.

38. Emiko Ohnuki-Tierney, "Brain Death and Organ Transplantation," *Current Anthropology* 35:3 (June 1994), 233–54.

39. Organized in 1993 by Yale Law School and entitled *Organ Transplantation and Human Rights: A Cross-Cultural Perspective*.

40. Ohnuki-Tierney, 1994, 233.

41. Ohnuki-Tierney, 1994, 236.

42. Ohnuki-Tierney, 1994, 241.

43. Ohnuki-Tierney, 1994, 243 (Michael Angrosino).

44. Ohnuki-Tierney, 1994, 245 (Carl Becker).

45. Ohnuki-Tierney, 1994, 248.

46. David Le Breton, *La chair à vif. Usages médicaux et mondains du corps humain* (Raw flesh: Medical and secular uses of the human body). Paris: Métailié (Traversées), 1993.

47. David Le Breton, *Anthropologie du corps et modernité* (Modernity and the anthropology of the body). Paris: PUF, 1990. *La sociologie du corps* (The sociology of the body). Paris, PUF, 1992.

48. Le Breton, 1993, Introduction, 14–15.

49. Le Breton, 1993, Introduction, 16.

50. Le Breton, 1993, Introduction, 16–17.

51. Le Breton, 1993, 267.

52. Le Breton, 1993, 271, 272.

53. Le Breton, 1993, 274, 275, 276.

54. A discussion on death in *Le cercle de minuit*, France 2.

55. Le Breton, 1993, 278, 280.

56. Le Breton, 1993, 280–1, 286–8, 290–1.

57. Le Breton, 1993, 291, 293.

58. Le Breton, 1993, 294.

59. François Dagognet, *La maitrise du vivant* (Mastery of the living). Paris: Hachette, 1988.

60. *France-Soir*, January 9, 1992.

61. David Le Breton, "Aspects anthropologiques des prélèvements d'organes" (Anthropological aspects of organ removal), *Lumière et Vie* 44:225 (December 1995), 17–26.

62. Le Breton, 1995, 24.

63. Le Breton, 1995, 24.

64. Le Breton, 1995, 24–5.

65. Alain Carpentier and Noelle Lenoir, "La transplantation d'organes" (Organ transplants). In Noelle Lenoir (ed.), *Aux frontière de la vie. Pour une éthique biomédicale à la française*

(On the boundaries of life: Towards biomedical ethics in the French manner). Paris: Documentation française, 1991, vol. 2, 15–36. Quotation on p. 27.

66. Monette Vacquin, *Frankenstein ou les délires de la raison* (Frankenstein: or the delirium of rationality) Paris: François Bourin, 1989.

67. Vacquin, 1989, 206, 208.

68. Jean-Yves Nau, "Clarification," *Le Monde*, December 14, 1988.

69. Jean Ziegler, *Les vivants et la mort* (Death and the living). Paris: Seuil, 1975.

70. Ziegler, 1975, 11.

71. Ziegler, 1975, 12.

72. Ziegler, 1975, 136, 137. Ziegler states that he is referring to "advertisement pages in issues of the American magazine *Hospital Management* in the years 1971 and 1972."

73. Ziegler, 1975, 178.

74. In 1975, the allowable delay was one hour for a heart, fifteen minutes for a liver, forty-five minutes for a kidney.

75. Ziegler, 1975, 206, 208, 212–13, 214.

76. *Nouveau Petit Robert* 1993, 2285. The dictionary points out that this modern pejorative usage has replaced the older one, in which "traffic" and "commerce" were synonymous.

77. *Transplant* 6 (December 1994), 274.

78. Christian Chartier, "Le 'marchand d'organes' néerlandais est sous les verrous" (The Dutch "organ merchant" is behind bars), *Le Monde*, October 26, 1989, 15.

79. Jean-Yves Nau, "Les trafics internationaux de rein se multiplient" (International trading of kidneys is increasing), *Le Monde*, February 15, 1991.

80. Thomas Gack, "Ein Scenario des Verbrechens wie in einem Gangsterfilm" (A criminal scenario like a gangster movie), *Hildesheimer Allgemeine Zeitung*, September 18, 1993.

81. Raj Chengappa, "The Organs Bazaar," *India Today*, July 21, 1990, 30–37.

82. A. K. Salahudeen, H. F. Woods, A. Pingle, and A. S. Dehar, "High Mortality among Recipients of Bought Living-Unrelated Donor Kidneys," *The Lancet* 336 (September 22, 1990), 725–8.

83. Tim McGirk, "Transplant Surgeons Steal Kidneys from Poor," *The Independent on Sunday*, April 2, 1995.

84. S. A., "Indian Organs, Foreign Bodies," *The (Delhi) Telegraph*, February 28, 1995.

85. Kai Friese and Saritha Rai. "Kidney Transplants: Business as Usual. The Organs Sales Continue Even as a New Act Takes Effect," *India Today*, March 15, 1995, with photograph of the demonstration.

86. Sandhya Rao, "Complex Issue: Implications of Organ Transplant," *Frontline*, March 10, 1995, 117–20.

87. M. D. Riti, "Great Kidney Rip-Off," *The Week*, February 19, 1995; Uli Rauss and Jay Ullal, "Organ-Klau in Indien: Nieren für die Reichen" (Organ theft in India: kidneys for the rich), *Der Stern*, February 23, 1995.

88. Harry Wu, *Communist Charity: The Use of Executed Prisoners' Organs in China.* The Laogai Research Foundation, January 1995. Document reproduced, pp. 13–15.

89. Ronald Bailey, "Should I Be Allowed to Buy Your Kidney?," *Forbes*, May 28, 1990; Keung Lam, "Kidney Trading in Hong Kong," *The Lancet*, 338 (August 17, 1991), 453.

90. Wu, 1995, 1.

91. Francis Deron, "Confessions 'arrangées' d'un dissident chinois. Harry Wu revient, en prison, sur ses révélations faites à la BBC" (Chinese dissident's confessions were 'arranged': Harry Wu, in prison, withdraws his revelations to the BBC), *Le Monde*, July 29, 1995.

92. Jean-Yves Nau, "Les autorités sanitaires veulent contraindre l'Institut Mérieux à mieux contrôler l'innocuité de ses produits sanguins placentaires" (Health authorities want to force the Mérieux Institute to keep better checks on the safety of its placental blood products), *Le Monde*, November 10, 1993.

93. My discussion is mainly based on a long article by Pilar Lorenzo, "La caza del 'desechable,'" *El Pais,* March 8, 1992. In France, the information gave rise to short articles in *Le Monde* and *Libération* of March 3, 1992 ("Columbia: Torture and Murder of the Poor"; "Columbia: Human Guinea Pigs"), March 5, 1992 ("Columbia: Inquiry into a Trade in Corpses"); and April 1, 1992 ("Columbia: More Murders for Organs").

94. I have worked from the English translation of transcripts of the program, entitled *Hora Clave*, produced by Grondona, and transmitted on November 25, 1993, and from a video of the first half of the broadcast. There were articles in *Le Monde* on March 14, 1992 ("Psychiatric Horrors in Argentina"); *L'Express* on March 19, 1992 ("Argentina: The Horror Hospital"); and *Figaro* on April 3, 1992 ("Argentina: The Secret Life of the Good Dr. Sanchez").

95. In the Argentine program, the controversy was between Dr. Lopez Blanco, president of INCUCAI, the organization in charge of transplants in Argentina, and Judge Heredia, the first judge to take proceedings in the affair, though he later passed the dossier to a successor.

96. *Organmafia Kolumbia*, Spiegel TV, broadcast March 23, 1992; *Organraub*, Spiegel TV, broadcast April 5, 1992.

97. "Los mercaderes de organos" (Organ merchants), *El Tiempo*, October 13, 1991; "Asesinados dos niños en La Virginia, Risaralda. Sus cuerpos fueron hallados sin organos" (Two children murdered in La Virginia, Risaralda: Their bodies found without organs), *El Tiempo*, March 4, 1995.

98. Daniel Pécaut, "Réflexion sur la violence en Colombie" (Thoughts on the violence in Columbia), in *De la violence* (On violence), ed. Françoise Héritier. Paris: Odile Jacob (Opus), 1996, 223–71.

99. Gilberto Dimenstein, *Brésil: la guerre des enfants* (Brazil: The children's war). Paris: Fayard (*Les enfants du fleuve*), 1991. Jacques Meunier, *Les gamins de Bogotá* (Urchins of Bogotá). Paris: J. C. Lattès, 1977.

100. Michel Huteau, Xavier de Lestrade, and Milka Assaf, *Gamins de Bogotá* (Urchins of Bogotá). Tribulation TV, broadcast on A2 (Special Envoy), March 22, 1990.

101. "El robo del organos es un mito que recrea las desapariciones" (Organ theft is a myth recreating the disappearances), *Pagina* 12, August 19, 1998. Psychology.

102. Nancy Scheper-Hughes, *Death Without Weeping: The Violence of Everyday Life in Brazil*. Berkeley and Los Angeles: University of California Press, 1992. (See chapter entitled "Everyday Violence: Bodies, Death and Silence.") Nancy Scheper-Hughes, "Theft of Life: The Globalisation of Organ Theft Rumours," *Anthropology Today* 12:3 (June 1996), 3–11.

103. Michael S. Serrill, "The Gray Market in Third World Children," *Time*, November 4, 1991.

104. Brigitte Trillat and Sylvia Nabinger, "Adoption internationale et trafic d'enfants. Mythes et réalités" (International adoption and child trafficking: Myths and realities), *Revue internationale de police criminelle* 46 (January–February 1991), 18–25. Quotation on pp. 22–3.

105. Maïté Pinero, "Enquête sur une abomination. Enlèvements d'enfants et trafic d'organes" (Inquiry into an abomination: Child abductions and organ trafficking), *Le Monde Diplomatique* (August 1992), 1: 16–17. Quotation on p. 17.

106. Eugene Robinson, "Some U.S. Couples Criticize American's Methods in Failed Peruvian Adoptions," *Washington Post*, March 13, 1992.

107. Todd Leventhal, "The Child Organ Trafficking Rumor: A Modern Urban Legend." Washington, D.C.: US Information Agency, 1994, based on an interview of P. G. in *Los Angeles Times*, April 16, 1994.

108. *Washington Post*, March 13, 1992.

109. Alain Feder and Antoine Garapon. *Enquête sur un éventuel trafic d'organes d'enfants* (Investigation into a possible trade in child organs). Paris: Féderation internationale des droits de l'homme, 1988.

110. Lionel Duroy, "Guatemala: anatomie d'un trafic d'enfants" (Guatemala: analysis of child trafficking), *L'Evénement du Jeudi*, March 12–18, 1992, 76–8.

111. William Assayag, "Des enfants volés pour des Français" (Children stolen for French people), *France-Soir*, August 14, 1992, 1, 3. Philippe Larue, "Trafic d'enfants. Les bavures de l'adoption" (Child trafficking: Disgraceful blunders in adoption), *Le Parisien*, August 18, 1992, 1, 2–3.

112. Denis Hautin-Guiraut, "Nouvaux-nés à vendre en Amérique latine" (Newborn babies on sale in Latin America), *Le Monde*, August 14, 1992, 7.

113. Martin Andersen, "Children Vanished as 'War Booty' in Argentina," *Washington Post*, July 9, 1985. Michael Specter, "Microbiology Reunites Families: Long-Lost Children's Genes Match Parents," *Washington Post*, January 17, 1989.

114. Steve Fainaru, several articles in the *Boston Globe*, July 14–16, 1996.

115. Caroline Moorehead, "Albanians Try to Prevent Baby-Trade Racket," *The Independent*, April 27, 1992. Titti Beneduce, "Bimbi comprati per gli organi" (Children bought for their organs), *Secolo* 19, April 28, 1992.

116. Leventhal, 1994, 6.

117. Al Mihalcea, "Copii din Romania torturati si ucisi in Occident" (Romanian children tortured and killed in the West), *Romania Libera*, February 27–28, 1993.

118. Yvon Samuel and Renaud Vincent, "Cet homme est-il un monstre? Un richissime dandy suisse accusé d'être un ogre" (Is this man a monster? An ultra-rich Swiss dandy is accused of being an ogre), *France-Soir*, February 1, 1993, 2–3.

119. *Evenimental Zilei*, July 31, 1993, and December 3, 1993.

120. Michael S. Serrill, "Poverty in the Subcontinent and a Camel-Racing Boom in the Gulf Combine to Create a 'Market' in Child-Jockeys," *Time*, November 20, 1989.

121. Vitit Muntarbhorn, *Droits de l'enfant. Vente d'enfants* (Children's rights: Sale of children). Geneva: United Nations, January 22, 1992, 83; January 12, 1993, 62.

122. Ofelia Calcetas-Santos, *Vente d'enfants, prostitution des enfants, et pornographie impliquant des enfants* (Sale of children, prostitution of children, pornography involving children). Geneva: General Assembly of the United Nations, September 20, 1995, 12.

123. Vitit Muntarbhorn, *Droits de l'enfant. Vente d'enfants* (Children's rights: Sale of children). Geneva: United Nations, January 12, 1993, 460–8; January 14, 1994, 23.

124. Ioan Maxim, *Rapport du groupe de travail des formes contemporaines d'esclavage sur sa 20ᵉ session* (Report of the 20th session of the Working Party on Contemporary Forms of Slavery). Geneva, United Nations, June 13, 1995, 14.

125. This document will be discussed below.

126. Ioan Maxim, *Rapport du groupe de travail des formes contemporaines d'esclavage sur sa 19ᵉ session* (Report of the 19th session of the Working Party on Contemporary Forms of Slavery). Geneva, United Nations, June 23, 1994, 19–20.

127. Vitit Muntarbhorn, *Droits de l'enfant. Vente d'enfants* (Children's rights: Sale of children). Geneva: United Nations, January 12, 1993, 29.

128. François Lefort (of the Raoul Follereau Foundation for Street Children), in Antoine Spire's program devoted to organ trafficking in the series "Voix du Silence," on France-Culture on September 3, 1994.

129. "Científicos de todo del mondo niegan que exista un commercio ilegal para transplantes" (Scientists of the whole world deny that an illegal transplant trade exists), *El Pais*, March 20, 1996.

130. As was said above, these mutilations, which are frequent, are due to a systematic policy of terrorizing and intimidating the population.

131. Professor Gilles Renard, Professor Marc Gentilini, and Professor Alain Fischer, *Rapport de l'examen de l'enfant Wenis Yeison Cruz Vargas* (A report on the examination of the child Wenis Yeison Cruz Vargas). Paris: Assistance publique, Hôtel-Dieu, August 10, 1995. Quotation on p. 5.

132. *El Pais*, March 20, 1996.

CHAPTER 3

1. Barbara Hofstetter, "Trafic d'organes d'enfants: que font les organisations internationales?" (The trade in child organs: what are the international organizations doing?). Lausanne: Institute of High International Studies, September 1994.

2. Peter Burger, "Organroof: feit of fictie?" (Organ theft: fact or fiction?), *Wetenschap, Cultur en Samenleving* 24:4 (April 1995), 27–34; quotation on p. 31.

3. "Trafic d'organes d'enfants!" (Trade in child organs!), *Orrizonti: Courrier de l'Antivivisection* (December 1993), 16–19.

4. Janice Raymond, *Women as Wombs: Reproductive Technologies and the Battle over Women's Freedom*. New York: Harper San Francisco, 1994 (1993).

5. Raymond, 1994, xii, xix.

6. Raymond, 1994, 145, 146.

7. We have already mentioned the work of Nancy Scheper-Hughes. Janice Raymond is quoting from a first version, "Bodies, Death and the State: Violence and the Taken-for-Granted World," presented at a symposium of the American Ethnological Society at Atlanta in April 1990.

8. Louise Palmer, "Baby Parts Myth Explained," *New Directions for Women* (March–April 1991). Noam Chomsky, "Victors I & II," *Z Magazine 3 & 4* (November 1990 and January 1991).

9. Raymond, 1994, 167.

10. Rolande Girard, *Le fruit de vos entrailles. Du bébé éprouvette à la guerre bactériologique. Le trafic des fœtus* (The fruit of your womb. From test-tube baby to bacteriological warfare. The trade in fetuses). Paris: Suger, 1985.

11. Michel Raffoul, "Chair à vendre" (Flesh for sale), *Jeune Afrique* 1988 (quoted by Raymond), and "Trafic mondial d'organes humains" (World trade in human organs), *Viva* (September 1988).

12. Raymond, 1994, 172.

13. Raymond, 1994, 208.

14. Shahpour Ravasani, "Decadence Devours the Guardians of Human Rights: The International Market of Human Life." *Echo of Islam: An International Socio-Political Journal* no.134 (August 1995), 8–30.

15. Léon Schwartzenberg, *Report of the Commission on the Environment, Public Health, and Consumer Protection on the Ban on the Sale of Organs for Transplant.* European Parliament, February 25, 1993. *Report in extenso on the Sessions (Intervention by Léon Schwartzenberg to Present His Report).* European Parliament, September 13–14, 1993.

16. Schwartzenberg, February 1993, 5, 11.

17. "Bimbi venduti? Conso scagiona l'Italia" (Children sold? Conso clears Italy of blame), *Corriere della Sera,* September 15, 1993. "Scandalo del trafico di organi. La Sanita apre un' inchiesta" (The organ trafficking scandal. Health Dept launches an investigation), *La Stampa,* September 16, 1993.

18. "Il Brazil blocca le adozioni sospete. Mai piu i nostri bambini in Italia" (Brazil stops suspect adoptions. Our children will no longer go to Italy), *La Stampa,* September 22, 1993. "Adozioni vietati agli italiani" (Adoptions by Italians forbidden), *La Reppublica,* September 22, 1993.

19. Marcel Scotto, "Le Parlement Européen condamne le commerce des organs. L'Italie dement que des enfants bréziliens aient été victimes de prélèvements" (The European Parliament condemns the trade in organs. Italy denies that Brazilian children have been victims of organ removals), *Le Monde,* September 16, 1993.

20. Dr. Pierre Pradier and Dr. Claude Herz, "Adoption. Quels traffics d'enfants?" (Adoption. What child trafficking?), *Le Monde,* October 9, 1993.

21. Léon Schwartzenberg, "Trafic d'organes et adoption" (Organ trafficking and adoption), *Le Monde*, October 31, 1993.

22. Arthur Rogers and Denis Durand de Bousingen, *Bioethics in Europe*. Strasburg: Council of Europe, 1995 (chapter entitled "Organ Transplantation: Ethical and Legal Problems"), 167–82.

23. Jonny Sågänger, *Organhandel: Kroppdelar till salu* (Organ trading: Body parts for sale). Stockholm: Alfabeta, 1994; quotation on pp. 325–6.

24. "Le pape dénonce les massacres et le commerce des enfants" (The pope denounces the massacres and the trade in children), *AFP Agence France Presse*, December 22, 1994.

25. Marco Politi, "Wojtyla a San Pietro: lezione di democrazia" (Wojtyla at St. Peter's: lessons in democracy), *La Reppublica*, December 23, 1994.

26. Cécile Ré, "Jean Dausset, Prix Nobel: c'est abominable" (Jean Dausset, Nobel Prize winner, says, "It's abominable"), *L'Humanité*, February 6, 1988.

27. "Dossier sur le don d'organes" (Organ donation dossier). ADOSEN, *Bulletin trimestriel d'information* no. 111, July 1995.

28. Didier Houssin, "Greffes d'organes: tour d'horizon" (Organ transplants: a survey). ADOSEN, *Bulletin trimestriel d'information* no. 111, July 1995.

29. Maïté Pinero, "Enquête sur une abomination. Enlèvements d'enfants et trafic d'organes" (Enquiry into an abomination. Child kidnappings and the organ trade) *Le Monde Diplomatique*, August 1992, 1, 16–17.

30. Delfeil de Ton, "Les harengs. Les lundis de Delfeil de Ton" (Herrings. Mondays with Delfeil de Ton), *Le Nouvel Observateur*, September 14–20 1995.

31. "Murderer Sold Daughter's Eyes," *The Times*, September 6, 1995. "Un égyptien s'offre une voiture avec le rein de sa fille." (Egyptian man treats himself to a car, thanks to his daughter's kidney), *Agence France Presse*, September 1, 1995.

32. *Time*, August 17, 1995.

33. This document was reproduced in Jonny Sågänger, *Organhandel: Kroppdelar till salu* (Organ trading: Body parts for sale). Stockholm: Alfabeta, 1994.

34. John D. Hall, "A Daughter's Last Gift," *Time*, September 5, 1994.

35. "L'enfant assassiné donné à la science." (A slaughtered child given to science), *France-Soir*, October 4, 1994. "Ils revivent grâce à lui. Nicholas (7 ans) a ressucité six Italiens" (Thanks to him, they live again. Seven-year-old Nicholas has given new life to six Italians), *France-Soir*, November 19, 1994.

36. Ariane Dollfus, "Le cœur de sa fille bat dans sa poitrine. Son père vit grâce à sa mort" (His daughter's heart beats in his breast. Her father lives, thanks to her death), *France-Soir*, June 14, 1995.

37. Lance Morrow, "When One Body Can Save Another," *Time*, June 17, 1991. Vittorio Zucconi, "Figlio mio, ti usero come deposito di organi" (My son, I'll use you as an organ bank), *La Reppublica*, June 19, 1991.

38. Nancy Gibbs, "The Gift of Life—or Else," *Time*, September 10, 1990. Morrow, as above.

39. "Arrivano i 'bambini donatori' nati solo per salvare i fratelli" (Here are "donor babies" born simply to save their siblings), *La Reppublica*, June 5, 1991.

40. "Une merveilleuse preuve d'amour" (A wonderful proof of love), *Détective*, August 10, 1989, reporting the second liver transplant in the world, for Japanese in Australia. "A Brisbane, des Japonnais meurent pour un foie" (In Brisbane, some Japanese die for the sake of a liver), *Courrier International*, December 1–7 1994, citing *Asahi Simbun*.

41. Jean-Yves Nau, "Une étude américaine sur des nouveaux-nés anencéphales. Des médecins souhaitent pouvoir prélever des organes avant la mort cérébrale" (An American study on anencephalic neonates. Some doctors wish to remove organs prior to brain death), *Le Monde*, August 17, 1989.

42. In Florida: "Anche un germoglio di cervello è vita. Bloccato in USA un espianto de d'organi" (Even a tiny piece of brain counts as life. An organ transplant forbidden in USA), *La Reppublica,* March 29–30, 1992. In Palermo: "Braccio di ferro sul sacrificio di Valentina" (An iron hand prevents Valentina's sacrifice), *La Stampa*, April 12, 1992. "Nessuna deroga per Valentina ma quella lege è da rivedere" (No exemption for Valentina, but the law will be reviewed), *La Reppublica*, April 15, 1992.

43. Except in the TV program mentioned, which, however, was only broadcast twenty-two hours afterwards.

44. *Agence France Presse*, March 28, 1992; *France-Soir*, March 30, 1992; *Unita*, March 29–31, 1992 (five articles); *La Stampa*, March 30, 1992 (two articles); *Nazione*, March 31, 1992.

45. Todd Leventhal, "The Child Organ Trafficking Rumor: A Modern Urban Legend." Washington, D.C.: US Information Agency, 1994. Quotation on pp. 32–3.

46. Sågänger, 1994, 341–2.

47. Ersan Arsever and Yves Lasseur, *Rumeurs*. Switzerland: Suisse Romande TV, December 16, 1988.

48. *Télérama*, April 4, 1990.

49. *Le Monde Radio-Télévision*, April 22–23, 1990.

50. Jurgen Roth and Marina Fuhr, *Organrauber: Menschen als Ersatzteilanger* (Organ robbers: Human beings as spare parts). Germany: ZDF TV, 1992.

51. Bruce Harris and Judy Jackson, *The Body Parts Business*. Canada: Alma, CBS, NFB, 1993. Great Britain: BBC, 1993.

52. Marie-Monique Robin and Jihan El Tahri, *Voleurs d'organes* (Organ thieves). France: Canal + Spain, CAPA Agency, 1993. A shorter version, renamed *Voleurs d'yeux* (Eye thieves), was shown by M6 in January 1995.

53. Maïté Albagly, "Interview with Marie-Monique Robin," *CIMADE Info* 14, 13, January 2, 1994.

54. Béatrice Bocard, "A Angers, tous les scoops sont primés" (In Angiers, all scoops are outdone), *Libération*, November 30, 1993.

55. Jean-Yves Nau, "Voleurs d'organes" (Organ thieves), *Le Monde,* December 5, 1993.

56. Béatrice Bocard, "Trafic d'organes en Amérique latine" (Organ trafficking in Latin America), *Libération*, December 8, 1993.

57. Marie-Monique Robin, "Trafic d'organes. On lui a volé les yeux!" (Organ trafficking. They stole his eyes!), *Télémoustique*, January 27, 1994. Her report also appeared in a Turkish paper, and she was interviewed in a fairly confidential information circular, "Trafic

d'organes. Contre le scandale du vol d'organes, un film témoignage" (Organ trafficking. A film testifying against the scandal of organ theft), *Savoir c'est pouvoir*, March 4, 1994.

58. Jean-Baptiste de Montvalon, "Le festival international du grand reportage d'actualité au Touquet" (International festival of major documentaries at Le Touquet), *Le Monde*, November 20–21, 1994.

59. Marie-Monique Robin, "Les voleurs d'yeux" (The eye thieves), *Science et Vie Junior*, December 1994, 14–20. The directors of the accused hospitals exercised their right of reply in the same journal in the issue of February 1995, 14–15.

60. Jean-Baptiste de Montvalon, "L'argent de la vue" (Money for sight), *Le Monde*, January 1–2, 1995.

61. Fabien Gruhier, "Des enfants sans regard" (Children without sight), *Nouvel Observateur*, January 4, 1995; Thierry Leclère, "Les yeux volés" (Stolen eyes), *Télérama*, January 4, 1995; Hacène Chouchaoui, "Voleurs d'organes" (Organ thieves), *France-Soir*, January 7, 1995; Olivier de Bruyn, "Quand les yeux ont le prix des yeux" (When eyes will cost someone their eyes), *Libération*, January 7–8, 1995; François Hauter, "La menace du chaos originel" (A threat of primeval chaos), and "Les Mengele de 1995 sont ophtalmologists en Colombie ou en Argentine" (In 1995, the "Doctors Mengele" are eye specialists in Colombia or Argentina), *Le Figaro*, January 9, 1995; Luc Biecq, "On vole les yeux des pauvres pour les greffer aux riches! L'enquête courageuse et bouleversante de la journaliste Marie-Monique Robin" (The eyes of the poor are stolen for transplants for the rich! A brave and distressing investigation by the reporter Marie-Monique Robin), *France-Dimanche*, January 15–22, 1995; Catherine Durand, "Trafic de cornées mis à jour" (Traffic in corneas revealed), *Le Généraliste*, January 17, 1995; Yves Durand, "Une enquête qui derange" (A disturbing inquiry), *L'Humanité-Dimanche*, January 19–25, 1995.

62. Barbara Hofstetter, *Trafic d'organes d'enfants: que font les organisations internationales?* (Trafficking in children's organs: what are the international organizations doing?). Lausanne: Institute of Advanced International Studies, September 1994. Quotation on p. 10.

63. Hofstetter, 1994, 7.

64. Extracts translated by the author from the TV production by Grondona and the letter of Dr. Patricia Rey.

65. Robert Sullivan, "The BIG Picture," *Life*, October 1993, 10–11.

66. Marie-Monique Robin, "Trafic d'organes. On lui a volé les yeux!" (Organ trafficking. They stole his eyes!), *Télémoustique*, January 27, 1994.

67. The massive documentation assembled by the Colombian investigation can be divided into *Plainte à la Defensoria* (Complaint to the defensoria), Hector Torres, October 23, 1993; *Eléments d'enquête* (Elements of the investigation), 1–119; *Rapport évaluatif* (Assessment report), 120–39; Fabio Delgado Sanchez, December 27, 1993; *Rapport du défenseur délégué* (Report of the defense lawyer), 150–3; Alejandro Pinzon Rincon, February 4, 1994. In the French edition of my book these documents were cited from their legal French translation.

68. *Rapport du défenseur délégué* (Report of the defense lawyer), 152.

69. Eléments d'enquête (Elements of the investigation), 19–26.

70. Professors Gilles Renard, Marc Gentilini, and Alain Fischer, *Rapport d'examen de l'enfant Wenis Yeison Cruz Vargas* (Report on the examination of the child Wenis Yeison Cruz Vargas). Paris: Public Assistance, Hospital Hôtel-Dieu, August 10, 1995. Quotation on p. 4.

71. Marie-Monique Robin, "La scandaleuse impunité des voleurs d'organes" (The shocking immunity of organ thieves), *Les Ecrits de L'Image* no. 7 (June–September 1995), 85–100; quotations on pp. 85, 99.

72. Béatrice Bantman, "Jenson, une image sans autre preuve" (Jenson, a picture without other proof), *Libération*, September 15, 1995; Isabelle Célérier, "Voleurs d'yeux: dix ans après, une difficile expertise médicale" (Eye thieves: ten years later, a difficult medical investigation), *Le Quotidien du Médecin*, September 11, 1995.

73. "Trafic de cornée: la polémique enfle autour du cas du petit Colombien" (Traffic in corneas; the debate increases around the case of the Colombian boy), *Agence France Presse* August 16, 1995.

74. Nathalie Gillot, "Polémique sur l'enfant avueugle" (Debate over the blind boy), *France-Soir*, August 12, 1995.

75. *Eléments d'enquête,* 40.

76. Actually, in January and February 1983.

77. Prix Albert Londres, *Résumé des travaux de la commission* (Summary of the work of the commission), March 20, 1996, 3.

78. Prix Albert Londres, *Résumé des travaux de la commission* (Summary of the work of the commission), March 20, 1996, 3.

79. Marie-Monique Robin, *Voleurs d'organes. Enquête sur un trafic.* (Organ thieves. An investigation into trafficking). Paris: Bayard Editions, 1996.

80. Tale 76 in the *Gesta Romanorum.* Quoted by Jan Brunvand, *The Study of American Folklore: An Introduction.* New York: Norton, 1986 (1968), 209.

81. "The Three Doctors," Tale 118 of the Brothers Grimm, quoted by Jan Brunvand, 1986, 207.

82. Brunvand, 1986, 208–9.

83. *La légende dorée de Jacques de Voragine* (*The Golden Legend*). Paris: les arts et le livre, 1929, quotation on pp. 367–8.

84. Alexandre Vialatte, "Et mon tout est un homme" (My whole word is "man"), *La Montagne*, November 23, 1965.

85. Philip French, *The Observer*, April 30, 1995.

86. *Elseviers Magazine*, August 20, 1988.

87. *Le Canard Enchaîné*, June 2, 1993. The author of *Game Over* was Gérard Guégan, writing under his pseudonym Freddie Lafargue.

88. *Phase Terminale* (Albin Michel).

89. Antoine de Gaudemar, "Interview de René Bellero," *Libération*, May 24, 1990.

90. Claire Devarrieux, "*La Classe de Neige*: suspense et épouvante" (*School in the Snow*: suspense and horror"), *Libération*, November 7, 1995. This novel by E. Carrère was published by POL in 1995.

91. *La Croix*, January 2, 1973.

92. *L'Humanité*, January 20, 1973.

93. Paul Planchon, *L'enfant d'Arturo* (Arturo's child). France: TF1, broadcast on May 11, 1995.

94. The series *Law and Order*. Broadcast on April 2, 1991, on NBC.

95. Broadcast on M6 on May 14, 1990, and April 24, 1993, under the title *Sale Affaire* (A dirty business).

96. Maurizio Ponzi, *Nero come il cuore* (Black as the heart). Italy: Canale 5, November 1991. Vittorio de Sisti, *Il Ricatto 2* (The ransom 2). Italy: Canale 5, March 1991. Paolo Levi and Vittorio Sindoni, *La Scalata* (The ladder), Italy: RAI 2, 1993.

97. David Marconi, *The Harvest*. USA: Arrow, 1993.

98. Michael Crichton, *Coma*. Canada: 1978.

99. Rainer Erler, *Fleisch* (Flesh). Germany: 1979.

100. Kryzstof Kieslowski and Kryzstof Piesiewicz. *Décalogue 10: Le bien d'autrui, tu ne convoiteras* (The tenth commandment: Thou shalt not covet thy neighbor's goods). Poland: 1989.

101. Almodóvar, Pedro. *La fleur de mon secret* (The flower of my secret). Spain: 1995.

CHAPTER 4

1. Charles Z. Wick, *Soviet Active Measures in the Era of Glasnost*. Washington, D.C.: USIA, July 1988. Quotation on p. 4.

2. Wick, 1988, 34.

3. Jakob Segal, Stéfan Heym, and Irène Fuhrmann. "Où est la vérité sur l'origine du sida" (What is the truth about the origin of AIDS?), *Vous et votre santé* (You and your health), January–February 1988, quotation on p. 19.

4. Todd Leventhal, "The 'Baby Parts' Rumor Erupts in Honduras." Washington, D.C.: USIA, April 23, 1993. Quotation on p. 5.

5. Todd Leventhal, "The Child Organ Trafficking Rumor: A Modern Urban Legend." Washington, D.C.: USIA, 1994. Quotation on p. 13.

6. Leventhal, 1994, 13–14.

7. Jonny Sågänger, *Organhandel: Kroppsdelar till salu* (Organ trafficking: Body parts for sale). Stockholm: Alfabeta, 1994.

8. This section was translated into French in the course of my study for the French Establishment for Transplants in 1996.

9. Sågänger, partial French translation, 27.

10. Sågänger, partial French translation, 41–2.

11. Sågänger, partial French translation, 44.

12. Sågänger, partial French translation, 49.

13. Nancy Scheper-Hughes, *Death without Weeping: The Violence of Everyday Life in Brazil*. Berkeley and Los Angeles: University of California Press, 1992.

14. Scheper-Hughes, 1992, 216.
15. Scheper-Hughes, 1992, 218
16. Scheper-Hughes, 1992, 229.
17. That is, squatters; most of the inhabitants are illegally in occupation of their land and houses.
18. Scheper-Hughes, 1992, 233.
19. Scheper-Hughes, 1992, 235.
20. Scheper-Hughes, 1992, 240.
21. Scheper-Hughes, 1992, 242.
22. Scheper-Hughes, 1992, 245.
23. Scheper-Hughes, 1992, 243–4.
24. Scheper-Hughes, 1992, 245.
25. Juan Ansion, *Pishtacos. De verdugos a sacaojos* (*Pishtacos:* From cutthroats to eye thieves). Lima: Tarea, 1989.
26. Juan Ansion, "Presentacion" in Ansion, 1989.
27. Eudosio Sifuentes, "La contuidad de la historia de los pishtacos en los 'robaojos' de hoy" (Continuity between the *pishtacos* story and the "eye thieves" of today), in Ansion, 1989.
28. Nathan Wachtel, *Dieux et vampires. Retour à Chipaya* (Gods and vampires: The return to Chipaya). Paris: Seuil (Librairie du xxᵉ siècle), 1992, 211.
29. Morgan Quero, "Les voleurs d'yeux" (Eye thieves), *Le Monde*, October 11, 1995.
30. Paolo Toselli, "*La famosa invasione delle vipere volante* (The famous invasion of flying vipers). Milan: Sonzogno, 1994, esp. 139–73.
31. Mary Douglas, *Purity and Danger: An Analysis of the Concepts of Pollution and Taboo*. London: Routledge & Kegan Paul, 1966.
32. Bengt af Klintberg, "Den Vandrande Njuren" (The wandering kidney), *Expressen*, May 26, 1991, Kultur p. 4.
33. Bengt af Klintberg, *Den Stulna Njuren. Sagner och rykten i var tid* (*The stolen kidney: Legends and rumors in our times*). Stockholm: Norstedts, 1994. Chapter on the stolen kidney, 15–20.
34. Rolf Wilhelm Brednich, "Unfreiwillige Organspende" (Involuntary organ donation), 77–80 in *Die Maus im Jumbo-Jet* (The mouse in the jumbo-jet). Munich: C. H. Beck, 1991. "Auf Nimmerwiedersehen" (Goodbye to the kidney), 53–6 in *Das Huhn mit dem Gipsbein* (The chicken and the toothpaste). Munich: C. H. Beck, 1993.
35. Jan Harold Brunvand, "The Kidney Heist," 149–54 in *The Baby Train and Other Lusty Urban Legends*. New York: Norton, 1993.
36. *De wraakvan de kangoeroe* (The kangaroo's revenge), 1993, and *De gebraden baby: Sagen en geruchten uit het moderne leven* (The roasted baby: Sagas and rumors in modern life), 1995.
37. Peter Burger, "Organroof: feit of fictie?" (Organ theft: fact or fiction?), *Wetenschap, Cultur: En Samenleving* 24:4 (April 1995), 27–34. The author kindly sent me the English translation of this article.
38. Peter Burger, "Ladrones de organos" (Organ thieves), *Enigmas del Hombre Y El Universo* 2:5 (May 1996), 67–74.

39. Peter Burger, "Organ Snatchers," *Magonia* 56 (June 1996), 3–7, 23.

40. Burger, 1995, 4.

41. Burger, 1995, 8–9, for all three quotations.

42. Burger, 1995, 6.

43. Patricia S. Turner, *I Heard it Through the Grapevine: Rumor in African-American Culture.* Berkeley & Los Angeles: University of California Press, 1993.

44. Turner, 1993, 151.

45. Bill Ellis, "Death by Folklore: Ostension, Contemporary Legend, and Murder," *Western Folklore* 68:3 (July 1989), 201–20.

46. Claude Lévi-Strauss, *La pensée sauvage* (*Primitive thought*). Paris: Plon, 1962.

47. Michel-Louis Rouquette, "La pensée sociale" (Social thought), 299–328 in Serge Moscovici (ed.), *Introduction à la psychologie sociale* (*An introduction to social psychology*). Paris: Larousse, 1973.

48. Nicole Belmont, "Folklore," in *Encyclopedia Universalis*, 1984.

49. Peter Lienhardt, "The Interpretation of Rumour," 105–131 in J. M. Beattie and R. G. Lienhardt (eds.), *Studies in Social Anthropology: Essays in Memory of E. E. Evans-Pritchard.* Oxford: Clarendon Press, 1975.

50. Salomon Reinach, "L'accusation du Meurtre Rituel" (The ritual murder accusation), *Revue des Études Juives* 25 (1892), 161–80; quotation on p. 177.

51. Yves-Marie Bercé, *Le chaudron et la lancette. Croyances populaires et médecine préventive* (*The cauldron and the lancet: Popular beliefs and preventive medicine*). Paris: Presses de la Renaissance, 1984. Quotation on pp. 208–9.

52. Antoine Tardieu, *Étude médico-légale sur les attentats aux mœurs* (A medico-legal study on offences against public morality). Paris, 1867 (5th edition; there were eight editions between 1857 and 1878). Quotation on pp. 100–101.

53. Artheur Goldstuck, "Rape and Race in the World of AIDS," 219–223 in *The Leopard in the Luggage: Urban Legends from Southern Africa.* Johannesburg: Penguin, 1990.

54. *Rajasthan Patrika* (Jaipur), January 3, 1995.

55. Ioan Maxim, *Rapport du groupe de travail des formes contemporaines d'esclavage sur sa 20° session* (Report of the 20th session of the Working Party on Contemporary Forms of Slavery). Geneva: United Nations, June 13, 1995. Quotation on p.11.

56. Bill Ellis, "De Legendis Urbis: Modern Legends in Ancient Rome," *Journal of American Folklore* 96 (1983), 200–8.

57. "Blood Libel," 1120–31 in *Encyclopedia Judaica*. Jerusalem: Macmillan, 1971.

58. Alan Dundes, *The Blood Libel Legend: A Casebook in Anti-Semitic Folklore.* Madison, Wis.: University of Wisconsin Press, 1991.

59. Claudine Fabre-Vassas, "La Pâques rouge" (Red Easter), 149–82 in *La bête singulière. Les juifs, les chrétiens et le cochon* (The singular beast: Jews, Christians, and the pig). Paris: Gallimard, 1994.

60. Robert Ian Moore, *La persécution. Sa formation en Europe X^e–XIIIe siècle* (Persecution: Its development in Europe from the tenth to the thirteenth century). Paris: 1991 (1987).

61. Moore, 1991, 143–9.

62. Benjamin Thorpe, *Northern Mythology*, vol. 3, *Netherlandish Mythology* (London, 1852), cited by Bill Ellis in *Foaftale News*, February 1994, 10.

63. Ache, "Brazilian Superstitions Respecting Leprosy," *Notes & Queries*, August 24, 1889, 145–6.

64. Julio Caro Baroja, *Ensayo sobre la literatura de cordel* (An essay on popular literature). Madrid, 1969. Cited on p. 105 of Nathan Wachtel, *Dieux et vampires. Retour à Chipaya* (Gods and vampires: The return to Chipaya). Paris: Seuil (Librairie du XXᵉ siècle), 1992.

65. Wachtel, 1992, 104.

66. Juan Ansion, "Presentacion" in Ansion, 1989, 9.

67. Reinach, 1982, 166.

68. Luise White, "Vampire Priests of Central Africa: African Debates about Labor and Religion in Colonial Northern Zambia," *Comparative Studies in Society and History* (1993), 746–72.

69. Luise White, "Cars Out of Place: Vampires, Technology and Labor in East and Central Africa," *Representations* 43 (1993), 27–50.

70. Luise White, "The Traffic in Heads: Bodies, Borders and the Articulation of Regional Histories," *Journal of South African Studies*, June 1997.

71. Richard Alan Drake, "Construction Sacrifice and Kidnapping: Rumor Panics in Borneo," *Oceania* 59 (1989), 269–79.

72. Maribeth Erb, "Construction Sacrifice, Rumors and Kidnapping Scares in Manggarai: Further Comparative Notes from Flores," *Oceania* 62 (1991), 114–26. Quotation on p. 124.

73. Edgar Morin et al., *La Rumeur d'Orléans* (Rumor in Orleans). Paris: Le Seuil, 1969.

74. Véronique Campion-Vincent and Jean-Bruno Renard. *Légendes urbaines. Rumeurs d'aujourd'hui* (Urban legends: Rumors of today). Paris: Payot, 1993. Quotations on pp. 303 and 305.

75. Letter from Victor Hugo to Josephine Butler, March 27, 1870, quoted by Edward Bristow on p. 36 of his *Prostitution and Prejudice: The Jewish Fight against White Slavery 1870–1939*. Oxford: Clarendon Press, 1982.

76. Edward Bristow, *Vice and Vigilance: Purity Movements in Britain Since 1700*. Dublin: Gill and Macmillan, 1977. Quotations on pp. 57 and 58.

77. Bristow, 1982, 37.

78. Bristow, 1977, 190.

79. Bristow, 1982, 41.

80. Bristow, 1977, 192.

81. Bristow, 1977, 193.

82. Bristow, 1977, 197.

83. Bristow, 1982, 46.

84. Victor Hugo, *Les Misérables*. Paris: Gallimard (Pléiade), 1951 (1862), 191–5.

85. Jonathan Swift, *A Modest Proposal and Other Satires*. New York: Prometheus Books, 1995, 255–6. Quotations on pp. 259, 260–1.

86. Drake, 1989, 275–7.

87. Don Bishoff, "Urban Legends Myth the Truth," *The Register Guard* (Eugene, Oregon), February 7, 1996.

88. Patricia Turner and Jan Brunvand. Personal communication on the occasion of my presenting an earlier version of this study at Berkeley, California, April 26, 1996.

89. Michel Demaison, "Le don qui sauve: une logique, une grâce" (The saving gift: logic and grace), *Lumière et Vie* 1995, 69–88; quotations on pp. 78–9, 84.

90. Gloria Pachon de Galan was Colombian ambassador in France from May 1993 to November 1995.

91. Santiago Gamboa, "Premio Albert Londres fue confirmado por solidaridad" (The Albert Londres prize was confirmed through solidarity), *El Tiempo*, March 24, 1996, 8D.

92. Thierry Leclère, "Au bénéfice du doute" (The benefit of the doubt), *Télérama* 2413, April 10, 1996, 30.

93. Lorraine Millot, "Quatre ans de prison pour faux reportages" (Four years in prison for false reports), *Libération,* December 24, 1996, 36. The report states that Michel Born was found guilty of seventeen cases of fraud.

94. Lorraine Millot, "Les reportages bidonnés sur les télévisions allemandes" (Lies in German TV reporting), *Libération,* February 19, 1996, 40.

95. JoAnn Conrad, "Stranger Danger: Defending Innocence, Denying Responsibility," paper given at the Contemporary Legend Conference at Bath in July 1996.

96. Personal communication from Peter Burger, December 30, 1996.

97. Donald Joralemon, "Organ Wars: The Battle for Body Parts," *Medical Anthropology Quarterly* 9:3 (September 1995), 335–56; quotations on pp. 340, 341.

98. Joralemon, 1995, 347.

99. Moulin, Anne Marie. "La crise éthique de la transplantation d'organes. A la recherche de la 'compatibilité' culturelle" (The ethical crisis in organ transplants: The search for cultural "compatibility"), *Diogène* 172 (October–December 1995), 76–96; quotations on pp. 79, 81.

100. Moulin, 1995, 95.

101. Jean-Pierre Mohen, *Les rites de l'au-delà* (Rituals of the beyond). Paris: Odile Jacob, 1995, 318.

CONCLUSION

1. Alain Boureau, *La papesse Jeanne* (Pope Joan). Paris: Aubier, 1988. *Le droit de cuissage. La fabrication d'un mythe XIIe–XXe siècle*. Paris: Albin Michel, 1995. The latter was translated as *The Lord's First Night: The Myth of the Droit de Cuissage*. Chicago: University of Chicago Press, 1998.

2. Boureau, 1995, 254.

3. Boureau, 1995, 256.

4. Neil Acherson, "Aliens Turned my Baby into an Olive and Other Rumours," *The Independent on Sunday*, July 22, 1990.

AFTERWORD TO THE AMERICAN EDITION, 2005

1. Peter Burger, personal communication, August 6, 2004. "Just the other week, the results came in of an urban legend survey among 1000 Dutch citizens, conducted on behalf of a popular science magazine. The existence of a mafia that kidnaps and kills people to harvest their organs is generally accepted: 32% are sure it is true, 47% say it is probably true."
2. Case in Mexico: Associated Press, March 27, 1998. Lynching occurred in Huejutla (state of Hidalgo); two dead truck drivers, said to have tried to kidnap four girls, aged four to twelve.
3. "Mob Kills Tourist, Bus Driver," *New York Times*, April 30, 2000; *Japan Times*, May 2, 3, 2000; "Two die as mob attacks Japanese tour group," *The Independent*, May 2, 2000; *Asahi Shimbun*, May 1, 2000.
4. "Satanic rites rumors linked to Guatemala attack," Reuters, May 4, 2000.
5. Anthropologists emphasize that conversion enables an enterprising individual to escape the yoke of community redistribution through the network of honorary (and costly) *cargas* linked to religion.
6. *The Independent*, May 2, 2000.
7. Adam Jones, "The Murdered Men of Ciudad Juárez," at http://adamjones.freeservers.com/juarez.htm
8. http://www.amnestyusa.org/women/juarez/
9. Debbie Nathan, "Missing the Story," *The Texas Observer*, August 30, 2002.
10. Sheila M. Rothman and David J. Rothman, "The Organ Market," *The New York Review of Books*, October 23, 2003, 49.
11. David J. Rothman, "The International Traffic in Human Organs," *The New York Review of Books*, March 26, 1998, 16.
12. Nancy Scheper-Hughes, "The Global Traffic in Human Organs," *Current Anthropology* 41, 2 (April 2000): 191–225; "Minding the Body: On the Trail of Organ-Stealing Rumors" in Jeremy MacClancy (ed.), *Exotic No More: Anthropology on the Front Lines*. Chicago: University of Chicago Press, 2002.
13. Véronique Campion-Vincent and Nancy Scheper-Hughes, "On Organ Theft Narratives," *Current Anthropology* 42, 4 (August–October 2001): 555–8.
14. Véronique Campion-Vincent, "Organ Theft Narratives as Medical and Social Critique," *Journal of Folklore Research*, 39, 1: 33–50.

INDEX

INDEX

INDEX